BATTLEFIELD AMERICA

A Citizen's Guide to Surviving the New World

BRIAN MALOY

Bean & Binder Publishing
Chicago, Illinois

Disclaimer: As an armed citizen, you are responsible for understanding the Local, State and Federal laws in all aspects regarding firearms, including using deadly force in self-defense, that specifically pertains to where you live, work, or travel to. You are expected to abide by these laws that are subject to change. This book, its content, the author, and his advisors only provide a platform for discussion of the subject matter. This discussion does by no means provide an absolute circumstance where deadly force should be used as all circumstances are different, requiring a different reasonable course of action.

© Brian Maloy 2024.

First Published December 2024
Digital ISBN: 979-8-9919223-4-0
Paperback ISBN: 979-8-9919223-0-2
Library of Congress Control Number: 2024923430

All rights reserved. No part of this publication may be reproduced, stored in or introduced into a retrieval system, or transmitted, in any form, or by any means (electrical, mechanical, photocopying, recording or otherwise) without the prior written permission of the publisher, Bean and Binder Publishing. Any person who does any unauthorised act in relation to this publication may be liable to criminal prosecution and civil claims for damages.

Credits:

Book cover	Amira Merrouche
Editing	Mike Valentino, Ashley Emma
Proofreading	Thomas Cross, Sara Keller
Interior design	Michael O'Donnell
Photographs	Dr. Ron Martinelli, Kurt Delia, & Delia Tactical International, LLC

Cover image credit: Amira Merrouche ©2024

Bean & Binder Publishing
Contact: info@beanandbinderpublishing.com

Dedications

To the Angels:

These brave men and women, born as mortals, who make the conscious decision to walk among the chaos of hell on Earth, are what most would call angels.

To my fallen brothers and sisters in blue:

You are not forgotten.

To the warriors who feel you are at the end of your ropes:

Taking your life is not the answer, regardless of how alone you may feel. I assure you that you are not alone, as your current perception is merely an illusion. This calling is not meant for modern humans to endure. Be strong, talk to someone, and realize that your journey in life has only begun. There is help out there. My ears are always open; consider me a friend! In the meantime, remember that isolation is a gift: Rise, transform, and then lead others to do the same.

To Angie:

May you be strong and resilient, as you navigate through this new, uncertain world. Finally, may you persevere under adversity. Pivot, but never quit! Always chase your dreams, and never chase the money!

Acknowledgements

I would like to take this opportunity to express my sincere gratitude to my friends, family, and colleagues who supported me during the forging of this book, as well as during the challenges, the triumphs, and even the defeats that inspired my journey to authorship. You taught me that our experiences in this truly short life will eventually lead us to the crossroads where we grow, and hard decisions must be made. We either shed into a better version of ourselves, or we travel far from where we are supposed to be until our tribe brings us back home, one way or the other.

To my confidants: Andy B., TC, Karin P., Luis and Lilian P., Ken and Mary T., Lisa T., Stephanie "Boss" P., and Mark Mod: Thank you for being the amazing humans you are and believing in me when I needed it the most.

To Angie: My kindred spirit, who followed me from the shadows of my past, whilst reminding me that the greatest treasures in life are the dreams that we have yet to manifest.

To Dr. Ron Martinelli: For offering your guidance and credence while giving me the courage to challenge the unprincipled few for the greater good of all.

To Larry Nichols: For generously examining the contents of this book well beyond the scope, while giving me the resilience to push to the finish line.

Lastly, to God: For helping me realize that my new calling was obscured deep within the one place I forgot to look.

Table of Contents

Dedications iii

Acknowledgements iv

Foreword vi

Prologue ix

Section One | The Impetus of Tribulation 1

Section Two | Duty Calls: The Rise of the Warrior 23

Section Three | Carrying the Burden 50

Section Four | T.A.A.R.S — Threat Awareness, Assessment,
    Response and Survival 152

Foreword

"In the blink of an eye."

FBI statistics over the past twenty-five years on gunfights between officers and suspects reveal that these armed encounters take place in 2.5 seconds. During this very brief period, an average of four rounds are fired from distances of between two and ten feet. Sixty percent of these shootings occur in environments of limited light to total darkness. Disturbingly, the studies show that trained officers miss their intended targets eighty-six percent of the time, while suspect adversaries with limited to no trained experience in pistolcraft hit officers sixty-eight percent of the time. That is a deadly disparity.

Street encounters where officers and citizens are forced to make deadly force decisions in self-defense and/or in the defense of others are not at all like the fantasized scripts from the TV series, "Miami Vice," "SWAT," "NCIS" or "CSI Miami Beach." In reality, officer and civilian-involved deadly force shootings often occur by surprise, in adverse environments, and absent any cover, where the armed defender has only milliseconds – literally the blink of an eye, to make a life or death decision to use or not use deadly force. Yet, when investigated and/or tried in a criminal or civil court, investigators, prosecutors, judges and juries will have days, months and sometimes even years to analyze, criticize, vote or rule on that deadly split-second decision.

Unfortunately for the person forced to use deadly force for self-defense, those who sit in review of these shootings do so from the abstract comfort of an office or courtroom. The reviewers and judges never experience any measure of the heart-thumping, mind-tingling stress the shooter experienced in the moment(s) force was used. Their review is also absent the negative human factors caused by an uncontrollable, instantaneous, rush of adrenalin that causes such tunnel vision, depth perception issues, loss of colors, diminished or complete hearing loss, time distortion and temporary to permanent stress memory recall amnesia.

Welcome to my world. I am a former police detective, forty-plus years law enforcement and civilian firearms instructor, and a forensic investigator certified in both federal and state courts nationally. I also investigate, analyze and occasionally testify in officer and civilian-involved shootings

– hundreds of them. I direct the nation's only multi-disciplinary Forensic Death Investigations Team comprised of forensic investigators, scientists and medical professionals specializing in controversial, high-profile death cases. Many of our cases you already know about: Trayvon Martin v. George Zimmerman, Officer Darren Wilson v. Michael Brown, "Hands up, don't shoot!" Cleveland Officer Michael Brelo, Mesquite, TX Officer Derek Wylie, GA Officer Zach Presley, Sacramento PD Officers v. Stephon Clark, the Robb Elementary School mass murders by an active shooter, AZ v. rancher George Alan Kelly and many others.

Getting deep into the forensic weeds with the help of a top-notch team, I have come to truly know the difference between media driven anti-police and anti-2A political rhetoric, and objective, forensic facts. The real truth of the incidents I have investigated versus the media and political "noise" in most my high-profile shooting cases would shock most people, which is the misinformation and deliberate public deception.

As a nationally recognized authority on the forensic and psychophysiological dynamics involved in self-defense shootings, author Brian Maloy asked me to consult with and then write the foreword to his first book, "Battlefield America." I am honored to do so.

A Look Inside this Book

Brian Maloy's "Battlefield America," is literally a compendium of important information on the use of deadly force in self-defense and the defense of others. Brian begins by discussing his own experiences as a street-savvy former Chicago PD officer. He then moves on to provide both opinions and insight to how the world around us in America has changed – and not for the better for honest, law abiding 2A supporters and patriotic Americans.

"Battlefield America," is a must-read resource book for anyone armed or considering taking on the heavy responsibilities of becoming an armed citizen. As those of us in law enforcement already know, there is no clear winner in a gunfight. While the ultimate objective in using justifiable deadly force is self-preservation and the protection of others, one must be mature enough to recognize that you must also prevail in criminal and civil courts of law. Prevailing means that you must ultimately be found by a prosecutor, judge and/or jury of your peers as having acted in a manner that is deemed to be "objectively reasonable." Brian's book sets the reader on the right path to accomplish this critical goal.

Human factors, psychophysiology, mental and physical preparation for becoming an armed officer or citizen, physical training, the basics of contemporary pistolcraft and analysis of actual gunfights provide a solid foundation upon which to build your mental library. Brian also provides important tips to post-incident processing and preparing for the criminal and civil investigations that will surely come after deadly force is used.

"Battlefield America," is the type of encyclopedia of self-defense that every law enforcement officer, serious 2A supporter and concealed carry citizen needs to have on their bookshelf. I thoroughly endorse the critical concepts of self-defense found in this excellent book. Stay safe out there!

Ron Martinelli, Ph.D.
Forensic Criminologist
Federal/State Courts Law Enforcement & Civilian Use of Force Expert

Prologue

Somewhere in the sands of time we have lost our humanity. Recent years have brought the greatest level of violence the free world has ever witnessed. But the one question that we all have in common is why? How can the leaders of the free world let their own country implode from the inside out? It is hard for us to fathom how any person can have such disregard for his fellow humans when we are just trying to live, raise our children, and be happy. When did this tribulation of America begin and when will it end?

I suppose the desire to know how it will end is more enticing. Of course, we did not get here overnight. This trajectory took time. The breeding grounds of these spineless, yet disturbed, emotionless sub-humans are still ripe. Where do we go from here? Criminals have been and always will be a problem that society must deal with, but there are greater evils at play now. Politics now take precedence over the wellbeing of all. Sadly, it will only get uglier and more violent before it gets better.

Violent offenders, including active killers and terrorists, do not always choose a firearm as a weapon of choice. Knives, explosive devices, chemicals, and cars, to name a few, can be just as deadly, if not more. Guns have always been here, but it is society that has changed as well as their twisted, godless values. Good will eventually win, but until that happens, we are going to have to defend ourselves, our family, and our community by any means necessary. I do believe the active killer phenomenon is a hard nut to crack. Whether the killer is pure evil or desperate in the throes of a severe mental health episode, the threat needs to be neutralized as quickly as possible, although the root causes must also be analyzed. Believe it or not, it is possible to identify and intercept a potential attacker prior to a targeted attack. The indicators are there, and the data proves this, so it is possible. I passionately believe that we are in the midst of a mental health crisis and have been for quite some time, but what would trigger such a disturbed person to take that next step and commit murder?

In the meantime, America's streets are more dangerous than ever, and the active killer epidemic is alive and well. Regardless of whether an active killer or terrorist walks into a library and starts shooting children on a Saturday morning or armed intruders kick in your back door while you are putting your young child to bed, Americans must be prepared to deal with it, no matter the circumstances. Although the dynamics of both threats are very different, when someone is pointing a gun at you, your co-workers, or your family, what's the difference? Furthermore, it is the fine armed citizen or the police who will be dealing with the situation, regardless of the type of lethal threat, who is pulling the trigger, and why. Also, it will be the organizations who may be liable if the proper protocols are not implemented.

America has changed, and we must change with it. I am an optimist. However, the perversion of those pulling the strings of chaos have no intention of relinquishing control.

Throughout this book, I also talk about how the ecosystem of law enforcement has dramatically changed, primarily fueled by politicians, the media, and their sponsors. This change influences the way the police respond. Training and instinct also affect the way they respond to violent lethal threats, whatever the source may be.

It is the police officer on the street who will respond and neutralize the threat, instinctively and systematically pushing forward regardless of where it is at. I have been in situations where I have watched officers walking in circles (including supervisors) until other officers, including myself, made the decision to make entry immediately upon arriving on scene. Why? Because we took the initiative, we were trained, and our fear was pushed aside as training and instinct took the lead. For me, this mindset took time to develop and did not happen overnight. In these types of situations, time is not on our side. Naturally, I have been afraid, but when you are trained the right way, after time your fear is put on the shelf so you can do your job like a well-oiled machine.

It's important for lawmakers and law enforcement organizations to dissect the 2022 Robb Elementary School shooting in Uvalde, Texas and other targeted attacks of the past because it not only brings to light some of the reasons these tragedies occur but reinforces the fact that training is the single most principal element of law enforcement. This includes civilians who legally carry firearms. Without resources and funding, quality training is simply not possible. Furthermore, without support from their community and their organization, police officers will not have the confidence to give the community the protection they deserve.

Law enforcement to the side, if you are a civilian who is authorized to carry a weapon, you, my friend, are the new front line of defense. Carry that burden on your side and in the appropriate holster. Once you have realized this fact, start training. It is not law enforcement that ultimately failed us. What failed us are policies set in place within society by politicians as well as the media who paved the path of destruction at the will of a few. Most police officers took the oath to serve and protect, and I can tell you first-hand that most would die trying.

Allow me to briefly discuss how my own journey began, not only with law enforcement, but with what inspired me to authorship. In the beginning of my journey in law enforcement, like others before me, I took the oath to serve and protect after graduating from the Chicago Police Academy. I was optimistic that I would be able to make a difference in the world, not knowing that as the years passed, I would be the one who changed. I remember the eagerness to learn the nuts and bolts of police work, and through my lack of wisdom at the time, I felt I was my only limitation. From the academy, I was assigned to the 4th District on the southeast side of Chicago. It was by far the most violent, yet diverse, district in Chicago that happened to border Indiana. Many native Chicagoans do not know that we border the Hoosier state along the Lake Michigan shoreline. That alone was strange to me as well as the rapidly changing environments that would happen within minutes. The 4th District morphed from a rural environment in the south end to a desolate industrial setting in the center to one of the most violent urban battlefields in the nation on the north, east and west end of the district. The 4th was also (and still is) home to a small Serbian and Croatian community which was nestled within close proximity of some iconic steel plants that have since closed decades ago. Subsequently, these plants employed an enormous number of Serbians and Croatians, many who lived in the area. I was fortunate to work with many of the grandchildren of these steel workers who became police officers serving the very community their grandparents worked and lived in years past.

On a cold and seemingly quiet night in this urban wasteland, the sun was setting, and the third watch afternoon shift had started. I enthusiastically entered the passenger side of the patrol car and began to document, as required, our "mission" for the night. Usually, the mission entailed "aggressive patrol" of high narcotics or gang areas within our assigned beat or sector. I asked the veteran officer (who was also my babysitter for the day as there was a shortage of Field Training Officers) who was in the driver's seat, "What's our mission of the day?" as I was filling out the required mission form.

He looked at me intensely as the red glare of the interior light shined on his face and said with an awkward one-thousand-yard stare, "To survive." The look on his face scared the hell out of me, and that was the moment I realized how dangerous a career I had chosen. For the next three years, I served side by side with my comrades in blue, aggressively patrolling the streets as they selflessly put their lives at risk while serving and protecting a thankless community from themselves. I always had compassion for the fine citizens in the community who were just trying to survive and keep their families safe. To me, it was where I was assigned, but to many, it was home, including many of my fellow officers.

After a few interesting details working on specialized assignments soon after the Twin Towers fell, I had been accepted into SOS, which was the controversial Special Operation Section. Here, I aggressively specialized in gangs, narcotics, gun investigations, counterterrorism operations, and active killer interdiction training, among other things. Although many of these officers were politically connected, most of these men and women were some of the best officers that the Chicago Police Department ever produced. Eventually, misguided community activists pushed for this unit to be dissolved. As a result, gangs, drugs, and gun violence once again took control of the city in ways unseen for years. With SOS off the scene, the tip of the spear was removed. In my opinion, this, as well as weak leadership from the department and city is what set a new trajectory for the lawlessness and turmoil we see today in Chicago.

Regardless of how bad crime gets in Chicago and other cities across America, aggressive police work is never an option in today's biome. The kinder, gentler peace-loving officer known as "Officer Friendly" seems to be working out just fine. Of course, I mean that with my usual dose of sarcasm. Aggressive police work is a delicate but necessary evil. In some respects, it is a "Band-Aid" to the hemorrhaging issues that communities endure but nobody wants to talk about. I have met with numerous community activists who agree with me wholeheartedly. Moreover, although I do feel that community policing is crucial, the approach used by law enforcement, especially in urban America, has been fruitless and for some very good reasons.

After several years in SOS, I decided to slow things down a little, returning to the patrol division and requesting a Northside district. After a stint in the 20th, I eventually transferred to the 18th District, informally known as the "glamor district" because many officers in that district had successful small businesses or were actors. I often saw many of my colleagues in commercials and movies while having my morning coffee, and it always brought a smile to my face.

On one spring evening while on duty in the 18th District, I decided to assist fellow officers with a disturbance. Upon my arrival, the disturbance escalated into a physical altercation. During that altercation, though I did not know it at the time, my life would change once again. It was not until I returned home that night that I realized that my gun hand (my dominant hand) had swelled to the point that I could not use it. I eventually learned that the ligament in my wrist had completely torn.

Months later, I endured surgery, and I found myself sitting in front of the fireplace with my hand in a cast, drinking too much wine, and reflecting upon my life while watching Chicago politicians try to explain why the murder rate has risen to numbers only seen in war. It was also noticeably clear in other parts of the nation that active shooters—or killers, as I call them—have also taken the very soul of America, and it broke my heart.

Feeling quite displaced myself, I spent numerous hours watching the news headlines as America started to take a whole new dangerous direction spiraling downward. Oh, let us not forget my biggest challenge at the time, which was my child's homework, and the useless nightmare called "Common Core" math.

Moving on, the headlines sparked questions in my mind. Questions like, "Have our warriors in blue become pacifists due to the media and politicians making them out to be the very plague from which they swore to protect us?"

I realized the issues, however, were much deeper in this country than we could have imagined. The long-debated racial disparities have been clouded by socio-economic differences, politics, the lack of education, community funding, family values, father involvement, and proper parental guidance in certain communities. When we add the lack of support for the police, unchecked and uncensored social media, violent movies, and video games, it is not particularly surprising that we have what we see now: American cities that are as violent as war zones worldwide, including Chicago.

Of course, we cannot forget the provoked civil unrest and riots prior to and during the Covid-19 pandemic that brought our cities to their knees, exposing the weaknesses of the elected leadership across the nation. Arson and looting ran rampant, especially during the tumultuous "summer of love" in 2020.

Then we throw in the growing epidemic of active and mass shootings that resurfaced after the lifting of quarantine restrictions as well as continued left-driven riots worse than this nation has ever endured. Yes, America, we have a problem, and it is not the police!

The final, life-changing event that drove me to authorship took place when I was driving my young child home from school, and he explained to me that they practiced hiding under desks in case "stranger-danger" comes into the school with a gun. What my child said to me struck a chord. It brought me back to my first days as a rookie police officer and ignited a fire that had not been lit for quite some time. Frankly, it infuriated me to think not even our children are safe. I cannot help but think about the good parents in underserved areas who send their children to school every day, or those who have already suffered losses after an active killing event. At what point do we stop and say enough is enough?

As Americans are navigating this uncertain time and the 2nd Amendment is still intact (despite constant attacks against it), it is imperative that responsibly armed citizens and law enforcement alike thoroughly understand the dynamics of neutralizing and surviving a lethal encounter. It is also crucial that those fine citizens who opt to carry a firearm or do so for a living master their weapon from the point when the lethal threat occurs up to the point that they neutralize it. This respectfully includes the physical, emotional, and mental aspects of conflict during and after the event. Police officers, seasoned and new, are not immune. They need to always remain vigilant. Master your craft and get home to your loved ones.

The training and resources available to law enforcement organizations are grossly deficient nationwide, as the domain that these warriors in blue must operate in has drastically changed. This is not only extremely dangerous to them while they are trying to perform their duties, but it has become devastating to the communities they are sworn to protect. Whether they are responding to an armed robbery, a home invasion, or an active killer in a school, their response must be rapid, lethal, and supported by all.

This book explores my professional and personal opinion about what I feel has brought us to this point in this country. I also dive into the foundation necessary to prepare yourself to be able to neutralize, detect and survive a lethal threat. This threat can be from an active killer, a terrorist, or another violent attack considering the unprecedented levels of crime in America. Furthermore, it is crucial that you or your loved ones have a complete plan to detect, intercept, respond to or survive a targeted attack, should one occur. This book also offers an overview of what I feel must not be overlooked in such a plan, such as situational and threat awareness.

Before we continue, allow me to apologize. There are certain things that I cannot stress enough and if I repeat some of the information every now and then, there's a reason for it. I'm sure you will find it somewhere deep in your heart to forgive me for the repetitive nature that I tend to have when passion takes over. Now that we have gotten this formality out of the way, let us break down an overview of the book.

Section 1 involves my theories on how we found ourselves living amongst a level of danger only comparable to war zones worldwide. But how did we get to this point? Powerful influences, whose only motivation is control, had orchestrated the finest illusion that modern humans have ever witnessed, ripping us from our roots and each other while allowing our adversaries to flourish. Furthermore, the greatest battle may very well be the battle for our minds, the minds of our youth and the spirit of America. Yes, extreme ideologies in any respect can be devastating to a civilized society, but the greatest battles are unseen, as we will discuss. It also discusses the limitations that police officers must operate in, preventing them from performing their sworn duties, with devastating effects to the community they serve, regardless of the threat's origins. As a result, while Americans pressure lawmakers to protect our foundation as a country, responsibly armed civilians must accept the challenge of making the thin blue line a little thicker by transforming themselves into warriors, mastering the skills necessary to engage and defend against an active lethal threat. Lastly, Section 1 lays out the groundwork necessary for a solid understanding of the other sections ahead.

Section 2 discusses the transformation into a warrior, understanding that it all begins with your mindset. This also includes the physical, emotional, and mental effects of lethal engagement as well as strategies for mitigating these effects, to not only survive, but neutralize the active deadly threat, if armed. Understanding the Acute Stress Response, stress inoculation, and the benefits of ingrained memory will help achieve this.

Section 3 delves into the controversial aspects of the 2nd Amendment, the necessary but seldom discussed knowledge required to safely carry, deploy, maintain, and store a firearm as well as the crucial topic of deadly force. Finally, we will break down some unique case studies where deadly force was used by armed civilians that I feel will benefit you on this journey.

Section 4 encompasses what I call TAARS, or Threat Awareness, Assessment, Response and Survival. TAARS is a robust, yet balanced model designed for those citizens who are in environments that are vulnerable to targeted attacks or those citizens that are not built for conflict—children, the elderly, those not able to carry a weapon or warriors that are caught off guard, which can happen. We will also examine two crucial studies meticulously researched by the National Threat Assessment Center, or NTAC, that I feel not only reinforces the principles discussed in this book, but additionally helps expose the risk factors and other vital data that all stakeholders must understand and act upon in today's America.

Finally, we will discuss the crucial skills of threat and situational awareness and then take a dive into an overview of my six-step Hybrid Threat Assessment and Response Guideline, which enables organizations to be in a stronger position to prevent, detect, respond to, and survive a violent targeted attack, like an active killer. For the warrior, understanding these components is imperative to detect, respond to, and if necessary, neutralize an active lethal threat.

Let's push forward and take this journey within these uncharted waters together. Like all storms, this one will eventually pass, but until that day comes, preparation is your mission and knowledge is your biggest weapon!

Let's Move!

SECTION ONE

The Impetus of Tribulation

1.1

Communities in urban America are and have been at war with themselves, and the police are just trying to make it home in one piece. With the police having their hands tied behind their back, the gangs control the circus, and the politicians are the clowns. Unfortunately, the law-abiding citizens are stuck in the middle. But wait, folks, there's more.

Our country is also at war with ideologies whose followers and motives are within reach of the American mainland. I was convinced that eventually, these war-driven ideologies would make their way onto our very soil, and now they have due to poor vetting policies and enforcement. These failed policies are from both sides of the political spectrum. This violent war, undeclared, is being waged not only by these misguided followers from abroad that we have freely allowed to enter, but also by a breed of homegrown offenders even tougher to seek out. This may be that quiet boy next door or a domestically grown terrorist organization waiting for the perfect moment to strike.

This closet misfit, social media addict, avid gamer, or politically and hate-driven threat to humanity whose only achievement will be to cause havoc to his fellow Americans is currently public enemy number one. Whether he uses a firearm or not, he will find a way to cause harm. He, she, or them is a ticking time-bomb that may go through life quietly and eventually end up in Corporate America, a factory, the military, or our schools undetected, despite the breadcrumbs left all along the trail.

There are great things at stake. Perhaps it is time to fight back in the only way we can: by being prepared for conflict should we encounter a threat and holding our elected officials responsible while we all figure out a long-term solution. Not if but when the day comes that we must protect our loved ones, fellow associates at work, and ourselves, what actions will be taken? And what about mitigation? What preventative measures, if any, can we take right now? Awareness and preparation are more than half the battle, but the proper warrior mindset will set the course.

Do not wait for tragedy to strike. The time to prepare is now. You might be at work and a disgruntled employee enters the facility and starts randomly shooting, or you are home in your bed at night and a group of armed strangers kick in your front door, hastily walking towards your son's bedroom.

Perhaps you are in urban America playing with your children in front of your home and a gang member carelessly shoots up the house of his rival gang who happens to be your neighbor, then turns his gun towards you. Regardless of what threat brings you to the point of being murdered, you are going to either engage the threat or run to fight another day. This is not about being tough. This is about survival and protecting your loved ones.

Remember, law enforcement is expected to help us survive in all these threat environments: an active killer or terrorist incident, crime suppression, prevention, response, and anything in between. At the end of the day, however, it is everybody's problem, no matter where we live, where we work, who we worship, or what color our skin is. We must resolve it together.

Although the political dynamic is vastly different as well as the underlying causes, I cannot with a clear conscience leave the disadvantaged and under-resourced behind, which predominantly are the African American communities of urban America. They have lived with violence for decades in their neighborhoods. Now that the rest of society is getting a taste of what they have always been dealing with for decades, conversations are finally starting to happen. The depleted morale of police officers and the poor funding of law enforcement organizations for training is adding fuel to the fire across the nation, affecting the way they respond to every crime. The tragedy in Uvalde proved this. There is a connection.

Whether you have a gun pointed at your head while driving home from work or watching the newest release at the movie theater, what's the difference? Although the underbelly of each dynamic is very different, the threat should be "neutralized" whichever way it comes. We must push our politicians and lawmakers to take action, and while they are attempting to dig us out of the hole they put us into, we need to learn how to fight fire with fire.

1.2

This ongoing and escalating epidemic of violence in the United States is affecting our communities, our families, and the future of America. This book offers forthright solutions in order to survive these new streets of what used to be the free world. While I was conducting my research for this book, all roads led me to the same place: the media and the corrupt politicians who didn't have the courage to do the right thing as they placed their own ambition before the very society who elected them. Of course, the real question is, who controls them and why?

The world has changed and so should we. How do we protect our interests, our homes, ourselves and our loved ones in this ever-changing and dangerous world? How do you protect your organization, home or family from a lethal threat, and more importantly, if one should occur, are you prepared? Are you willing to stop the threat by any means, or will you be the next victim?

Sure, you think you have a plan that was well thought out, but what about the low man on the ladder in your organization, your wife who works at a hospital, or your son or daughter going away to college next fall? Are they ready? Do they know what to expect should a violent threat occur? You must ensure they are prepared to survive and neutralize the threat if it happens. It's your job to make sure they are.

In May of 2022, an 18-year-old male, entered the Robb Elementary School in Uvalde, Texas, with a rifle and murdered 19 students, 2 teachers, and injured 17 others after barricading himself in a classroom. During this heinous attack, which lasted over one hour and 17 minutes, children called 911 and some called their parents. Some parents even arrived and evacuated their children from the school. The police, who were in the building within minutes, withdrew instead of pushing forward to neutralize the threat, giving the offender more time to barricade himself within a classroom, killing yet more innocent children as well as the wife of one of the responding officers. Border Patrol agents, including their tactical operators, eventually responded and successfully neutralized the threat as well as provided field triage to survivors.

For days, the police community stayed quiet on public platforms, but thankfully the silence was broken within the profession. Nothing is more uncomfortable to a police officer than Monday morning quarterbacking his own. It's painful because we are a brotherhood of warriors. Police officers are modern humans yet operate within a primal and almost extinct realm of existence creating what some call the blue line. It's NOT a normal job, and it takes a special type of person to do it. Many officers, like myself, became police officers to change the world for the better, and little did we know that in time, it would be the world that changes us. What also changes is the way the police respond to these types of attacks.

Department policy and poor training were the key factors in why the local police response was so poor in Uvalde. As a result, the loss of life was inconceivable. Answering these "why" questions is just as important as figuring out what empowered this monster to walk up to the school (which was unlocked) and commit such heinous acts of terror. Let us also add that the shooter shot his grandmother prior to entering the school. Like countless other active killers, the red flags were evident throughout his life, including on social media where he repeatedly threatened women.

Let's be clear: when there is an active shooter within a building or area of operation, the number one priority is to neutralize the threat. There is no need to ask for permission, and policy needs to be thrown out the window.

Nothing replaces good realistic training, instinct, confidence, and a little initiative.

Let us touch on one more active killer incident that happened as I was wrapping up the completion of this book. This was a horrific active killer event amid the long-awaited post-pandemic 4th of July Parade in downtown Highland Park, Illinois, in 2022. Seven lives were lost and at least 36 were wounded on that day.

The lone gunman was a Highland Park, Illinois native, a self-proclaimed rapper with potential ties to radicalized organizations, according to some sources. He had a semiautomatic rifle in his possession that he legally purchased and used a fire escape to climb onto a roof to an elevated fighting position. He then rained hell upon citizens celebrating the Fourth of July parade, 15 minutes after the parade began. At this point, many are speculating why he chose the 4th of July and why the parade. To him, was it symbolic of his distaste for American values, or did he take advantage of the fact that gunshots sometimes sound like fireworks to the untrained ear? A glimpse of the investigation revealed he was possibly infatuated with the numbers 4 and 7, hence July 4th. When the shots rang out, many citizens at the parade thought it was just fireworks.

He temporarily was able to escape, and while this monstrosity was still at large and actively being hunted by law enforcement, I had an opportunity to watch a video that he uploaded previously to a social media platform. The video displayed a professionally edited and cinematic red flag, displaying the intentions that were to play out on this horrible day in great detail.

To me and others who viewed it, it was obvious what his intentions were, although likely he did not know when or where he would fulfill what he called his "destiny." Even more shocking, if it is possible, much of his video was recorded in what looked like a school classroom. This video was chilling, and within a few hours of the shooting, the video was removed by the social media platform **after being available for 8 months**. It is interesting how it was able to slip through the cracks for this long of a period when these same platforms do not hesitate for a moment in violating our First Amendment rights. We all know the answer to that. Why didn't any of the viewers sound the alarm to the authorities?

I would be curious to learn what other social media platforms were host to these red flags, including how many teachers, family members, and friends observed these threats evolve throughout time with the Highland Park active killer and others of the past. You would be surprised how many targeted violent attacks could have been prevented had someone said something.

Later in the day, this offender was apprehended by police officers in the vicinity of North Chicago, Illinois, after a brief vehicle chase. As I was watching the events play out, I thought it was strange that the killer successfully escaped, which told me that he had a well-planned exit strategy. It was later learned that he was disguised as a woman and drove to Madison, Wisconsin to potentially commit another act of terror, as he had in his possession another rifle.

Like every other shooting, it did not take long for the politicians to use this opportunity to politicize the gun control movement. The truth is that if he opted for a vehicle as a weapon, he may have caused even more casualties. It is not the gun. It is the evil pulling the trigger.

What made him act on the 4th and not wait until the fall when school was back in session? It could have been his infatuation with the numbers 4 and 7, however, that would leave another possibility for a spring shooting on the 7th of April, perhaps during a school year.

I believe this and many other questions will be answered in the near future, because unlike many active killers of the past, this attacker survived. With his survival comes the potential for intelligence and for this reason alone, I am hopeful this will help push us in the right direction. We might even get lawmakers to do their job and pressure social media platforms to aggressively monitor the red flags, and report these indicators to the proper authority.

Furthermore, what institutions was he part of and how was their threat assessment plan structured to detect and intervene in order to prevent a targeted violent attack? We must backtrack and figure out where we missed the signs and why these red flags were overlooked by administrators and law enforcement; the truth is, the indicators are almost always there. We will dig deeper into this discussion in Section 4.

The soul of America was once again stained on the very day that gave us our independence. It makes you ask the question of whether we are really free.

The situation in America is out of control, but the one thing I've learned is that everybody is afraid of something, even the bad guys.

1.3

If you told the American public on September 11th, 2001, that 20 years later, our President would make the abrupt decision to pull out of Afghanistan, leaving advanced American armament and military hardware in the hands of those with the ideologies of who attacked us, I believe they would be rightfully infuriated. I know I was. That was a slap in the face to every victim killed in the attack and their family members, including those who bravely served in the armed forces in both Iraq and Afghanistan. Let's not forget the 13 additional warriors killed by the suicide bombing attack during the withdrawal and the 2.9 billion dollars in cash that the UN has generously given to the Taliban since, which is shameful. Those funds would be more useful to assist the homeless veterans across America and Europe who served in that region. We have more control than you think, folks.

We can't erase history. We must not. If the American media made the effort to ensure the public did not forget about these horrible atrocities that the terrorists rained upon our country on September 11th, 2001, the public outcry would not have allowed the Biden administration to make that decision as uncalculated and irresponsibly as it was made. Even some of the more liberal media outlets were embarrassed. Media outlets should not be polarized but they are. Middle of the road, uncompromised centrist thinkers like myself find this extremely frustrating. As divided as our country is and has been, maybe some humility is what we all need to come together finally as one country, one America.

Moving on, these political puppets underestimated the voice of America, which includes the cries of the under-resourced in both urban and rural communities. Historically, it was our differences that made us the amazing country we are. Our ability to agree to disagree is what kept us on track with this experiment called America.

Not only is it open season on the police, but our very way of life is under siege. Our schools, all religions, and communities have been under attack and immensely polarized. I suppose we are expected to step aside and let the sociopath take our life, let certain extreme militant organizations take our home, and let the media and politicians divide our society at the will of a few.

We must lock hands as one nation and one people, regardless of our differences. If we do that, the soil of our land will remain fertile. Of course, when I say soil, I mean the deep-rooted foundation that created the growth of our country and not the farmland bought by the Chinese government to control our food supply. These politicians should understand it's about being the leader that We the People elected them to be.

I have faith in humanity, but there are certain truths you cannot erase, as much as we would like to. If I were to erase only one aspect of history, it would be the substandard leadership that plagued some of these cities during the course of their provoked civil unrest of the recent past, but we cannot! We must remember what and who brought us to this most vulnerable place in time. Hence, should we ever be once again at the crossroads of humanity, we know what we must do.

All storms pass and so will this. **The danger of erasing history is that it allows the wrong people to rewrite it.** History, being unforgiving, will judge us, and as we all know, history does eventually repeat itself if we do not make it a priority to remember it.

The crisis in Ukraine is an example of this. Regardless of your personal views on that conflict, who would have thought the Russians would ever storm their borders and ignite a war in Europe, unearthing memories of humanity's dark past of World War II. This, of course, is the great risk to which we are not immune. The Robb Elementary School shooting in Texas holds this truth as does the symbolic killing in Highland Park, Illinois, on the 4th of July, robbing us of our independence. Both killers embraced mutated and warped ideologies then acted upon them. Seems like war to me, and I am not so sure America is winning.

One of the greatest challenges as a nation is the threat to our democracy. Of course, our adversaries, seen and unseen, pay close attention to this, but so do our closest allies as their sovereignty is dependent on our strength as a nation, our military capabilities, and our leadership.

Yes, the media is powerful, but how deep does this parasite really go? The more unstable our value system, the more opportunity that ideologies far from the ones that created the fabric of our great nation will germinate.

Sometimes the greatest threats are the ones that hide deep within the shadows of our own society. Carefully cultivated extreme ideologies, the demonization of religion, indoctrinating our children with malformed perspectives, the attack on freedom of speech, and the attack on the Second Amendment may very well be our biggest battleground.

At the end of this tribulation of America, and after the few bad souls stop pulling the strings of chaos, we all want the same thing: peace, safety, and a secure future for our loved ones.

These are strange times. American culture has taken a dangerous turn as political aspirations and power struggles have taken precedence over the well-being of its citizens as our adversaries curiously watch.

The quarantine during the Covid-19 pandemic is testament to this. Most people were inside, of course, unless you were burning down cities. When the restrictions eased, we started to see active killers in the headlines again and violent crime reaching an all-time high. As a result, the attack on the Second Amendment was at full speed once again.

You must remember that a law-abiding citizen is going to obey the law, regardless of what he has strapped to his side. The violent criminal, the terrorist, or the active killer will always get his hands on a weapon one way or the other. If it is not a gun, it will be something else that will create the butchery he is seeking. Perhaps we should attempt to ban knives and cars also. With the gas prices in 2022 being what they were, certain political "leaders" were right on course.

1.4

The constant degradation of the police nationwide due to civil unrest has directly affected underprivileged communities and also how they respond to targeted attacks. Crime and active killer attacks are at record highs because it is almost impossible for law enforcement to do their job. Furthermore, the constant demonizing of the police has impacted not only their morale, but the quality of police service in all the communities that they are sworn to protect, and it is frustrating.

Many folks in these urban communities are now realizing that the true suppression stems from decades of inadequate resources, a broken value system in the home, and a consistent lack of police support, all for the purpose of ensuring that coveted vote. These citizens living in the tougher parts of America are worth a hell of a lot more than their vote. This is degrading, but it ensures that the wrong people control where their vote goes.

Regarding defunding the police, who suffers then? The good families in these tougher communities trying to survive these uncertain times would suffer the most, initially. They have always struggled with keeping their children safe, long before the rest of society felt their pain.

Then when the same defunded police organization who patrols their community responds to an active killer in a school on the other side of town, how effective do you think these under-resourced and emotionally drained officers would be at neutralizing the threat? Fund these departments so they can train properly, then support them!

Politics and the media are dangerously affecting the safety of all of us, no matter where we live. Who would have ever fathomed that these factors, as well as the tensions with law enforcement stemming from urban America, would have ever affected how the police respond to an active killer on the other side of the country? My critics doubted my logic, and then Uvalde happened.

Police departments already have a tough time keeping their officers mentally and physically fit, well versed in the law that they must enforce, and proficient with the perfect amount of force under an imperfect political system and under unpredictable circumstances. They are given tools like a firearm, a CEW (like a Taser), chemical spray, and an ASP or a baton (primitive but effective). Then they are expected to deploy those tools within the boundaries of the departments or State's Use of Force modules, usually while somebody is trying to kill them. Then, folks, they are judged. Whereas criminal's rights are handled with white gloves, the police officer who was forced to make a split-second decision will have lost his job within hours while the media invokes chaos at the will of their sponsor's political agenda.

The politicians failed us, but the media—which is the most powerful entity in the world—has put gasoline into the fire, and it is a true indication of how much control can be bought with the blood of innocent people. The old saying goes, "If you control the newspapers, you control the people."

Due to this, police officers are more powerless now than ever, and it is up to the responsibly armed and trained citizen to step forward to fill the gap and hold the line. Furthermore, lawmakers must address the underbelly of targeted violence, no matter where it happens.

Police officers have always been scrutinized; however, the times have changed in other ways. The consequences of police officers making the "wrong" decision could be devastating to them, their family, and eventually, their communities. What is the wrong decision? I have seen police officers, time after time, operate within the set rules and guidelines of their use of force modules within their department policies but still lose their jobs, face suspensions, or be victims of legal or financial proceedings. What do we have now? Politicians are screaming to defund the police and community activists who, instead of attacking the root problems in their communities, criticize the police who in many cases were justified in their actions. Of course, then we are left with insecure, undertrained police officers who are afraid to draw their weapon, enter a building with a purpose, and give the active killer hell, then send him there.

Remember, although possible, it is difficult for a country to deploy their Armed Forces without public support. In a twisted way, police departments operate the same way. Without public support, a police organization will not get the funding they need for good training and resources. Also, its officers will not likely put their hearts and minds into public safety with confidence should a violent crime or active killer event occur. Showing up to the fight is important, however, it's their job to finish it with speed, accuracy, and confidence while being supported by their organization and the community.

Be confident that the violent criminal or active killer is trained and ready to act. As time has proven, you do not have to have a weapon or the space to train for combat. We have video games! Video games are extremely effective in terms of training, within reason. Certain violent games not only dehumanize the value of life, but they "inoculate" the player for conflict. Video games are accessible to everybody, and the quality is so advanced that the military and police utilize them for training, ingrained memory, and stress inoculation. We will get into more detail in Section 2 regarding ingrained memory, stress inoculation, fight or flight, as well as my recommended training strategies needed as hinted above.

Hesitation is dangerous for everybody, but can we really blame them? Officers are judged right after the evening news and most police departments follow suit, relieving the officer of duty pending a criminal investigation. Well, that is until an unqualified and compromised elected official gets involved and oversteps their boundaries, terminating the officer within 24 hours, violating a police union contract, and not allowing the post-shooting investigation to run its course.

There are other risks. That same officer might be in that movie theater or school event with his children or yours when that active killer comes in with guns blazing. What then? Or the officer just received a 10-day suspension because a misguided community activist deemed his use of force inappropriate while neutralizing a violent armed robbery offender. The officers who make split-second decisions and operate within the boundaries of the department's use of force guidelines should always be supported by the department, its supervisors, and citizens in the community. There is always a "gray area" because police officers learn to function under emotional stress and instinct that is mitigated through constant training and their mindset. With seconds to react, sometimes these warriors make mistakes. The poor training resources available to law enforcement contribute extensively to these mistakes.

I'm afraid that departments will have a tougher time finding qualified young officers to take the reins and keep society safe. The veteran officers at this point have had enough and are retiring in droves. Cities will be forced to hire under-qualified young recruits driven by the political environment that brought society to this point in the first place. I already see it happening in many urban police organizations, including Chicago. Quality hiring pools for law enforcement are shrinking at an alarming rate. I am concerned this will pave the path for well-trained private security forces, AI or drone technology strategically placed where we need them. Of course, we all know that the politicians who got us into this situation to begin with will have their own well-funded security protocol set in place, as most already do.

Ultimately, "We the People" will be the ones that will have to protect our loved ones, our friends, and our neighbors whether we like it or not. Within the few years that this book has taken me to write, I have already observed this come to fruition. There has been a shift as armed citizens have stepped up to not only assist officers in need, but swiftly neutralize an active killer during a targeted attack, saving American lives well before first responders arrive.

As many states now allow citizens to carry firearms, I suggest that you not only carry one but become extremely effective in its use. If the day should come and you must decide between life and death, you will be happy you were prepared, and you will go home to your family in one piece. Even if you make it home unscathed, you will never be the same.

Do we really want civilians to be armed and trained well enough to outperform police officers? That has always been controversial. Honestly, most police officers are uncomfortable with it, but we do not really have a choice at this point. The threats are countless, and being surrounded by well-trained citizens has done more good than harm. My opinion has changed from the point I started drafting this book until I completed it as I witnessed the blood of Americans continue to hemorrhage.

Most civilians that carry weapons are capable, law-abiding citizens, and I feel they should be tactically trained to handle modern-day threats. We should not be afraid to train them to neutralize an active lethal threat. As Uvalde proved, the outcome would have been quite different if a civilian were trained well enough to make entry and engage the attacker.

1.5

Let's paint a picture of the world we now live in. Imagine that you are sitting in a meeting with your CEO and other executives going over the business of the day when you suddenly hear gunfire and screaming down the hall. A previously fired employee and now active killer is interested in expressing his deepest feelings to the CEO with an M4 carbine rifle. As the sound of gunfire gets closer, your heart beats faster, you lose your hearing and fall due to your knees buckling, noticing several of your coworkers now at eye level with you, huddled under the table attempting to hide. You grab your mobile device but realize that your fine motor skills have diminished, and you are not able to dial 911. You see your assistant frozen as if time has stopped. Unbeknownst to you, she is unable to move out of fear, and for her, time did stop. You are now helpless as the memories of your children run through your head and you realize you may have only seconds to live.

Luckily, your colleague and mother of two, while in her unlocked office, was able to call 911 and tell the dispatcher that there was an active shooter in the building before being discovered by the killer and executed with her mobile phone in hand, orphaning her children. Unfortunately, when the under-gunned (and under-trained) first responders arrive, you might be dead.

The leaders of the organization probably didn't think about the down and dirty details if an attack like this were to occur. Making sure that the building or entry point is secure may have helped. The truth is, however, regardless of how detailed the plan is, extraordinarily little can prepare untrained citizens, and even the police, for that type of chaos. An armed, off-duty National Guardsmen and company executive who was carrying a firearm concealed at work that day may have neutralized this threat immediately if given the chance. We cannot predict something like this happening, but we can prepare and educate ourselves on the different scenarios and the best course of action should one ever occur.

If the organization does not include a balanced TAARS plan, then the organization, regardless of whether it is a company, school, hospital, church, or even a police department, will not survive the moment, not to mention get the organization or community back on track.

The company, and even the police, may very well be liable for the death or injury of citizens who may never make it back to their families because proper procedures were not established and practiced while the politicians point the finger across the aisle.

I understand that the scenario described above is disturbing, however, I can assure you of a few things. By the end of this book, you will be in a better position to not only identify indicators left by a potential attacker well before it gets to that point, but you will have the confidence to stop the attack by either deploying deadly force with or without a firearm, and at the very least, place yourself and others in a better position to survive.

Making sure that every staff member, officer, family member, executive or teacher understands the TAARS plan is important, but even more so, being able to function during and after the disaster is crucial. This includes active killer training drills using actual simulation and the strategies discussed in Sections 2 and 4.

Keep in mind that there is a 3–10-minute window from the time the police are called until they arrive, and when they arrive it will become even more violent. Until we get a grasp on this epidemic plaguing America, I have the first recommendation of many: do not be a victim. Become a warrior whether you are armed or not.

Where do you start? Start with your mindset. Oh, and start training with a firearm, including tactically, and then start carrying it. If you are more of the passive type or are against firearms, the sections ahead offer valuable insight that can increase the chances of your survivability and those you love. Remember, neutralizing a lethal threat during a targeted attack is imperative, but merely mends the underlying issues, which must also be addressed. This is a multilayered problem that requires multiple approaches, which we will discuss ahead in the book. This problem is a tough one and is impossible to solve with a blanket solution.

The world has changed. It will continue to change, and we must change with it. We can only speculate—as I do through experience—why these violent crimes and active killings occur, but there is hope, as several NTAC studies have indicated.

These tragedies are not about gun control because if an active killer wants to wreak havoc, he or she will find a way. You do not need a firearm to kill people. Look at the tragedy in Waukesha, Wisconsin, in November 2021 during a Christmas parade. The offender, who had an extensive criminal history, drove an SUV into a crowd of people, killing six and injuring 62.

Let's also look at the incident at Ohio State University in 2016. The terrorist drove his vehicle into his targets, then exited and began to stab the stunned students until neutralized by a police officer. He was a terrorist with an extreme ideology who had the desire to hurt Americans. This type of targeted violence and warfare will continue to happen. Sure, he used a knife, but what if he had entered the country undetected through the southern border and had the ability to build explosive devices, a skill he acquired whilst fighting against our troops overseas? It is possible, and I can assure you, adversaries with such knowledge have already made their way here. They understand war because they have been in war. They also understand that Americans feel immune and distant to the possibility of such atrocities, which gives these terrorists a clear tactical advantage.

Listen closely, people. The bad guys will always find some type of weapon or way to do harm. Do not feed into the politics of the gun control argument. Guns do not kill people. People kill people. I can certainly understand the desire to keep our society safe. However, taking guns away from law abiding, trained citizens is not the answer. Another critical point to understand is that although an attack may be carried out by methods other than a firearm, the only viable force option may be that of a firearm to quickly neutralize the threat, which could be a knife, a car, or an explosive device. In fact, due to the tougher protocols set in place to acquire a firearm, it would almost make sense to plan the attack by other means to stay off the radar and avoid exposing the plan, terrorist cell, or associates. We will leave the conversation there, but you understand my point.

If the motivation to commit murder or violence against citizens is there, they will find the means to do so. That aside, criminals will always have access to firearms if they take the time to look for them. Firearms are extremely easy to find on the street, the black market, or to 3D print with the right knowledge. They do not care about the gun laws because they have other things on their agenda, like selling drugs, committing acts of terror, murder, armed robbery, planning targeted violence, and protecting their gang turf so the drug enterprise can keep cash flowing within the shadows of certain communities.

In Section 3, we take a deeper dive into the 2nd Amendment, but I feel that well-trained, law-abiding citizens should be able to protect themselves, their family, and their community during a deadly lethal threat.

With regards to background checks, I get it. I understand it does not seem fair. I mean, if a bad guy could carry a weapon without the background checks and proper credentials, why should the rest of us bother? This argument has been long debated. In the recent past, many states have evened the playing field, creating more pathways for citizens to carry firearms, thereafter, turning the wolves into prey.

1.6

There have been many incidents when armed citizens have intervened, saving the lives of police officers who have been either disarmed, outgunned, or losing the fight. In 2017, an Arizona State Trooper was ambushed while responding to a call. The offender fired multiple times at the officer, striking him in the chest and shoulder, causing his right arm and dominant hand to become incapacitated. The hero citizen who was driving by the scene observed the offender smashing the officer's head into the ground repeatedly. The citizen then pulled to the side of the road and obtained his firearm. The offender, who did not obey the citizen's verbal command to stop, was immediately terminated by the citizen, ridding the world of this evil soul. The good citizen saved the officer's life and likely more lives thereafter that the offender had not yet had the opportunity to take. I have learned that if a person is able to take an officer's life, or at least try, then they can kill anybody.

Police officers in the field cannot lose a physical altercation because that could result in the officer being disarmed of their firearm and ultimately their death and possibly others. This also applies to the fine American bearing arms, and due to this, some retention training as well as tactical training under stress should also be strongly encouraged, if not required.

In 2017, in rural southeastern Indiana, an armed citizen observed a man attempting to disarm an officer during a struggle. The citizen fired one round, striking the offender, who later died at the hospital. Thankfully, the citizen was cleared of all criminal charges from the State's Attorney but was eventually sued civilly by the family of the offender. This good citizen saved the officer from getting disarmed and likely killed with his own weapon. The toxicology report of the offender revealed he was under the influence of narcotics during the time of the incident. Unfortunately, this hero citizen didn't have insurance or protection in place, but thankfully the case against her was dropped in 2019.

I hear stories like this from time to time, and I can't stress enough how important it is to have the proper protection in place should a shooting occur. Making the decision to engage a violent offender, especially while assisting a police officer who is on the verge of losing his life, in my opinion, is nothing short of amazing. Just protect yourself along the way. Understand the use of force parameters, train hard, and yes, explore the legal protective options that work for you! In terms of insurance options, I encourage you to explore USCCA, US LawShield or CCW safe, which are the bigger players in the industry. An alternative to a policy would be an organization like the Armed Citizens Legal Defense Network, which has a different approach that is worth checking out.

Moving on, keep in mind that law-abiding, armed citizens also have several advantages over criminals in respect to carrying a firearm. One advantage is that they can practice openly (at the range or a safe, designated area, of course) without conviction and without always looking over their shoulder wondering if they will get caught by the authorities. They can also have accessibility to numerous tactical classes taught by experienced professionals to enhance their firearm skills and confidence. The most important advantage, however, is the element of surprise. Most active killers, terrorists, and violent criminals would not expect a well-trained and armed citizen to engage in combat with them. How many times have we seen an active shooter commit suicide before the police confront him?

The clear disadvantage to the good citizen is that the active killer has absolutely no intention of losing the fight and may already expect to die during the engagement one way or the other. The violent criminal, likely a habitual criminal, also has nothing to lose as he would be sent back to prison, violating his parole or probation. Two clearly different mindsets that are both extremely dangerous.

How do you confront such evil who is mentally prepared to do you harm and has absolutely no intention of losing? The short answer is that you must transform yourself into a warrior!

1.7

The worst thing in life is to take another life, no matter the circumstances. It is ugly, violent, and goes against our nature. The bad guy does not hesitate to harm or kill his prey. For us, this does not come naturally. Regardless, we must train to be more lethal than our adversary. Ironically, violence is also what gave us our freedom in 1776. Nations and people with radical ideals have been trying to take it away ever since.

Prior to a lethal encounter, you must make the decision to survive and prevail during a violent engagement before that day comes. In other words, consciously give yourself permission to engage an attacker should the moment ever present itself and thoroughly understand the lethal force authorized under the federal, state, and local laws.

Make peace with it. If you are a law enforcement officer, your organization will have a use of force protocol, which would allow you to use other less lethal force options if deadly force is not appropriate. If you work for a good law enforcement organization—and they have a backbone—they will stand by you if you were within the use of force guidelines specified.

The world is rapidly changing, and I feel the use of deadly force to preserve life is becoming increasingly accepted and supported by American society. In the past, these opinions were frowned upon, but times are changing, and people are becoming more desperate for action. The rapidly increasing crime rates, the ongoing active killer phenomenon, and the incline in terrorist attacks, domestically and worldwide, are all affecting the way we live, work, and play.

I was recently at a local grocery store, and I overheard a man saying that he was flying to Spain with his wife and was in the process of updating his will in case he was killed overseas by terrorists. Likely, tourists coming to America from other countries are equally as concerned with the active killer events as these tragedies are covered by media outlets worldwide.

Be conscious of the fact that the active killer epidemic is a global problem, not just in America. How would gun control advocates justify their position here in the United States if the active killer incidents involving firearms were happening in countries that had an incredibly low gun ownership base?

In today's America, as I have hinted, the underlying problems are obscured to the naked eye, but the most dangerous threats are closer than you think. How quickly we forget the past. Radical Islamic terrorism used to be public enemy number one in America. Give it time, folks, because you may be stunned if you knew how many radicalized "citizens" and poorly vetted immigrants who are on the terrorist watch list are living within our communities, driving our streets, learning our vulnerabilities, shopping at our grocery stores, and living next door. If that man I spoke to in that grocery store knew what I knew, he would most definitely move to Spain.

This is a disgrace to the wonderful immigrants of all religions that want a peaceful life and the American Dream, many of whom are my closest friends. Radical terrorists are not only embedded deep within America but across Europe, Asia, and the globe. When the time is right, these radical terrorists, foreign or domestic, homegrown, or inserted, will strike once again. And believe me when I tell you, they are here to stay.

Although I am limited in how much I can discuss, I will say that I have been in their homes while working in law enforcement and they were intentionally positioned within proximity of the most casualty-producing vantage points in the nation. Do not be disillusioned and think that our next attack will be with an airplane.

The FBI, the nation's premier law enforcement agency, has been under some intense scrutiny, and for good reason. However, most of these brave men and women are dedicated patriots and are the front line of defense against these types of attacks, among other threats to our nation. The scrutiny, of course, involves the recent controversy of redirecting investigative resources and manpower in places like the Catholic church or with parents who voice strong, influential, or opposing opinions.

At first glance, this is concerning, but with the limited information available to the public and the scope of these investigations unknown, I will remain neutral. Being raised Roman Catholic myself, I will say that getting chased by an irate nun for stealing the wine before mass is terrifying, but that's a story for another time!

I will, however, add one more component, and this is regarding domestic terrorists. They are just as dangerous, with a hell of a lot more firepower and should not be underestimated as the Oklahoma City bombing proved in 1995 after 168 American citizens were maliciously killed.

The border crisis is a horrible problem in many different respects, but you rarely hear anything about terrorists mixing in with these illegal immigrants during the border crossings, which has happened for years. Now, with the migrant crisis amidst, violent encounters with American citizens and the police have skyrocketed, adding yet another layer of uncertainty in major cities across the country, stretching resources past their capacity.

Yes. Terrorists successfully infiltrate the United States, undetected from the southern border with the support of the cartels. So, if the fentanyl is not bad enough, known criminal organizations are facilitating the infiltration of radicalized terrorists as well as military aged men from adversarial countries, like China, who wish to destroy our country from the inside out, buy our farms and control our food, medicine, and economy. Who needs a Trojan Horse when you can just walk through the back door, or in many cases, the front?

Do not think for a second that a terrorist cell within the United States is not taking notes and observing the active killer events and how it destroys the very souls of Americans. Ultimately, our destruction is really what they want. All I will say is that it will not be easy for them, however, recently in the Fall of 2024 as this book is being published, such planned attacks have been detected and prevented by law enforcement. According to the FBI, an ISIS-planned mass attack was foiled and was to take place on Election Day in 2024. You must understand that these attacks are easy to plan, but hard to detect. Law enforcement has their hands full and from the looks of it, so do the rest of us!

Ironically, other than mentioning this last planned attack by ISIS on Election Day, I wrote this segment of my book well over two years ago! No, I do not have a crystal ball, but the clues are hiding in plain view so pay close attention to the world around us! Yes. The indicators are everywhere, as well as our adversaries, so be prepared.

Even more frightening, if a cyberattack occurs in conjunction with an organized attack, it can simultaneously isolate not only citizens, but those responsible for taking action from the first responders to the country's leadership. Sure, ISIS may or may not be capable of a cyberattack, but their handlers, Iran, is more than able to. If such a coordinated attack occurs, who are we left with? Well, it might be you, your training and your organization's protocols. So be prepared for this rarely discussed possibility.

1.8

Stand up, people, and live your lives, but let those who want to hurt you know that if they try to, you will respond in kind, as it may be the only language they understand.

On this note, I would like to discuss one last incident which took place in July of 2022 at a mall in Greenwood Park, Indiana, where one young man stood up and became the "blue line." An active killer entered the mall and proceeded to a bathroom near the food court in order to assemble at least one assault-style rifle. Upon assembling the rifle, this disturbed nonhuman exited the bathroom and opened fire in the food court, killing three innocent citizens. A lawfully armed citizen, under the Constitutional Carry Law, drew his firearm, positioned himself behind good cover, and at 40 meters, fired 10 rounds, ridding the world of this disturbed killer (with 8 rounds on target), saving the lives of many. As this citizen was moving towards cover, he was motioning for citizens to seek a safer position, while he simultaneously engaged the killer. This fine man's actions saved countless lives.

The killer came prepared to inflict carnage, and the hero citizen came mentally prepared to stop him and did within two minutes. It was later learned that the killer had in his possession two assault-style rifles, one pistol, and at least 100 rounds of ammunition. The investigation at first glance did not show a social media trail as many killers have done in the past. Further investigation revealed that he not only had a presence on a popular social media forum but displayed a strong interest in other past active killer events on the platform, with a particular interest in firearms and Nazism.

Like in that Indiana mall, civilians who legally carry firearms will become the new frontline and first responders. They will be the new frontline of safety and the primary deterrent of this growing epidemic in this country, whether it is an active killer in a mall, an armed robbery in urban America, or a terrorist opening fire on a church or school. You must start somewhere. Start here. Then transform.

With that being said, welcome aboard, Mr. (or Mrs.) Citizen, you just made that thin blue line a little thicker.

SECTION TWO

DUTY CALLS: THE RISE OF THE WARRIOR

2.1

The journey begins. We never know where the battle will take us, but our training may just be the only thing that gets us home. In the midst of potential conflict, there are no guarantees. Those warriors whose job it is to keep the wolves at bay know this. They also know it's worth the risk. Why would a mortal take such a dangerous, thankless, and underpaying job? Many police officers are some of the most intelligent, educated, capable, and bravest souls I have ever met. Law enforcement was likely not their only career option.

For most of us, wearing the badge was a choice, fueled by the hopes of making the world a better place. After time, it was the world that changed us, one way or the other. Navigating through man's wicked disregard for his fellow homo sapiens is bad enough, but then coming home to your family with a smile and pretending the world is rainbows and butterflies is the tough part. While walking out the door to go to work, the thought is always there of not returning and it always makes you hug your children a little harder. Without the proper training and mindset, that very thought of mortality and hesitation may get yourself, your partner, or others around you killed that you were sworn to protect.

If and when we make it back home, we are never the same. This is the quest of the modern-day warrior that is sworn to protect us. The warrior in blue is spat on, ambushed, and ridiculed on a daily basis by society then they are demonized as one by an ignorant few when they fight back or when they don't. This undertaking is also now carried by every American citizen of modern America, one way or the other. So, at this point, we have an idea of how we got to this dangerous place in time. The question is, where do we go from here?

The act of pulling the sword from the stone is the easy part. Using it effectively in a lethal engagement is a different story. Not all warriors are alike, and our journey to such an awesome responsibility takes time. Some are well-trained while others are not. Some are extremely physically fit, and some are not. Some run in the direction of gunfire and others run the other way. The three truths in my mind that they all have in common are that they are limited by the confines of their mortality (they can die), their training dictates how effectively they respond, and their mindset either flies the craft or crashes it.

This section will create a pathway to warriorship and lay out the foundation to help you navigate in that direction. Whether you engage an active lethal threat during an attack or run the other way, you may still have to get past a bad guy with a weapon trying to orphan your children.

Give yourself permission to respond when engaged with an active lethal threat. When you strap that firearm to your side, whether you are law enforcement or a civilian lawfully carrying concealed, make the conscious decision to use it should the reaper arrive. If you engage an active killer or another lethal threat, you need to inflict a greater amount of violence upon the offender than he has projected upon you or others during the event, whether you are armed or not. I know this sounds horrible, and it is. For many, fighting isn't always the answer. At times, a more viable option is avoiding the threat when the exit is right in front of you. There is no right answer because every circumstance is different. Most do not have the luxury of choosing, but police officers must push forward. That's their job. Threat interdiction must be executed with speed, while aggressively pushing forward and inflicting a greater amount of violence than the bad guy is inflicting.

The warrior, in any capacity, is expected to win in every threat environment. No matter how powerful the opponent seems, the true warrior understands that everyone has a weakness and losing is not an option because that means death or serious injury. Winning at all costs is the driving force of the warrior. The bridge to winning is preparation and the regimens set in place along the way.

Soldiers, depending on their job function, and police officers, are trained mentally and physically to function within this capacity. They understand their human limitations, and for a brief time during conflict, they set those limitations aside to do their job.

They make physical training a part of their daily ritual. They mentally conjure up scenarios of possible threats and then mentally or physically solve how they would react to them through training. Then they train, train, and then train some more until it is second nature. The idea behind constant training, or drills, is to be able to react or perform on autopilot under stress. They also understand how their body reacts under conflict and learn to function at levels that still allow them to maximize the use of their body, mind, and firearm, putting emotion to the side while lowering their heart rate. Warriors understand emotion will poison their logic and performance. Succumbing to the emotional, physical, and psychological effects of conflict may even get them or others around them killed. It will prevent them from focusing on their mission and even walking, shooting, thinking, or driving straight. This can be terrifying and deadly if the proper foundation and training regimen is not executed. Conflict is the gift that keeps on giving, even after the event. The foundation needs to be strong, balanced, and maintained at all times.

2.2

Prepare yourself to engage a lethal threat in any capacity. How you engage the threat is influenced by training, and staying in the fight is dictated by your mindset.

Have a plan and start with yourself. We all have tight schedules but try to stay in shape. Perhaps start off taking brisk walks and increase the intensity from there. Meditate in whichever way you feel comfortable. Both exercise and meditation will help you sleep better as well. Sleep deprivation will slow your reaction time and hamper your logic in every aspect of your life, regardless of the circumstances.

Also, it is important that you practice breathing. Tactical breathing exercises allow you to lower your heart rate and blood pressure in case you are wounded. The faster your heartbeat and blood pressure, the faster you will succumb to your wound. Meditative breathing is important in terms of self-awareness and preparation, but tactical breathing, which we will discuss ahead, is imperative during conflict and will save your life.

Take a self-defense class. This country is host to an amazing amount of talent that brings an array of martial arts styles from all over the world. Learn the basics of fighting as this may come in handy during lethal or non-lethal situations.

Learn how to shoot, even if you are against the use of firearms. You may find yourself in a situation that will require you to fire a weapon, and if that is the only way you can get home to see your smiling children again, or even save them, you will be glad you set your personal views to the side in order to survive!

In recent years, citizens in Chicago and other unsuspecting communities nationwide have been granted the opportunity to carry a handgun with the proper licensing. As I have stressed in Section 1, the training is not extensive enough, and the average person in times of conflict cannot even use their mobile device to call 911. God help the untrained soul who draws on an armed home invader or active killer. The good citizen would be lucky if he managed to pull his weapon out flawlessly and successfully engage his target without the proper training. On the contrary, I have stood next to the worst (and the best) shooters known in my lifetime during the qualification courses on the police gun range. In short, go to the range and practice. Tactical classes are a valuable tool and widely available to the public. I would encourage police officers to do the same, even if off duty.

Many police departments do not have aggressive training programs available for the patrol officers for a variety of reasons, such as lack of funding, poor leadership, political influences, "defund the police" movements, or allocation of resources, to name a few. This is especially true with smaller police departments. The danger is clear because it is these patrol officers who will usually be the first responders on scene during a targeted attack. An active killer's assault during a targeted attack is over within minutes, so seconds count. Waiting for a specialized unit to arrive can take time which may cost lives, as we learned in Uvalde. Every patrol officer should be trained just as well as any tactical member, including aggressive threat interdiction tactics and field triage for gunshot wounds or other skills needed during or after a lethal engagement. I truly feel that active killer tactical response training, aggressive tactical firearms, and gunshot triage as well as annual physical fitness tests should be mandated for law enforcement nationwide.

Emergency medical services, or EMS, will not be allowed to enter and offer assistance until the pending threat is no longer present in the area of operation so it's important that police officers have enough knowledge to sustain life under certain conditions.

2.3

The personal attributes of a warrior are intriguing. Warriors seem to have a certain type of primal personality. They understand that successfully functioning within this realm is a lifestyle. This transformation does not happen overnight, however. I will sound like a broken record when I say that developing a consistent training routine is crucial. A young police recruit has all the time in the world to train, but life happens. Kids, side jobs, and a spouse can really take time and energy away from the training. **It's interesting how, as our life progresses with family or other responsibilities, we don't make the time for the one thing that can get us back home again.** Make training a priority, no matter where life takes you.

When I say lifestyle, it's not just the tactical or firearm aspect of training. For me, preparation encompassed a holistic approach that included intense physical exercise including cardio, routine tactical training sessions, meditation, nutrition, and sleep. This sounds great when you are young and single without the responsibilities of life. Aside from life responsibilities, our body changes with age, injuries, or chronic stress. Adjust as you need to and ensure you develop or maintain the skills you need to engage and survive a lethal threat.

Striving for a balanced approach will not only transform you into a warrior, but it will improve your overall health and quality of life. The confidence from this transformation affects other parts of your life, not just in conflict. The person sizing you up will pay attention to how you carry yourself, looking for weaknesses and the opportunity to cause harm to you, your family, or community.

We all work somewhere. Most of us love to go to the movie theater. At times, we need to go grocery shopping, sit in stop and go traffic, or buy clothes at the mall or outlets. As we go about our everyday life, please understand that most people are small fish in a sea of sharks or, as some have described, sheep in the midst of wolves. The very interesting but true fact is most sheep know who the protectors are. Do not think for a second that the wolves do not know, too. Sometimes that is enough to keep them at bay. Other times it's not and action is imperative. I'd like to share two examples of this happening to me personally while off duty.

I used to live in a high-rise building off of Lakeshore Drive in Chicago. The building had a pool, and there was a very nice couple in their mid-80s that I used to speak to in passing from time to time. Nobody knew I was a police officer because this was not considered an area that would normally support the police unless they needed them. Because of that, very few residents knew what I did for a living.

One day, I was in the pool swimming and a genuinely nice elderly woman and Holocaust survivor asked loudly across the crowded pool if I was a police officer. I became slightly defensive yet still polite, immediately asking why she would ask that. She replied with, "Because you look like a protector." I chuckled and said, no but thank you for the compliment. I was not the only confident man at the pool that day in extremely good physical shape, but I could not fool her. Still suspicious, she swam in one direction, and I took a nosedive underwater in the opposite.

Another example of this happened right down the block from that building when I was coming home from work and decided to get gas for my car. An aggressive citizen was walking from car-to-car shouting at people, and then when he passed me, I glanced at him, and his eyes widened with a stunned look on his face. He told me I was "either a police officer or I'm crazy!" He then walked off while looking over his shoulder at me as I was pumping gas into my car.

Some who know me would argue this fine citizen was right on both accounts, although I must admit it takes a certain type of person to take the job. It is a thankless, underpaying job, but when duty calls, most answer it.

Confidence is important because it is a key ingredient when engaging an active killer or even causing a violent criminal to bypass you to look for a weaker, feebler target. Keep this in mind as we move forward.

Mental, emotional, and physical balance is crucial, and mindset takes the lead. Some would argue over which is more important: mindset or training. Confidence is part of one's mindset in any circumstance. Sometimes confidence can be the very thing that will help us avert conflict in the first place. When conflict does occur, especially a lethal encounter, your training will take over and then your mindset will give you the resilience to endure the engagement or survive it. This delicate balance is essential to prevail during and after conflict.

This balance, as well as training, mitigates the strange things that happen to our mind and bodies when stress plays a factor, as police officers and soldiers already know. Under the stress of conflict or a targeted attack, one may temporarily lose hearing or see "tunnel vision." The elevated heart rate will affect the fine motor skills, among other things, needed for effectively deploying a weapon system and making sound decisions. You may experience the engagement in slow motion and have a very different perspective of what happened after the event. Your eyes may dilate or develop a keener field of vision.

These are all attributes of the fight and flight response, better known as Acute Stress Response, which dates back to our more primal past as humans. We will dig deeper into this section about the stress response and how to mitigate this to effectively engage or survive a lethal threat. As stated earlier, the answer is not always to fight, depending on your proximity to the threat, your function, your ability to engage, and other factors.

In Section 1, I mentioned an incident that occurred in November of 2016 at Ohio State University. Ohio State University sent out an alert via Twitter stating, "Buckeye Alert: Active shooter on Campus. Run, hide, or fight. Watts Hall. 19th and College." Not all souls are created equal in the ability to do any or all of the three, and my guess is that the brave person who sent the tweet knew that.

Just prior to that Tweet being sent out to students and staff, a Somalian radical Islamic terrorist and student used his vehicle to plow through a group of people. The terrorist then exited the vehicle and began to stab whomever he was able to until he was shot and killed by a police officer. As a side note, I was shocked when I heard a faculty member, who was struck by the vehicle, had stated to the media not to judge until we knew what the whole story was. Understanding every piece of the puzzle is crucial, yes, but this is an example of how much tolerance many Americans have for this type of threat, even after he had been almost killed. If our countrymen can forget the horrific attack on September 11, 2001, then they can forget anything, as the botched withdrawal from Afghanistan proved.

The police officer, being the trained warrior he was, took action, eliminated the threat, and prevented more harm to the students and loss of life. He was also well versed in the amount of force needed and authorized. The terrorist regretted bringing a knife to a gunfight, but at the end of the day, things fell into place, and we had one less terrorist to worry about. This is a good example of how sometimes a firearm is the only way to stop a non-firearm inflicted targeted attack.

Figure 2A
Courtesy of Dr. Ron Martinelli

That aside, never underestimate the deadliness of a knife. Knife wounds are devastating, and it takes seconds for an assailant to charge and lethally strike a potential victim or officer, leaving little time to respond. Creating distance is crucial while giving verbal commands to stop while clearing your holster and stopping the threat if he continues to aggress forward. We will touch on this further in Section 3.

I know we are jumping ahead a little as Section 3 and some of Section 4 will talk about the basics of deadly force (keeping in mind that all states have different laws). What is consistent is the scrutiny, whether a civilian or a police officer deploys his firearm. With the nation giving praise to the hero who neutralized the active killer in that Indiana mall, I am hopeful that we are on the right track.

2.4

Let us briefly talk about running or fighting. Also, be mindful that hiding is usually not a good option for reasons that we will discuss ahead. I will repeat, however, that if there is an active killer attack taking place, priority number one for a police officer or trained civilian is to neutralize the immediate deadly threat in any way possible.

For those who are protectors and trained to engage in conflict, running can be hard, if at all even possible. Remember, part of being a warrior is knowing when to fight. That is, if you even have the luxury of choosing. Most people do not. This is why preparation is so important. We never know what will happen after walking out the door.

If the tables were turned and an off-duty police officer had a knife and the assailant had a gun, unless the officer was cornered or had a tactical advantage to use the knife, maybe a better option would be to call the on-duty police in order to provide intelligence to the responding officers or help others escape. This depends on the circumstances, of course. Remember, weaponizing our resources is at times necessary. Not everyone carries a firearm, and a little improvisation goes a long way.

Perhaps the off-duty officer is with his family and his first thought is to relocate them and then engage the offender or retrieve his firearm from the glove box of his car (regretfully). Proper information and intelligence can sometimes be as important as engaging the threat, although in the middle of an active shooter event, engagement and eliminating the killer should be priority number one. We want to eliminate the threat and not give the monster time to barricade himself in a stronger fighting position with hostages or victims in need of immediate medical assistance. Giving him time to think or kill more innocent victims is not an option.

Systematically pushing forward while engaging him with speed and a greater level of violence is necessary. Keep in mind that many active killer situations in the past have been lone shooters, but there is always a chance there are more threats including additional gunmen or explosive devices and traps. The immediate threat may be terminated, but it does not mean that there are not more around the corner. Breathe, keep focused and scan the area of engagement with your finger off the trigger, unless you are highly trained, because mistakes happen under stress. "On trigger, on target" is the safest practice with the business end of your weapon up and forward, ready to engage any deadly threat while advancing onward. This, accompanied with the proper **real-world** training and mindset, will ensure the first responder has the confidence to neutralize the active lethal threat during such a targeted attack. Armed citizens are not exempt from this expectation.

2.5

If you are a civilian and carry a concealed weapon, chances are you applied for a permit within your state, following whatever procedure is required. Some states offer Constitutional Carry, which we will get into in Section 3. In Illinois, there is a list of requirements including 16 hours of training which includes classroom and range instruction. It is a two-day course in two, eight-hour blocks of instruction. The first day may consist of the basics of marksmanship, weapons safety, fundamentals of use of force, weapon maintenance and storage. The second day would consist of more use of force instruction, some dry fire, live fire exercises, and then a qualification course. Many of these instructors are very experienced professionals who understand the value of having extensive tactical training. Prior military or law enforcement usually would be able to waive the second eight-hour block of training.

As of 2024, these are the basic requirements in Illinois that will allow a citizen to carry a weapon on their person. I feel that tactical, retention and inoculation training should also be included as well as understanding what happens to the human body during conflict, or the Acute Stress Response. **Your proficiency with a firearm is absolutely useless if you cannot manage and push through the effects of the fight or flight response.**

Times are changing, and professional modern-day warriors have the tools and training available at their fingertips to mitigate the effects of the body during the Acute Stress Response. The knowledge of these primal gifts of ancient man that are handed down from our ancestors is indispensable. Experiencing these effects during conflict without knowing they can happen is terrifying and deadly. Now, there are numerous opportunities for civilians to have the same advanced training which was historically exclusive only to law enforcement and the military.

How many times in the past have soldiers and police officers stated that if they only knew what to expect in conflict that they not only would have performed better during the engagement, but they would have been more prepared to recover emotionally and physically afterwards. Let us take a deeper dive into humans in relation to the fight or flight response, stress inoculation, ingrained memory, and strategies to help mitigate the effects and succeed during an active lethal threat.

As said earlier, the body goes through several changes during lethal conflict or an aggressive confrontation. An accelerated heart rate, loss of fine motor skills, blurred vision, tunnel vision, loss of bowel or bladder control and the inability to take decisive action are just a few things that can happen. Let us add the dilated pupils, the hearing loss, the shaking and dry mouth, and our earthbound bodies become the very thing that can get us or people around us killed. Oh, did I say everything can happen in slow motion also? Yes, let's prolong the misery even more! How ever did our prehistoric brothers in arms, or spears, do this?

Hyperarousal, or Acute Stress Response, is more commonly known as "fight or flight" response. It was first described by Walter Bradford Cannon who stated that, "animals react to threats through a general discharge of the Sympathetic Nervous System, preparing the animal to "fight or flight." In modern times, it is generally agreed that there are about five responses that humans go through during conflict. We will dive deeper into this ahead.

When I was an extremely new police officer with just months on the street, I, as well as other police units, responded to a call of a "disturbance with a mentally disturbed citizen," as they called it. Upon arriving, we spoke to a woman who said that her son, who was about 40 years old, was in the basement and off his medications. Myself and another officer proceeded down the stairs into the basement, and we were greeted by a screaming man who was pacing back and forth while very agitated. Our objective at that point was to transport him to the hospital so he could take his meds.

In the back of my mind, I felt my prior military experience, along with my limited police skills at the time, would help me get through most situations until I learned the long-term skills needed to survive the streets. I could not have been more wrong.

The other officer tried to calm him down but without success. This disturbed man then lunged at me with a box cutter. Most experienced officers would have used deadly force at that point, but I opted for my chemical spray. I sprayed him twice as he laughed, then he turned around whilst he swung the box cutter aimlessly in all directions, preventing us from getting close to handcuff him. He hastily walked a few feet to a table where he picked up a can of spray deodorant and a lighter. At that moment, I suddenly faded off into space, recalling my childhood from the 1980s. Like every member of the Gen-X community, we raised ourselves from unusually young ages, jumped ramps that we set on fire as Evel Knievel did and survived by drinking water from garden hoses. We also made flamethrowers out of lighters and cans of deodorant! As I abruptly snapped back into reality, that's when things got hot, and my fight or flight response kicked in. Being a newer officer, I was not confident to deploy deadly force upon a citizen under unusual circumstances like this. I assumed the veteran officer, who was using me as cover, felt the same.

Suddenly, the makeshift flamethrower screamed overhead within inches of my hair, and my fine motor skills were diminishing. At that point, I would have been justified, once again, to use deadly force with my firearm as we were in danger of death or great bodily injury, but the only thing I was able to see clearly was the exit.

The other officer screamed at me, asking what we should do, and I said, "Run like hell" as we ran up the stairs and out the door. SWAT (Special Operations) eventually responded and successfully resolved the situation. The next day, a commander called down to my district to commend me personally for my use of restraint and professionalism. I was not sure what hurt more, my ego or the singe marks on the back of my head. All I know is that the department was incredibly happy that I did not shoot him.

I played that event in my head over and over. My limited experience on the street and my lack of confidence in using deadly force against an offender with a weapon other than a firearm made me second guess myself. Lacking confidence during life-or-death circumstances can get the warrior killed. That was the first and last day I ever ran from a fight.

2.6

Another example from my past on the street with the Chicago Police Department was when I was assigned to what they call the Mission Team. The Mission Team was a plain clothes detail where newer officers are attached to a violent crimes detective unit which gives them an opportunity to work in a more aggressive capacity, gaining valuable investigative and tactical skills.

While I was assigned to this unit, I had the dismay of returning to that district on the southeast side of Chicago where I was initially assigned out of the academy. While roving the district in a covert car, working on an unrelated case, we observed some uniformed officers on a traffic stop with two gang members in front of their squad car. Their hands were on the hood, and they were being interviewed by the officers conducting the stop. I recognized the officers on scene and as always, we slowed down, exited our vehicle, and provided back up. Based upon what the gang members were wearing, I assumed they were part of a certain gang.

During the street interview I was having with this gang member, rapid gunfire started roaring from an undisclosed, elevated location. It wasn't uncommon to hear gunfire within our proximity as gang members were always shooting at each other, but I soon realized we were being ambushed. As the shots rang out, I heard the buzzing of multiple gun rounds whiz past my head and torso in slow motion. The sounds of the gunfire then became silent as I drew my weapon, looking for a target while seeking cover behind our vehicle. Within about a minute, the gunfire stopped, and we observed the shooter jump from a garage and run. We immediately gave chase while I felt the adrenaline pumping through my veins and felt like my legs were like Jell-O.

That wasn't the first time I was shot at, but that was definitely the closest I ever came to getting hit at that point in my police career. We soon apprehended the offender and subsequently realized there were two offenders on top of the garage during the close ambush. The punk that we caught was providing cover fire for the one that escaped. Not only did I experience hearing loss, or auditory exclusion, while the event was happening in slow motion, but my recollection of the event was also extremely distorted. Afterwards, I was wired because of the adrenaline that was left over after the event took place. This is quite common with police officers because of the sudden adrenaline rush and remaining adrenaline that has yet to be dumped. After the enormous amount of paperwork, which took all night long, I returned home the next morning to get ready for a friend's wedding, still wide awake and wired. With time, I learned that the best way to remedy post-conflict adrenaline is with exercise, which releases (or dumps) the remaining adrenaline chemical in the body, and also with sleep, which will allow a better recollection of the event.

Adrenaline is a useful tool during conflict, but you must learn how to minimize the effects while engaging a bad guy. Mitigating this and other factors during such an engagement involves many moving parts including stress inoculation, tactical breathing, ingrained memory and, you guessed it, mindset.

Before we go any further, let's discuss tactical breathing. Whether you are a first responder, an armed civilian engaged with an active killer, a staff member of an organization under a targeted attack, or an administrator executing the response and survival plan, tactical breathing can save your life and those you are responsible for protecting. It may even help you maintain some sense of control with your teenage child, spouse, or other thespians in your life who feel that their primary purpose is to increase your blood pressure.

Throughout this book, we talk about the benefits of this type of breathing. With that being said, I'm going to discuss two simple strategies to effectively lower your heart rate so you can optimize your performance, slow down the bleeding if you are wounded and mitigate the effects of the Acute Stress Response.

- **The first strategy is simply to breathe deeply in through your nose for a duration of about three seconds. At the top of your breath, briefly pause and slowly exhale through your mouth completely, then repeat 3 to 5 times or as needed. You will notice a difference immediately.**
- **The second strategy is like the one above except this time when you are at the top of your breath, take a second smaller breath in through the nose, pause and then exhale through the mouth. You can also repeat these 3 to 5 times or until you feel more relaxed and notice your heart rate decreasing.**

Whether you are at work, home, or on the range, practice these techniques with any stress you may encounter, so when you really need to use this strategy, it will kick in automatically.

2.7

Let us talk about stress inoculation. First, stress inoculation involves training strategies specifically designed to help the warrior overcome the psychological, physiological, and emotional factors that play a significant role in the human body's response during conflict. Stress inoculation helps the warrior become familiar with stress responses and successfully overcome the associated challenges so performance can be maximized.

In the past few decades, some police departments have been utilizing scenario-based training with paintball guns for this purpose. Paintballs are painful, but effective. It allows the officer, when struck with the paintball, to feel the pain and keep on pushing forward under stress. Airsoft has been utilized the same way. Currently, there are some extremely realistic looking paintball and airsoft guns that would be ideal for training, ingrained memory, and stress inoculation. This training method was and still is optimal and cost effective, which is why vendors promote the more expensive simulation options. Taking it a step further, explore marker rounds, which marks your target either by using a training firearm or by using a barrel conversion kit which will convert your weapon into a training tool.

Preparation for engaging a lethal threat is a lifestyle in your warrior journey. My recommended training strategy that I will not deviate from is the natural training model. Nothing replaces force-on-force training in a "natural training environment." Keeping training as realistic as possible is crucial.

Technology-based training platforms do have a limited place within the training realm. In my opinion, many of them, although impressive, are counterproductive. Integrating these platforms within the entirety of the training program is plausible, as long as it does not replace the realistic scenario-based, real world training experience. Many of these tech-based platforms are extremely expensive, taking away valuable funding that should be used for good, old-fashioned hands-on training and better gear. Training that develops instinct and the ingrained memory to get the job done and return home safely should never go out of style. Law enforcement training is a fast-paced and booming industry.

In more recent times, another interesting example of stress inoculation is the use of a shock belt or bracelet while in scenario-based training. Usually, the shock belt or shock bracelet, designed to create stress in the trainee, is used in conjunction with a realistic laser tag suite of training weapons geared for military and law enforcement use during scenario-based training sessions. Although some schools of thought push back on this training strategy, it is believed to be effective in ensuring the warrior is trained and prepared for conflict, especially when biometrics like heart rate are monitored.

Just recently I met a gentleman named Tim Richardson who created an interesting stress inoculation tool called The Gunshot Box. Tim, who has a theater prop background, invented this brilliant device that safely replicates gunfire in a training environment and can be integrated within the existing simulation training platforms like virtual reality and realistic force-on-force training for departments or the military. It could also be included within the training spectrum of organizations like churches, schools, and companies to help them get acclimated, or inoculated, to respond to the sounds of gunfire, putting their plan into action.

Yes, I'm giving Tim a bit of a plug here, but I give credit where credit is due. I'll be interested to see the evolution of this product throughout the years. It's simple but effective because it taps into who we are as humans, forcing us to react and function instinctively in conflict. Ultimately, that's what this is all about. We must expect the unexpected, and this unknown should be reflected within our training. Minus a few exceptions, we cannot always control the threat, **but we can control** how we react to the threat when the time comes.

It is important to understand that gunfire does not always sound like what you expect. Sometimes it is muffled or even sounds like a popping or fireworks, so instructors must make sure when using any inoculation method that the trainees understand this. It is also important to understand that while in the denial phase during an attack, prior to realizing that it is, in fact, gunfire, the Acute Stress Response will sneak up on you in the most unexpected way. We will get into this more in Section 4.

2.8

Ingrained memory is no less important. Stress inoculation and ingrained memory work together as it helps create a flow state and enhances performance during a lethal engagement. As stated, the way you train will set the foundation for how you perform in conflict. Not only will training help you mitigate the stress of conflict, but it will also help you create what is called ingrained memory. The proper term is ingrained memory, but for decades, the law enforcement community has referred to this as "muscle memory" which is incorrect. For the sake of argument and explanation, let's expand upon this a little.

According to the Oxford Dictionary, muscle memory (ingrained memory) is the "ability to reproduce a particular movement without conscious thought, acquired as a result of frequent repetition of that movement."

In other words, what we are doing is religiously practicing a specific motor task which stamps it into our memory so that should we have to react we will perform without thinking about it. This happens as if we are on autopilot.

Warriors are not the only ones who should adopt this training strategy. Organizations like schools, companies, hospitals, and churches should create response and survival protocols with the goal of developing the ingrained memory needed if a targeted attack occurs. They should practice the protocols, along with the inoculation methods, with local law enforcement, the rapid response security team on site, or qualified consultants who specialize in the space.

If the training routine is poorly practiced, it can be deadly. "Dry firing" is a great example. It is a useful tool to make sure you have the fundamentals of marksmanship, mastering skills like breathing, trigger pull, sight alignment, stance, and grip. On the contrary, some of the dry firing training platforms available on the market still have some shortcomings, which create "training scars." Training scars are negative and potentially hazardous responses that are infused within the training process that unexpectedly emerge during conflict or stress. Ingrained memory can be a blessing and a curse, which is why it is important to understand this early in your journey.

Let's say that you have a dry fire laser training platform, in any form, that requires you to rack the slide every time you dry fire the weapon. Being the noble warrior in training that you are, you practice after work every night. You come home, walk past your loyal wife, kiss the dog, and then you go down in the basement, safely clearing your weapon and inserting the training laser within your chamber and begin to practice. Here's a newsflash, folks. Repeatedly racking the slide in repetition each time prior to pulling the trigger can cause a training scar. When the time comes to actually use your firearm under stress, you are going to revert to your training and likely rack your slide, extracting a valuable round (or rounds) from your weapon, losing seconds and your life.

Of course, even though racking a live round into a chamber always seems a little intimidating, let's keep that one for the cowboy flicks, unless of course you're in the Israeli Defense Force (IDF). Interestingly, the IDF has a unit that is required to carry an unchambered weapon because of its specific function, but because of their training, they are flawlessly able to engage their target with speed and accuracy.

There are some realistic options on the market for dry firing and laser-focused target practice. Spend the money and consider using them along with the tactical courses I preached about.

How we train will directly affect how we react under stress. It's the truth, and it is deadly if you don't realize this earlier in your journey. Eventually, your training will become instinctual as your ingrained memory creates a fluid reaction during an engagement, almost as if on autopilot.

It's like getting into your car after work and your mind wanders. Before you know it, you're pulling up in front of your house, not recollecting the drive home. You did it instinctively because day after day you took the same route. As unsafe as it sounds (and clearly is), we almost always make it back in one piece.

Many police departments and training academies, (including the military) have training platforms that allow the officer to stand in a room and react to realistic, responsive scenarios that are projected via video on a screen or virtual reality. It is a scenario-based platform, and the officer uses a mock weapon that fires and records the dynamics of the officer's response. Although the after-action evaluations are impressive, I do see some potential "training scars" that can occur with continuous use of these overpriced training options.

Movement restrictions or positioning and visual or target acquisition limitations are just some of the factors. Whether you are a civilian, a soldier, or a police officer, real world tactical training is not only more effective, but creates the proper ingrained memory and limits the "training scars" that can occur, subsequently resulting in deadly mistakes during a lethal encounter. This is the only way to train, and it's cost effective!

Furthermore, situational and threat awareness as well as target acquisition and engagement, although preached, is not conducive within these modern-day tech-based platforms because the simulation, including the graphics, is not realistic. Movement is limited and most of the weapon systems do not function like a real weapon, although many have come a long way in the recent past and are only getting better. What's the alternative? You guessed it. Good, old-fashioned hands-on training, in my experience, will always be first and foremost.

There is periodically a time and place for training platforms like virtual reality, augmented reality, and other simulated training tools. Again, virtual reality definitely has its limitations, and augmented reality technology is in its rudimentary developmental stages at this point in time.

On the other hand, some of the after-action or post-conflict evaluation software, I must say, is impressive, as many of these platforms are able to recreate the movements of the officers or participants which display valuable data like the response time, the number of fired rounds, and the bullet trajectory during the engagement.

As targeted attacks are becoming more violent and frequent, law enforcement, military and civilian training regimens should reflect these threats. Technology-based simulation training is not the answer.

I do eventually foresee augmented reality being integrated with the natural training environment, among other tactical uses, which makes sense and stays within the boundaries of my training theorems. We are not there yet, but this technology is rapidly evolving.

I have some final thoughts before we push on. From a training perspective, stress inoculation and ingrained memory are just as important as mindset, because when properly implemented through training, they become coalesced, or unified. It's all seamlessly connected.

There are a few more important things to remember. When we play games like laser tag, paintball, or airsoft, when we get hit, we stop. We stop because it's a game. We also stop sometimes because it hurts. Other times, we stop because the tech-based simulated training session abruptly ends for the next trainee to begin.

In a training environment, regardless of the training mechanisms used—whether it's paintball, airsoft, or advanced professional laser tag—you must train to continue to fight after you get hit. The fight does not end after you are struck by gunfire. In many cases, it has just begun. Stress inoculation training combined with the proper ingrained memory and tactical breathing will not only increase your chances of successfully terminating the threat, but it will also lower your heart rate, blood pressure, and keep you within the desired performance range of 115 beats per minute to about 145 beats per minute. Anything less than 115 BPM and greater than about 145 BPM will dangerously affect your performance and dramatically decrease your chances of neutralizing the threat. If you are struck by gunfire or wounded by any other means and are losing blood, proper breathing techniques (tactical breathing) will slow your heart rate and increase your chances of survival.

The most highly trained professional warriors, especially tactical operators, can function beyond 145 BPM because they are masters of their craft. I am sure now you can understand why monitoring biometrics within a training environment is so useful and highly recommended.

2.9

Honestly, the best police training I have ever had was in the Chicago Police Academy when we physically conducted traffic stops and physically acted out solutions in scenario-based training sessions. Then, we physically walked into a room that looked like a bar or a residence during an actual scenario with role players. It allowed us to enhance our skills under stress as well as use all our senses while interacting with the role players, just like we would in the field.

The training program was truly phenomenal, and the instructors were extraordinary. They were good at their job, and they made us better. Reluctantly, let me share a funny story regarding a training session in the academy and how ingrained memory unexpectedly kicked in for me as a new recruit. I was strongly advised by my fellow comrades not to share this embarrassing event, but realizing that we all must start somewhere, it was necessary to both prove a point and offer a little humor in the process at my expense.

It was a scenario-based training session, and I was expected to walk into a room that looked like a bar. Of course, it was one of the classrooms converted into a training environment, but it worked for the lesson we needed to learn. We had a duty belt complete with handcuffs, an extra magazine, and a holstered weapon with simulated blank ammunition. We were instructed to walk into the "bar" and handle the unknown disturbance.

Upon walking into the room, there was a group of men to my right and a man standing at the bar having a drink about 10 feet in front of me. Before I could even utter a word, the man at the bar pulled a weapon and fired several rounds at the men to my right. I quickly cleared my level one training holster keeping a low profile while rapidly shooting and moving low and to my left while instinctively seeking cover.

After I emptied my magazine and quickly reloaded a fresh mag into the weapon, the offender of the day dramatically fell to the ground. I proudly handcuffed the poor instructor who had been tossed around like a rag doll all day long by young, aggressive recruits during the scenario training. I rose from the ground with a smile on my face with my head high and proud.

Well, since I was used to carrying a rifle with a sling while in the Army and rarely trained with a pistol, I failed to re-holster my weapon and inadvertently placed it on the ground while handcuffing this "offender."

The instructor who was evaluating me asked me where my weapon was. I frantically looked for it and soon realized he had grabbed it from the ground while I was handcuffing the "offender." He handed me back the pistol with a smile on his face and asked me if I was a police officer anywhere else prior to joining CPD because of the way I reacted during the scenario. I told him if I were a police officer anywhere else, I would have remembered to put my pistol back in my holster. I left there that day with a little more humility and an even bigger lesson learned. "Muscle memory" made me look like a rockstar and then it got me killed!

2.10

To manage the effects of conflict during the Acute Stress Response, it is important that we are cognizant of the dynamics in greater detail. This topic is not poolside reading, but it is paramount to understand, so onward we go.

In times of conflict, lethal or a perceived threat, the Sympathetic Nervous System prepares the body to fight or flee by infusing a massive dose of adrenaline which increases the breathing, increases the blood pressure, stops the digestive function, and increases the heart rate rapidly. It regulates the energy the body needs to function under stress. The Sympathetic Nervous System is part of the Autonomic Nervous System, or ANS. This is better known as the SAM Response, or sympathetic branch, in which a gland near the kidney called the Adrenal Medulla is stimulated, releasing the adrenaline. This adrenaline release then activates the Acute Stress Response.

It's also worth mentioning that part of the SAM Response involves chronic stress, or the HPA Axis. The HPA Axis involves three glands. The Hypothalamus gland stimulates the Pituitary gland, which produces ACTH. The ACTH in turn stimulates the Adrenal Cortex gland. The Adrenal Cortex produces cortisol, and cortisol suppresses the immune system.

This type of stress involves a constant feeling of pressure or worries over an extended period. Some causes of this type of stress could be a test, bills, relationships, or any of life's overwhelming challenges. For the police, chronic stress can also result from the aftermath of a conflict, a lethal encounter, low morale within the police ranks, poor leadership within the department, political pressure, and lack of public support. It is said that cortisol is the silent killer. For myself, mindfulness, meditation, good sleep, exercise, and breathwork works wonders. If prayer is your go-to, go for it. I urge you to make meditation part of your daily ritual in one way or the other. The benefits are rewarding, you will feel more balanced, and your stress levels and cortisol will decrease.

After conflict or the perceived threat has ended, the PNS, or the Parasympathetic Nervous System, activates slowly to relax the body. The PNS is part of the autonomic nervous system and is informally known as the "rest and digest system," or the "feed and breed" system. This process helps bring the body back to the center point, lowering the heart rate, and restoring the digestive system and respiration after the release of acetylcholine through the vagus nerve. The vagus nerve runs from the brain through the face and thorax to the abdomen and controls bodily functions like digestion, heart rate, and the immune system.

The PNS process is automatic after fear or conflict, however, meditation and breathwork are invaluable under these types of circumstances. I would like to briefly discuss a little hack I have used in the past for the vagus nerve reset. This will help relax you and reset your vagus nerve as you will feel the results almost immediately. Lay down on your back and hold your hands interlocked behind your head. If you cannot lay down, sit relaxed with your hands interlocked behind your head. Take three slow, deep breaths three seconds in through your nose and three seconds out through your mouth. Then what you are going to do is keep your head straight and move your eyes to the three o'clock position. Then you are going to wait for a sigh, a yawn, or a swallow. This may take a few seconds or a few minutes, depending on your levels of stress, however, it is an effective tool that will reset your vagus nerve! I used this technique countless times in a squad car after stressful situations while working with the police and in other parts of my life where chronic stress plays a significant role. I encourage you to try it. In this crazy world we live in, we can use all the help we can get.

In regard to the Acute Stress Response, I would like to bring to your attention an interesting study called, "Mediation of the Acute Stress Response by the Skeleton," which was published in 2019 in Cell Metabolism.

This study suggests that it is osteocalcin (bone), not adrenaline, that surges through the body which triggers the "fight or flight" response. I am by no means a scientist, however, I thought this was fascinating and a true reminder of how little we know as humans about ourselves and our body. Regardless of how we are flung back into our primal endowment of fight or flight, the one thing we can all agree on is that this gift has a profound effect on how we react to lethal conflict.

2.11

Now that we have touched on the basics of the Acute Stress Response, let's discuss our heart rate specifically, as well as the remaining three responses that we should be aware of.

Above 140 beats per minute, the sympathetic nervous system goes into survival mode. At about 145 beats per minute, you start to lose your complex motor skills, and at about 170 beats per minute tunnel vision can set in.

Anything above 170 beats per minute is said to be our fight or flight response in all its glory, which can result in the emptying of the bladder or bowel.

This fear-induced response is much different than the elevated heart rate that one would have through exercise. When we are operating within a tactical capacity, we want to be between 115 and 145 beats per minute, which is an **optimal performance range.**

As said earlier, advanced tactical operators who are in phenomenal physical shape and are well-trained can function well above 145 beats per minute.

A solid ingrained memory foundation, physical fitness, continuous stress inoculation training, and-real world experience all contributes to these elevated levels of functionality under stress. These are true warriors in every respect and should be revered. Packed with knowledge and real-world experience, I encourage those with such talent to put it back into service, training the law enforcement community in threat interdiction, including active killer neutralization. Start with your local police organization and take it from there.

Moving on, I had the privilege to observe and hear over the police radio many intense car chases where the officer shouts at the dispatcher, letting her know he is in a vehicle pursuit. Usually at that point, it's up to the supervisor to determine if the pursuit is safe to proceed based upon the crime the offender committed and the condition of the pursuing officer. They consider their condition, meaning his state of mind, because of the stress response or physical status of the officer if he was injured or in a lethal encounter prior to the chase. Many times, the officer's heart rate is so elevated that auditory exclusion settles in, and the officer cannot hear the supervisor or the dispatcher who is attempting to get more information about the pursuit. It would be probable that other acute stress responses like loss of motor skills and tunnel vision would have been present also, hindering the officer's ability to drive at high speeds, maneuver around obstacles and engage the bad guy.

Currently, these types of chases in many urban settings, like Chicago, are generally not allowed. Of course, at one point in the recent past during the reign of Chicago's most incompetent mayor, police officers were not even allowed to pursue an offender by foot, castrating the little morale and brawn they had left and empowering criminals to carry their weapons on their person.

Getting back on point, I have also heard officers in high-speed chases over the radio who were calm, systematic, and collected like a DJ on a smooth jazz radio station. I was always impressed with those guys.

As for myself, it took time, but eventually it was business as usual and a lot of tactical breathing to keep my heart rate optimal for performance, allowing me to drive straight and engage the assailant after the pursuit. Whether the pursuit was by vehicle or foot, controlling the heart rate was imperative because if or when you catch or engage the bad guy, chances are it will only get even more violent.

So, we've touched on the effects of the acute stress response, specifically fight or flight, as well as the heart rate ranges for optimal performance during a violent engagement. But wait. We left a few out that I feel are worth discussing. For those who live in the space between, we still have posture, submit, and freeze. Many of us have encountered these types of responses at some point in our life.

Posture is an interesting one. Animals by nature make themselves look bigger to deter an aggressor from taking action or causing harm. Attempting to make the aggressor think the potential victim is more dangerous than he really is in order to avoid conflict is the goal. Police officers use this strategy a lot to prevent conflict from escalating into a more dangerous situation. Good verbal communication and good posture usually can have a positive outcome. Feather rustling against a 6'5", 300-pound, agitated bodybuilder doesn't always work but making ourselves look tougher than we really are can help us look intimidating enough to avert a fight. Sometimes a well-kept uniform with a confident and professional demeanor can do the trick.

As the great James Brown once said in his song, "Payback," "I don't know karate, but I know crazy." If posture doesn't work, things go to hell very quickly, and losing is not an option.

Then we have "submit" and "freeze." Submitting to an aggressor means generally backing off. For example, that same 6'5", 300-pound man aggresses towards you, and you tell him you won't fight him while backing off, letting him clearly know that you are afraid. Submitting to his aggressive actions at times will be enough to stop the potentially violent encounter. For the police, submitting is never an option and running away seldom is.

On that note, many officers have been forced to use deadly force due to the fact that the offender or aggressor was unusually strong, and the less-lethal options were unsuccessful during the engagement. Many times, certain narcotics like PCP can give the average human superhuman strength, speed, and endurance.

I learned this the hard way when an average-sized man jumped out of a stolen car and led me on a five-block, extremely fast paced foot chase. Upon barely catching up to him, I grabbed him, and after telling me he was not going to jail, he effortlessly threw me on the hood of a car that was about four or five feet away. After uttering an expletive, I hastily removed myself from the hood of the car and the fight was on. Long story short, I had to explain to a citizen why his car window had a hole the size of a head in it and "Superman" who was high on PCP, went to jail.

Either way, it is never comfortable deploying a firearm on an unarmed assailant, but each circumstance is different, especially when there is a risk of being disarmed from your firearm or your less lethal weapon system. Even losing control of your less lethal weapon systems would result in you becoming incapacitated, disarmed of your firearm, and subsequently killed. Most untrained civilians, newer police officers or the public do not understand this deadly possibility.

The last response that I would like to discuss is freeze. In the wake of conflict, one can "freeze," or what some would call "tonic immobility." The term "a deer in headlights" seems appropriate for this response. The muscles tense up and the parasympathetic nervous system is activated, instinctively conserving your resources. Continuing aggression by the aggressor may even cause one to faint, as the heart rate and blood pressure drops excessively. This response is fascinating to me as one can completely shut down physically but be consciously aware and alert of his surroundings during the encounter.

The human body is captivating, as it seems we were built for conflict. As times change, so do our perceived roles within a civilized society. The warrior knows deep down that modern society is anything but civilized with predators lurking in the shadows to prey upon the weak. Now more than ever, it is the heroes in blue and the standup citizens like in that Indiana mall who will keep the monsters at bay. To do this successfully, there must be a process set in motion. This process of warriorship starts before conflict and is a lifelong journey. It starts with mindset, and it ends with mindset. The path in between is not comfortable and requires determination and a clear direction.

When this transformation happens, you will change, and people around you, near and far, will know it. Some will despise you, others will respect your courage, and all will call upon you when the reaper comes.

SECTION THREE

Carrying the Burden

3.1

Little did our Founding Fathers know when they drafted the Second Amendment that it would one day ensure that Americans were able to defend themselves from their fellow citizens in the wake of a mutated value system and a government that has left them to the wolves.

Moreover, I would also bet that the Founding Fathers would never have guessed that the future leadership of this once great country would have allowed those with extreme ideologies, foreign and domestic, to flourish as our country's foundation and values are ridiculed and demeaned. To make things even more frightening, many of those in public office (who are attempting to take these rights away when the aforementioned threats are lurking just outside our front door) claim that the Second Amendment is outdated and should be drastically modified or removed. Where does that leave those of us who just want to live safely in peace, provide for our family, and be happy in a country that is far from the one we knew not so long ago?

America has had many dark moments, and I would certainly include this as one of them. The division of God and Country, the demoralization of our foundation, the constant degradation of our rights including free speech and the right to bear arms has caused more damage than any foreign adversary could ever hope to inflict. The old saying "divide and conquer" comes to mind. American politicians, the media, and their sponsors made it easy for our adversaries, regardless of whether they are homegrown, imported, or foreign.

I never thought this kind of assault would come from our fellow Americans—if you can be so kind in calling them such. Both the extreme left and the extreme right in this country have done us no justice. In the meantime, the Second Amendment is in place, and for those who are willing to carry this burden, I strongly recommend you carry this "burden" on your side and, of course, in the appropriate holster!

This section is intended to offer information and guidance that complements whatever tactical course you may take. There is only so much time within that training curriculum and the instructors do the best they can with the time they have by giving you the hands-on training you need. Most of those tactical instructors understand that tactical training is an ongoing journey, and there is always something new to learn. The reality is, nothing replaces experience, and we all have something unique to bring to the table of knowledge.

Towards the end of this section, we will discuss the components and deployment of deadly force as well as some uncomfortable cases from the recent past from which we can all learn. Again, keep in mind that all lethal encounter situations are different, and every state has different laws regarding the dynamics of the use of deadly force allowed within their boundaries.

This section is not intended to replace the hands-on training that I preach about throughout this book, but it is merely for the purpose of creating a foundation from which to grow. I want you to consider it sort of a "ground school." Every pilot starts off in a classroom before they enter the cockpit. While ground school generally does not teach the pilot the hands-on experience of flight that is necessary to be proficient to fly the aircraft, they learn the essential tools to create a foundation for this journey to begin. Honestly, that is the purpose of the entire book, but this section is imperative because if you pick up the wrong habits, it could be lethal for you or others around you. Remember ingrained memory? It is something to keep in mind.

I feel it is important to understand the gravity of this responsibility that our Founding Fathers, unforeseen, created in the midst of a very different threat nearly 250 years ago. To be completely honest, I would love to live in a world where we did not have to look over our shoulders or rely on those who are sworn to protect us, whilst their hands are tied behind their backs as they helplessly watch the wolves get closer to the sheep. Instead, we are forced to depend on an incompetent government that constantly impedes our safety and then ridicules us when we protect ourselves and our loved ones. With that being said, let's push forward.

We touched lightly in the previous sections about the immense responsibility involved with carrying a firearm as well as some passive tips. In the segments ahead, we will dive deeper into this undertaking that some call a privilege and others, like myself, call a responsibility. This section, especially the firearms segments, are designed to enhance the skills that you may already have as well as provide crucial knowledge to stakeholders within an organization that is susceptible to targeted attacks if deploying such a weapon is the only bridge back to your loved ones, even if you do not agree with the use of a firearm. This includes the legal and moral fundamentals of deploying deadly force. Before we do that, let us talk about some controversial topics that need to be up front and center. Constitutional Carry is the perfect place to start.

3.2
Constitutional Carry & The Right to Bear Arms

Section 3 is extensive. Due to this, it will be a little more structured, so you will be able to go back and reference some of the information during your own journey. Keep in mind that this is an ever-changing dynamic, so make sure you stay on top of all the latest and greatest in the firearms world. With the laws changing on a constant basis, you will need to continuously educate yourself depending on the state you live in and where you travel. If you travel from state to state, make sure you understand that state's gun laws to keep yourself safe and out of trouble. With that being said, I would like to talk about one of the most controversial topics in the firearms world:

Constitutional Carry. I have my opinion and, as always, I will express it. It is a conversation that needs to happen. I will also play devil's advocate to myself and try to explain my logic. I would love for you to embrace the topic and keep an open mind. This is a very gray area as the Second Amendment clearly states, **"A well-regulated Militia, being necessary to the security of a free State, the right of the people to keep and bear Arms, shall not be infringed."**

Constitutional Carry, or otherwise known as permit-less or unrestricted carry, allows a citizen to carry a firearm unrestricted and without a permit or training within a specific state, based upon the Second Amendment mentioned above. Generally speaking, handguns are the main topic of focus during the legislative processes that take place. Long guns and knives usually don't fall under most state Constitutional Carry laws, but the laws do differ from state to state. As of 2023, there are over two dozen states that have passed laws for Constitutional Carry. Most of the states allow this from the ages of 18 and above, and a few states allow this type of carry for citizens 21 and over. Vermont allows Constitutional Carry from the ages of 16 and up. I'm going to leave that one alone for now. Some of the states require a weapon registration whether Constitutional Carry is allowed or not. I personally think this is a great idea because you would be surprised how many people lose their weapons through negligence or theft.

On a responsible note, most states do not allow a convicted felon, or a citizen convicted of domestic violence to carry a weapon under any circumstance. This does not mean that they will abide by this law. Criminals are criminals for a reason. Obviously, the consequences for them carrying a firearm are substantial if caught, but somebody must catch the offender, and it will probably be the police one way or the other. That "minor" traffic violation that causes the officer to initiate a stop can be a violent convicted felon who has a gun under his seat. Such a stop no longer seems minor and can become deadly. It is a risky job.

I would like to relay a quick story for those who live in more of an urban setting. Years back, I drove to the Rocky Mountains in Colorado and spent a week in a small cabin enjoying the fresh air, the strong smell of pine and the best tasting spring water I ever had! I quickly became friends with a man that lived next door who had a 14-year-old son. After a few beers and some heated conversations about politics, his son walked into the living room and told his father that he was going to his friend's house for a few hours. His father told him not to forget his rifle. The man looked at me and said that black bears and mountain lions come out at night. The boy took the rifle and walked out the door. This boy grew up with firearms and hunted with his father on a regular basis. Carrying a firearm in that area was not only a way of life, but it was also about survival; a boy just wanted to walk down the road to visit his friend, knowing that it would be dark upon his return. I must admit that it still threw me off because you do not hear that every day.

Let's touch on some perspectives regarding the argument for not only Constitutional Carry, but armed civilians in general. I will attempt to tread lightly, however, I have not thus far, so why start now?

There are many schools of thought on this. Let us discuss a couple that stand out for me. We have the far-right gun advocates who believe because the Constitution states that citizens have the right to keep and bear arms, that this is enough to strap a weapon to their side and go about their daily business. No background checks, no training, and no problem! Of course, we cannot leave out the far-left anti-gun activists who forget that it takes an actual human to pull the trigger and that if the crazy bastard could not get his hands on a gun, he would use a car, a knife, or anything else to achieve his desired level of death and mayhem.

Then we have our local, state, and federal law enforcement officers. Their perspectives reflect the experiences they encountered within the communities or jurisdictions they are sworn to protect. I mean, in all fairness, when they see the level of devastation that involves firearms (or when they get shot at enough times), it is usually substantial enough to make them think, "Hey, you know, maybe it's a good idea we get tougher on the gun laws, Constitutional Carry, etc."

I have heard this over and over while working as a police officer, and at the time, I agreed. Looking at the world now with a different set of eyes, I realize that the police, as well as responsibly armed civilians, need to operate under a different set of rules in a vastly different world. Now, until society realizes that the police are the good guys, it is the fine citizens who may have to take point, as discussed in the previous sections. Let us get back on point from the perspective of a street cop.

Local and state law enforcement officers conduct hundreds of traffic stops a month. Some traffic stops are for basic traffic violations which sometimes would substantiate enough probable cause to take the investigation further, depending on the situation or circumstance. Other traffic stops are higher risk because either a crime has been committed, is in the process of being committed, or will be committed. Usually during these types of high risk stops, the officer's threat awareness is elevated, and he is expecting some sort of engagement one way or the other. In my mind, it was the small traffic violation that was always higher risk because the driver or passengers usually expected us to be caught off guard. This is when the training really kicks in because during a lethal encounter, the response needs to be automatic and fluid, as discussed in the previous sections. Training and ingrained memory are always put to the test during these types of unexpected situations that can and do happen when you least expect it.

Traffic stops aside, the most dangerous call for service that a police officer can respond to is a domestic call, even when violence has yet to occur with the parties involved. Emotions are extremely elevated during these types of encounters, and if there is a firearm involved or accessible, things could take a violent and unexpected turn within seconds of the officer exiting the squad car.

Domestic encounters are unpredictable and can turn a normal, rational person into a dangerous, irrational person within seconds, depending on the circumstances. Let us just use our imagination for a few minutes and allow me, if you will, to practice my romantic novel writing in case I decide or I am forced to change careers after this book is published. Who would have thought the discussion of Constitutional Carry could be so exciting? I surely did not when I started this section.

So, you work two jobs to pay for your mortgage and to send your young children to a private school. Your beautiful spouse (you know, the one who you walk past every day on the way to the basement prior to dry firing every night), unselfishly decided to take a hiatus from her lucrative career to raise your two children. You are in love and your amazing spouse knows it. You are in so much love that you decided to come home from work early to take her out to a romantic lunch before the children get out of school. Of course, I feel that fairy tales do happen, however, in this situation, it clearly does not. You enter your home with a beautiful bouquet of roses and hear some interesting noises coming from the bedroom. Your heart races as you walk towards the noise that you have not heard since last month while you were intimate with your spouse. Behold, the door opens, and you see your amazing, dedicated, and beautiful spouse on top of your neighbor, doing things you have not done since your wedding night. I have never been in this situation, but I can only imagine what I would want to do to that neighbor, but it takes two to tango. Having a firearm strapped to your side at that moment can turn this unthinkable situation into a lethal one.

I have responded to some equitable calls during my time as a Chicago police officer. It's betrayal in the worst possible case, and I can only imagine the emotions flowing through the head of those involved. How does it end? Does the loving husband, who just recently read this book, start "tactically breathing" in order to regain emotional, mental, and physical control of himself? Or does it go the other way and make the evening news?

Honestly, it can end in several ways, but no matter the ending, the fine officers called to the home are in the middle of someone else's shitstorm, and there is a weapon involved. Every second is unpredictable and because of this, things can go south very quickly. Most advocates for Constitutional Carry or even concealed carry haven't experienced the chaos that happens in this type of environment. You have to keep in mind that carrying a firearm is not only a debated right of the Second Amendment, but it's a business. A very lucrative business. Ask Big Pharma. If the cure paid more than the medication and hospitalizations, I could promise you we would have little illness in this world. The Covid-19 pandemic proved that. Who would have thought we would have so many vaccine options in such a quick period of time? Do not think for a second, it was a miracle. The firearms industry, although essential, is no different.

There are several factors that go through the minds of law enforcement during the Constitutional Carry discussion and the above examples are the more common concerns. Many law enforcement officers feel that allowing more citizens to be armed would only create more risk to them or those around them for a good reason.

That argument to the side, a criminal can always get their hands on a firearm one way or the other. This fact is almost as frightening as an untrained citizen carrying a weapon, concealed or open, because weapon retention is a practiced skill among other skills that are necessary to effectively deploy your weapon.

That hero in that Indiana mall is an example of how Constitutional Carry was a success. I truly feel that carrying a weapon is an awesome responsibility that should be taken seriously.

In 2022 following the Uvalde, Texas, school shooting, lawmakers finally came together. A bipartisan package was proposed to extend the age from 18 to 21, implement red flag laws (which identifies potentially dangerous people who shouldn't own a weapon), funding for school safety, enhanced mental illness resources and more extensive background checks. I personally feel that special funding for rapid response interdiction training for first responders should be in the mix as well.

I will keep an eye on it, but I think the process will take time, and it does not seem to have all the answers. Bipartisan support for the police may also be a great start.

Constitutional Carry, and even the idea of armed civilians, is a heated debate that should be continuously discussed. I try to remain neutral as much as I can, understanding that every situation is different. I feel that more good than bad has come out of responsibly armed and trained citizens exercising their Second Amendment right. In whichever pathway leads you to carrying a firearm, the rest of Section 3 will help point you in the right direction.

3.3
The Bridge to the Abyss

I want you to remember one thing: this book is not intended for the criminal or the rogue vigilante. I certainly understand the taste for revenge, but at the end of the day, both the criminal and the vigilante end up in the same place: either dead or in prison. In most cases, the vigilante is the criminal and in other situations, he may be painted as one by the media even if he operated within the parameters of the law. According to the Oxford dictionary, a vigilante is, "A member of a self-appointed group of citizens **who undertake law enforcement in their community without legal authority**, typically because the legal agencies are thought to be inadequate."

Defending yourself or others under an **exigent circumstance, like an active deadly threat,** certainly does not fit the definition above. You have to remember that restraint is the one thing that separates us from the monster, and the appropriate use of force with proper deployment of your weapon system will be what stops him.

Unfortunately, some hero citizens have been labeled as such because many anti-gun advocates didn't have anywhere else to take the argument.

Honestly, if an attacker walks into a public library on a Saturday morning randomly shooting children, and the studious librarian who happens to be a well-trained and legally armed citizen neutralizes the bad guy within seconds, what else is there to say? Before those far-left anti-gun advocates attempt to demonize the librarian alongside the Second Amendment, the State's Attorneys may have their shot depending on their political pressure. This is as disheartening as it sounds, and America is increasingly starting to look like a Third World country every day.

Let me reiterate this again: aside from being tactically trained and well-versed in the laws regarding use of force as well as abiding by the parameters of the firearm laws of your state, the next most important thing you could do is have the self-defense legal protection I have been preaching.

Ahead, as we plunge into some important discussions and strategies that I feel are imperative while carrying a firearm, keep in mind that all skill levels will be reading this book, which may perhaps be a citizen who never picked up a firearm, or a highly trained instructor with real-world experience. As I have hinted, even if you do not carry a firearm or are against doing so, I do feel that it is a good idea to at least be a little familiar with the basics. I was undecided about adding these next few firearms related segments because I wanted to stay on point with the scope of the book, but I feel that this book would not be complete without discussing some of my perspectives that determined my survival while working on the streets with the Chicago Police Department. Back in the academy, I was told by an instructor that knowledge is more powerful than a firearm and is our biggest weapon. As the years flew by, I learned that he was right, but the best way to gain this wisdom is through experience, which usually happens under dangerous circumstances. If we are lucky enough to survive, it is our duty to teach others how to do the same.

Figure 3A Kurt Delia from Delia Tactical International leads the way!
Courtesy of Kurt Delia & Delia Tactical International, LLC

Before we slide into the firearms segment in 3.4, it is important to mention that the photos ahead are courtesy of Kurt Delia, a retired law enforcement officer and the founder of Delia Tactical International, LLC. Delia Tactical specializes in teaching the crucial skills of breaching, armored mobility, threat vulnerability, protection, tactical driving, and rescue operations to both military and law enforcement personnel, including first responders. The company also boasts an array of breaching tools and products used for such operations, ensuring that the most elite operators are mission ready and the bad guy has nowhere to hide. It is an important job, and I am grateful that I had the opportunity to collaborate with Kurt during this project. Let's move!

3.4
Open Carry vs Concealed Carry

Figure 3B An example of Open Carry
Courtesy of Kurt Delia & Delia Tactical International, LLC

I am sure this late in the game, you know the difference between open carry and concealed carry, but let's start the conversation with just that. Concealed carry is when you carry your firearm, generally under clothing, in which your weapon is hidden, and nobody knows you are armed. Open carry, on the contrary, is when one carries their firearm openly or partially open, depending on the state and how they classify it. Most of the time, citizens who carry openly will do so with their sidearm in a holster just outside the clothing where it is visible. I have seen civilians utilize open carry with assault rifles within a community, which I always thought was interesting. Let's order a burger and fries with an M4 Carbine strapped over my shoulder. To each their own. I do not judge until their intentions or threat level changes.

I've heard some interesting arguments on both ends of the spectrum for those who support open carry and for those who support only concealed carry. I think there is a time and place for both. I disagree with the majority of the arguments that support open carry, however, playing devil's advocate, I'll throw this into the mix for the sake of conversation. It is believed by some that if a citizen carries a weapon openly that this alone may deter a criminal or active killer and prevent a shooting or violent crime. I think in some cases this may be true, depending on the intent or experience of the criminal. If armed robbers enter a jewelry shop and see staff carrying a sidearm, that may be enough to deter the robbery. Or, it may have the opposite effect, which we will get into below.

Either way, I would imagine it would stir up some interesting Second Amendment conversations. I would also imagine that citizens who are open carrying in an area like Colorado or Georgia where it's widely accepted would have less issues than in areas where open carry is permitted, but the community is not accustomed to seeing it. This could cause a problem if law enforcement is called, and it would likely set the majority of that community on edge.

There are a few things to keep in mind. All states have different rules regarding open carry. Some states require a license, and some do not, which is called permissive carry. Many states strictly prohibit open carry and although several states do allow open carry, many cities within those states have ordinances and laws that prohibit this type of carry. It's always important to do your research.

In my opinion, open carry puts the citizen at a tactical disadvantage. In the majority of cases, the bad guy is going to have a weapon on his person concealed because he understands that the element of surprise will work to his advantage, especially in a gun-free zone. The minute the bad guy observes a citizen carrying a weapon, chances are the fine citizen exercising his Second Amendment rights openly will be ambushed and disarmed. Whether they want to commit an armed robbery or commit murder, the element of surprise (not knowing if the good guy has a weapon) will be what puts the bad guy at a clear disadvantage. Another thing to keep in mind is that many of these shootings happen in gun-free zones because the bad guy knows most law-abiding citizens are going to abide by those rules.

As I have mentioned earlier, there should be a protocol set in place in order to neutralize this type of threat in these gun-free zones, even if it is a less-lethal option. Less-lethal options are not my favorite, but it is better than nothing. Moving ahead, I am 100% in agreement that a firearm should be carried concealed unless the situation dictates open carry. Blend in, be discrete, and if your weapon is exposed in public, the business end of it should be pointed towards your target. If you are on your property, or your farm, or someplace where it is not as obvious to the public that you're carrying a weapon, then perhaps.

Now, having your firearm readily available outside of your clothing does contribute to a faster draw and deployment of your weapon system. Most law enforcement, especially patrol, are already operating within a fishbowl. Sadly, police officers get ambushed every day. With that possibility, quick weapon access can save the officer's life. For me, deploying my weapon system was second nature, but I had to practice my deployment sequence every now and then in terms of carrying concealed under my clothing. Whichever way you carry, have a plan and system set in place should the day come that you must engage an active lethal threat to save your life or others around you.

3.5
Quick Reference Information When Carrying a Firearm

As discussed in Section 2, understanding the physiology of what happens during conflict not only allows you to prevail during a lethal threat, but it will help you deal with the post-event psychological and emotional aftermath. This knowledge, combined with the proper tactical training, will place the odds in your favor for success in lethal conflict. While these are two very important realms of mastery that I recommend you learn, there are many components in between that you should know. Some would reasonably argue these components are as important as tactics or understanding the body and mind during conflict.

Police officers go through an academy. Most of the time, these recruits have well-trained and knowledgeable instructors that give them an enormous amount of information from their personal experiences on and off duty.

Usually, after a training academy, officers get assigned to an area surrounded by yet more police officers, many of which are senior members of the organization. Most officers learn the do's and don'ts quickly of carrying on and off duty, whether it is open or concealed.

Civilians or police officers in smaller organizations do not have that luxury. I felt compelled to create a quick reference list of important tips, suggestions, and required knowledge that I feel is extremely important. To be completely honest, there is an endless amount of information that should be understood while carrying or deploying a firearm, however, these are some of the more important elements that stand out for me. Some of this information is reiterated or summarized from the previous segments and sections for a very good reason.

Brian's Pre-Engagement Survival Tips

- Read this book cover to cover, because "knowledge is power."
- Carry a semi-automatic firearm.
- Pick the proper holster, keeping deployment in mind as well as retention.
- Make sure the holster is specific to the firearm you are carrying.
- Make sure your holster covers the trigger whether you carry concealed or open.
- Pick a durable belt and put your holster along with extra magazine pouches on it.
- Do not keep your firearm too close to your extra magazines while on your person. Utilize your non-dominant hand and carry the extra magazines on the opposite side of your firearm. This will allow you to keep your weapon straight and on target while reloading. This will also allow you to keep your eyes on the threat and utilize both hands as compared to shifting your body. Some people like to keep their extra magazines on the same side or attached to the holster. Keep it separate unless there is a specific reason, or you have the skill set.

- Regardless of where you keep your extra magazines, infuse it within your deployment sequence training.
- Take as many tactical shooting classes as you can.
- Research and choose a self-defense legal protection strategy.
- If you carry your weapon concealed, always blend in with loose clothing.
- Never let people know you are armed and be discreet.
- Try to avoid unnecessary conflict, arguments, road rage, etc. Most police officers are mandated to take police action on or off duty, but as a civilian, unless there is an immediate lethal threat, just call 911.
- As a civilian, if time permits, call 911 prior to or after an engagement. Most of the time lethal encounters happen extremely quickly, leaving very little time to handle anything else. Segment C in the deadly force section ahead discusses this further.
- Do not engage and deploy your weapon unless it is absolutely necessary.
- Again, carry extra magazines. I would recommend at least two extra magazines. Weapon malfunctions can occur which would normally require you to quickly strip the magazine to the ground and perform remedial action. It is not recommended you pick up the magazines from the ground, taking your eyes or firearm, off your threat. We will touch on this ahead.
- Always have a round chambered, unless a specific reason dictates otherwise. If you decide not to, practice deploying your firearm after chambering a round. This would be an ingrained memory nightmare, so stick with one plan.
- If your firearm has a safety, though many do not, practice deploying the weapon after engaging the safety as part of the deployment sequence.
- Keep the same deployment sequence consistent and practice it on or off duty, with open carry or concealed. This will build the proper ingrained memory needed to quickly and accurately engage a lethal threat.
- Whether you are off duty or a civilian who is armed, always inform the on-duty officer you are armed and where the weapon is. Never

put your hands anywhere near the weapon. At that point, follow the officer's instructions.

- If you are an off-duty police officer, on-duty police officers are always the ones with the authority, regardless of your rank or position.
- Avoid adjusting, or babying, your weapon in public. It's always a dead giveaway. If you really feel the need to, go to the washroom to adjust your firearm.
- Take into consideration with how you wear your weapon. In the summertime or warm weather, you would have to wear loose clothing when your weapon is concealed, whereas in the wintertime, you have a little more flexibility depending on where you live. Obviously, carrying in Texas would be a lot different than doing so in Michigan. If you travel, be prepared to adjust your clothing and carrying methods.
- Make sure you are familiar with the laws in the area or areas you plan on carrying your firearm in. Laws change from state to state and city to city. Do your research beforehand.
- Be aware of gun-free zones and be aware of those who may take advantage of that.
- Perform regular maintenance on your weapon.
- Have a deployment plan for your firearm when your weapon is stored away at home or elsewhere.
- Select a firearm that is perfect for you and your hand size.
- Practice with the ammunition that you carry in your firearm normally.
- Train for situational and threat awareness and when to engage.
- Give yourself the mental validation to engage should that day ever come to stop a lethal threat to save your life.
- Explore optics and specialized sights with your weapon of choice.
- Always keep your weapon in the same place on your person.
- Always carry the same weapon and if you do switch firearms, make sure you train with it and take the steps needed to carry and deploy it for the sake of ingrained memory.

- Keep your attorney's information available as well as all your credentials needed in order to legally carry your firearm.
- Above are some of the most important tips that stand out in my mind aside from the other important content mentioned throughout this book. In the discussion ahead, we are going to discuss some information that is necessary in order to properly deploy your firearm and engage an active lethal threat. Before we get to that point, though, we have a little housekeeping to do. We're going to discuss basic weapon maintenance and storage. I know it sounds uneventful and mundane, but it is a crucial and necessary part of this subject matter.

3.6

Basic Firearm (pistol) Maintenance, Storage and Accessibility

The saying goes, "if you take care of your weapon, your weapon will take care of you." It is very true. There are some very important things, however, you must keep in mind. Environmental factors should be taken into consideration when it comes to maintenance. Warm, dry climates may affect how often you lubricate your weapon or even how often you clean it. Armed citizens or officers in the high desert may have factors like sand, while those in some of the colder climates may have to deal with condensation after leaving a heated location and then going into the elements. This condensation can affect the mechanisms within the firearm, hampering its functionality.

Another factor you must consider in terms of how you maintain or clean your weapon may depend on your function or lifestyle. Is this your primary everyday carry? Is it part of your job capacity? How often do you go to the range?

Regardless of your job capacity and how or why you carry your weapon, you will eventually have to clean it. Below are some tips and recommendations regarding maintaining and cleaning your weapon. I highly recommend you talk to your range instructor, tactical guru or local gun shop for further tips and clues that are more directed towards your specific circumstances and needs.

Speaking of gun shops. Although many folks that work in gun shops are knowledgeable, some of the old-timers just like to hang out there. It doesn't mean they know all the answers. Be careful who you talk to and make sure you get the right information.

Before we move on, I couldn't help but think of an incident at a gun shop that had an indoor range in the back. Some of the old-timers that "worked" there used to use the range every now and then. I used to frequent that range before I became a police officer and continued after the academy. One day, my buddy from the academy and I decided to do some shooting at this civilian range that wasn't too far from our homes. While he and I were in our specified firing ranges flying though our ammunition, one of the "range employees" (a gun enthusiast who just hung out at the gun shop) was firing his .22 caliber semi-automatic pistol a few lanes away. Shortly after, this "employee" decided to exit the firing lane with his finger on the trigger while he was attempting to clear the weapon. I moved out of the line of fire right before he pulled the trigger and fired a round that landed within two inches of my friend's foot. While my friend danced a jig, I busted out my nervous laugh while grateful I moved out of the way. My poor buddy, who clearly did not have the same sense of humor as me, was just in shock. The gun shop staff entered the firing range and immediately disarmed this gentleman who was completely frozen and embarrassed. That was the last time we were at that range. The moral of that story is, be careful who you talk to. Nobody is perfect and we all make mistakes, but the wrong mistakes can be deadly, regardless of your experience. Let's move on!

Below are some of my recommendations regarding firearm maintenance:

- Always safely clear your weapon prior to maintenance.
- If available, use a bullet trap or clearing station.
- Either way, make sure you do a visual and physical inspection to make sure your weapon is clear.
- Separate your ammunition from your immediate location where your weapon is being cleaned to avoid mistakes.
- Carefully disassemble your weapon.

- Use a microfiber rag for the bigger parts of your weapon and Q-tips for the smaller parts like grooves, etc.
- Feel free to gently use a bore brush for the barrel to loosen up the carbon and then follow it up with patches and an extremely light coat of oil within the barrel. There is some debate regarding using a bore brush. Follow the recommendation of your gun manufacturer.
- Lightly apply oil where necessary
- Do not over-lubricate your weapon and keep the oil away from the mechanisms (like the striker pin, firing pin, etc.) that make contact with the cartridge.
- Avoid using carbon/brake cleaners (but some people swear by them).
- Carefully reassemble the weapon.
- Perform a functions check ensuring everything is working properly and it is reassembled correctly.

Firearm maintenance is not a complicated topic, but some of the simple tasks can be overlooked and even lethal if improperly implemented. Above are some basic recommendations that will keep you safe and keep your firearm functional. If you deploy your weapon because of a lethal encounter or firing at the range, I recommend you clean your weapon as soon as possible. Otherwise, an unfired weapon should be cleaned about every one and a half to three weeks depending on the factors mentioned above.

Storage and Accessibility

If there's anything I think I've stressed throughout this book it's that sometimes the small things are not so small. The devil is in the details. Every circumstance, skill set, and environmental factor is different. Some of us are well trained with firearms and some are not. Some of us live alone, some of us have teenagers with emotional issues or perhaps small children in the home who like to get into mischief. Some of us have very emotional spouses, and the thought of having a firearm accessible to them is frightening as others may have that emotionally unstable jealous boyfriend on probation with a temper. Regardless of the circumstances or environmental factors that exist within our personal or professional life, the bottom line is that if the firearm belongs to us, we are responsible for every aspect of it, including the actions of those who have access to it. This can be a roommate, our children (or visiting children), partner, or spouse. Believe it or not, we can even be responsible if the bad guy obtains the unsecured weapon within our home or abode depending on the state you live in.

There have been numerous cases where children obtained an unsecured firearm from home and brought it to school or other places, causing harm to unsuspecting citizens. Sometimes, the children are too young to understand the consequences of their actions and at other times, they have the intention to commit murder. Whether this is the case or not, the person who owns the firearm or who has direct control of the firearm's accessibility is ultimately responsible. Another thing to keep in mind is that some states are very specific with the way you are required to store your weapon for this very reason.

There must be a balance between safety and accessibility.

If somebody breaks into your house and your fight or flight kicks in as discussed in Section 2, will you have the physical ability to obtain your weapon and deploy it properly? Have a storage plan that works for you, your company, or your family. Yes, I said company. Responsible business owners or company executives who would rather store a weapon in the facility than on his person are responsible for that weapon regardless of where it is. Just remember, when an active killer enters the facility or office, you need to be able to safely access the weapon quickly under stress in order to neutralize the threat. Many people fall victim to home invaders because they're not able to access the weapon in time under stressful conditions!

There are many different storage options when it comes to safes. There are key options, biometrics release options, your standard combination or number locks and even magnetic locks. As I mentioned earlier, every personal circumstance, environmental factor, or state law is different, but having a gun safe with a quick access option with little time to think would be the way to go.

Are you going to remember your combination in the heat of the moment? Or that damn key! Where did you put it? I lose my car keys at least once a week. If you're anything like me, this probably isn't a good option. If a home intruder or burglar sees a safe, where do you think he (or they) is going to go after he murders your spouse and rapes your daughter? My guess is the safe, especially if the safe is visible. If your firearm is in the safe, the situation might even get worse if at all possible if the bad guy gets his hands on it.

The magnet safe is fascinating to me. Usually this is a hidden trap safe as part of a shelf or piece of furniture or even in the wall that is opened by following the specified sequence. Many times, there may be an inconspicuous object with a magnet attached to it that deploys the opening mechanism for the safe, making the weapons retrievable. Now, children are very curious creatures regardless of their age. Depending on the circumstances and your child's age or experience with firearms, like that young man out in the Rocky Mountains I mentioned who took his rifle with him before leaving the house, this may or may not be a good option.

In my opinion, in terms of using a safe, the best option is a discreetly placed biometric release safe. Using a fingerprint or hand scanner, which would release the locking mechanism on the safe, allowing you to gain access to your weapon within seconds, seems like the most viable option to me. Regardless of your physical or mental condition, you will be able to obtain your weapon under stress. Some of these biometric options have the ability to store other biometric data from multiple people, so you can add family or those you trust. Even this option has its loopholes. Pick the option that works for you and your family. As mentioned earlier in this book, whatever option you pick, make sure you practice accessing the weapon so you could keep yourself, your family, or your staff safe from themselves or the bad guy.

The Principles of Weapon Deployment

3.7
The Symmetry of Lethal Engagement

Section 2 discussed the physiology of conflict and the different things that could happen to your body during a lethal engagement. As you have learned, building proper ingrained memory and having a consistent training plan will not only help you mitigate the effects of the Acute Stress Response, but it will give you a tactical advantage when deploying your firearm. When it comes to deploying your weapon system, the attributes of ingrained memory and a consistent training plan are crucial. As we discuss this ahead, keep Section 2 in mind.

If there was one ingredient that I could install within your mind when it comes to weapon deployment, it would be consistency. As hinted above, be consistent with what you carry. Be consistent with the type of ammunition you carry within your weapon system. Be consistent with your holster. Be consistent with where you put your holster on your person. Be consistent in how you grip, aim, and fire your weapon system. **Just like with tactical training, consistency will help create the proper ingrained memory that you need in order to successfully engage a lethal threat under stress.**

The strategies you utilize to deploy your weapon is no less important. Changing the way you deploy your weapon system can be a fatal mistake. Looking ahead, we will discuss many different facets, some less common, of weapon deployment. As always, I will voice my opinion and support the arguments with why I think these procedures should be followed. On the contrary, many of the ways that we carry and deploy our weapon system is of personal preference.

Many people have different opinions and arguments, likely for a good reason: their experience. Every job function is different, and every level of experience can be very personal if most of this type of experience was gained under dangerous circumstances, as mine was. Many folks may not agree with everything I discuss and that's OK. Do what works for you, but whichever way you carry and deploy your weapon, keep it consistent. If you disagree with my perspectives or that of your tactical instructors, ask questions and figure out the best solution for you.

Ahead, we're going to start with discussing the more popular types of carrying methods and strategies, primarily focusing on those citizens opting for concealed carry. Before we get into this discussion, I'd like to point out that if you decide to open carry, make sure you take retention and accessibility into consideration. **When I say retention and accessibility, I mean not only the way you negotiate the deployment sequence from the holster (drawing the weapon), but also the bad guy's accessibility to your firearm.** If the bad guy gains control of your firearm, there is a good probability that he will turn it on you or others around you. Either way, it's your lifeline, so protect it.

Police officers are faced with this type of situation and threat whenever they mingle with citizens on a daily basis. They are aware of the risks that can happen in a split second. No, they might not always be in that domestic encounter we discussed above. They just might be talking to that "good citizen" who happens to have a warrant for homicide, unbeknownst to the officer. A weapon retention situation can happen unexpectedly and instantaneously. If the bad guy is stronger, faster, or under the influence of a narcotic, you can have a serious problem. The way officers position their bodies and their hands when they speak to citizens all revolve around placing themselves into a better tactical position should things go to hell. They do it on a constant basis, building yet another attribute of the ingrained memory equation, enhancing their performance should a lethal threat or a retention situation occur.

Citizens who openly carry their pistol may not always be in that constant state of awareness like police officers are (contributing to the officer's elevated cortisol levels). With that being said, there are various levels of tactical disadvantages that you would have. One being, as mentioned earlier, making you the first target. You would also have the disadvantage of not knowing when somebody would catch you off guard and try to disarm you. There is a science behind it, and if it is not understood and practiced, it can be lethal to you or a liability nightmare. Make retention training part of your tactical training, whether you open carry or carry your firearm concealed, because you do not want to place yourself in a position to get disarmed.

At one time or another, most officers have fought to retain their weapon in their holster during their career and understand the consequences if the bad guy obtains control of it. Many police departments have pushed less-lethal weapon options in their policies for these types of circumstances, and if you have some distance from the bad guy trying to disarm you or the officer's partner has the ability or the time to use a less-lethal, then this may be a viable solution. There is a certain point of no return, however, where deadly force becomes the only option. Much of the time, it is the solo officer on a quiet road in the middle of nowhere losing the battle while a bad guy is trying to disarm him. Or perhaps she is a city officer in a dark alley. It's a violent dog-eat-dog situation and the unarmed bad guy could very well put himself in the predicament of being neutralized as he is attempting to gain control of the officer's firearm. Most civilians don't understand these types of circumstances. Unless you are there, this is a gray area, and it is very easy to judge. Now, I am not a fan of body cameras because it's yet another hurdle for the officer to do his job as he is always under scrutiny. It generally takes away the officer's discretion in monotonous situations. In a retention or deadly force incident, however, it may benefit him because the video would clarify what happened.

Moving on, there are various steps they must take in order to negotiate the holster and deploy their weapon system, depending on the holster's level of retention. The difference is most officers are trained. Most civilians are not trained. Keep this in mind if you open carry.

If there's any recommendation I strongly advise, it's carrying your weapon concealed. If you're adamant about carrying a weapon openly, make sure you have the proper retention system in place with a good holster that requires specific steps in order to draw the firearm. As I discussed like a broken record earlier, make sure you practice with this holster and use it consistently to support good, ingrained memory. Also, make sure your holster covers the trigger, use a good sturdy belt, and take that retention class.

Now that I've touched on this, let's move on to the discussion regarding different types of carrying methods and strategies when carrying your firearm **concealed.**

3.8
Firearm Carry Methods and Strategy

The way you carry your firearm will depend on your job function, the shape of your body, your reasoning for carrying the firearm, environmental factors like climate, type of community you live in or travel to, and the threat levels of your surroundings where you are operating. There are several other factors that would dictate how and where you carry your firearm, but these are the major ones that I feel are important.

As mentioned above, blending into your environment while carrying your firearm concealed as well as taking accessibility into consideration is the key takeaway here. Again, when I refer to accessibility, I am referring to not only your ability to obtain the firearm from your person, but also somebody else's ability to disarm you! The more popular methods for carrying your pistol are on the hip, the small the back, and appendix carry.

Now, no matter which way you carry your weapon around your beltline, it will be uncomfortable. We have bones there. Having a hard metallic object encased within another enclosure called a holster pressing against those bones hurts and is uncomfortable. With that being said, I'd like to offer you a friendly reminder not to baby your weapon or reposition in public.

Before we jump any further, let me mention that all of these forms of carry, as well as the different stances, grip methods, styles of shooting, and sight alignment strategies are easily available to the public. Because of this, I have decided to use only the pictures that I felt were necessary and instead, focus on articulating to the best of my ability the logic behind my thought process, which I feel is more important. Most folks understand the basics, but they are seldom told the reasoning behind the instruction. Off we go.

Figure 3C An example of carrying a firearm in the 3 o'clock position while right-hand dominant
Courtesy of Kurt Delia & Delia Tactical International, LLC

So, when you carry on the hip, whether it's the 9 (left side) or 3 o'clock (right side) position depending on if you're left-handed or right-handed, you would have to make the decision on whether or not you want to carry **outside of the beltline or within the beltline**. There are some amazing holsters on the market that accommodate both methods of carry. Depending on the climate you live in, your body type or the situations mentioned above, you have to make that personal decision. In colder climates, since you would be likely wearing a jacket, carrying a firearm outside the beltline may be a viable option. Remember that you would eventually have to take off that jacket, so having a loose-fitting shirt that covers the entire weapon system is recommended. Carrying your firearm within the beltline, meaning between the belt and your undergarments, is a lot more discreet and hugs a contour of your body, but it is not as comfortable. Whether you carry the firearm inside or outside of your beltline on the hip, make sure it's not cross-drawn and make sure the handle, or grip, is not facing out, which would make it easier and more appealing for the bad guy to attempt to disarm you, should he see or know you are carrying a weapon.

Before we continue, for the sake of explanation, when I refer to the grip (handle) of a firearm, I am referring to the part of the firearm that your dominant hand grasps, which includes the front strap, the side panel and the back strap. The front strap of the grip is the front of the grip, whereas the back strap is the rearmost part of the grip. The side panel is, of course, the sides of the grip.

Figure 3D Drawing a firearm from the 3 o'clock position
Courtesy of Kurt Delia & Delia Tactical International, LLC

Moving on, if your job function or the situation dictates that you carry cross draw, then do what works for you but make sure you practice deploying your weapon system in that fashion. I am not a fan of the grip facing outward, but every situation and circumstance is different.

Another popular way to carry your weapon, widely used by off-duty law enforcement, is **concealed** in the 4 or 5 and 7 or 8 o'clock positions depending on your dominant hand. This 4 or 5 o'clock position is the small of the back of the body resting just to the right of the hip almost right above the buttocks (with the magazine well pointing toward the spine), for those who are right-handed. Please note that the magazine well is where the magazine is inserted into the grip.

Obviously, for your left-handed dominant citizens, carrying it **concealed** in the 7 or 8-o'clock position is your option, again, with the magazine well facing the spine. Whether you carry outside the beltline or within the beltline, these are fairly comfortable positions for your firearm to be placed on your person.

Before we touch on the less popular forms of carry, let's discuss appendix carry. Appendix carry generally entails carrying a weapon within the beltline between the outer garment and inner garment and on or just off center from the navel (belly button), roughly between the 11 to 1 o'clock position. At first thought, men get a little squeamish about this type of carry because the business end is facing towards the male anatomy. With humans being as clumsy as they are, we can only imagine what could happen should a round accidentally go off while carrying in this fashion or trying to deploy your weapon during a lethal engagement under stress.

Figure 3E   Appendix Carry at the 12 o'clock position
Courtesy of Kurt Delia & Delia Tactical International, LLC

Figure 3F Appendix Carry at the 11 o'clock position, cross draw
Courtesy of Kurt Delia & Delia Tactical International, LLC

Remember in Section 2 when we talked about losing your fine motor skills during the fight or flight response? Experienced police officers or military who were trained to mitigate these primal gifts of ancient man are likely in a better position to rapidly deploy their firearm under exigent lethal circumstances. Sure, there may be times you'll have a few seconds to consciously think about clearing your holster before an engagement, but much of the time you will not. Now, there are holsters available in the market that allow you to shift from appendix carry to other positions around the beltline. Research these options and choose the best option that works for you. Appendix carry is more comfortable while driving and is overall much more discreet.

Your body type and clothing can drastically affect all methods of carry. The skinny person has a little less meat around the hips and may experience a different level of comfort as compared to somebody with a little more weight. Obviously, somebody a little heavier would have issues with wearing a belt and the weapon may be faced inward while on his person.

I would like to briefly touch on a few other less utilized forms or methods of carry. Let us begin with the famous ankle holster. As mentioned earlier in this book, there is a time and place for everything. Accessibility and retention should be your priority when you opt for any type of carry. However, sometimes circumstances may dictate an ankle holster. I know an officer who was working undercover and opted to carry a smaller weapon on his ankle in a holster due to the type of assignment he had. His cover was blown, and he found himself alone with a few very mad people in a secluded location. While they were discussing how to kill him and where to dump his body, he was trying to figure out how to access his firearm from his ankle holster. He eventually secured his weapon and sent these unsuspecting deplorables to the not so pearly gates of hell. He went home to his family that night thankful he was in one piece, literally.

When I was a rookie police officer, I opted for a backup weapon on the ankle. That was short-lived after a foot chase went awry. As I was chasing the bad guy through a yard, I hopped the fence and as I was on the top of the fence getting ready to land on my feet on the other side, I went one way and my weapon detached from the ankle holster and flew the other. Being that I was always finding myself in a foot chase, usually at night, I decided to relocate my backup weapon to another location on my body.

Another less common method of carry is with the shoulder holster. This type of carry was and still is popular within the investigation community because it's comfortable and can be worn under a suit jacket or sport coat discreetly. It is accessible and extremely comfortable. This type of carry was definitely made for TV because it showcases the persona of a detective or investigator smoking that cigarette while sitting in his office late at night typing out that report. What's not to love about that?

I have, in my past, worn a shoulder holster depending on my function. The obvious downside is that if the holster malfunctions, the weapon could fall right out into the public view. Also, the grip is facing outward and can be accessible to the public, creating a retention issue. If officers or citizens carry the weapon in the shoulder holster under loose clothing or a jacket of some type, if a hand-to-hand situation takes place, the bad guy is within an arm's reach of your weapon, potentially disarming you with the business end already towards you. You will have more control of the weapon somewhere along the beltline, as discussed above.

There are innovative garments out there that support some unique methods for carrying your weapon. I've seen specialized shirts, pants, vests and jackets that have a holster within the garment, allowing quick access to the weapon. Again, as with the appendix carry, during an unexpected exigent lethal threat, ingrained memory can affect how you obtain your weapon on your person, and with your vital organs in the approximate area of where your weapon is holstered, a lethal mishap can take place.

Figure 3G   Concealed Carry fanny pack
Courtesy of Kurt Delia & Delia Tactical International, LLC

I have personally utilized body holsters under my clothing where the weapon is placed in a specialized holster on a large elastic belt that hugged the contour of my body. It is simple, inconspicuous, comfortable, and effective, but again, retention can be an issue if exposed to the public or if it is known you are carrying a weapon. I utilized this type of carry while working undercover as a bank teller in an armed robbery investigation during the course of a bank robbery spree.

Figure 3H   This is a body holster for concealment close to the body. This specific holster as well as other concealment options are sold by a family-owned company called Ghost Concealment out in Utah
Courtesy of Kurt Delia & Delia Tactical International, LLC

I also used one while working undercover during another armed robbery investigation as a maintenance engineer in a high rise because a suspect of an armed robbery duo was believed to have lived there with a friend. It was discreet, close to my body, accessible to me and very comfortable. I had the bad guy fooled until the doorman decided to point out the suspect in the middle of the lobby. The suspect saw that he was pointed out and after we both scowled at the doorman, he ran like a bat out of hell, leading me up 7 flights of stairs within a stairwell and into an apartment until I apprehended him. Because of the circumstances I was operating in, it worked. Well, at least until the doorman blew my cover! Ironically, the suspect's partner in crime walked into a police station with his attorney an hour later to turn himself in because of the way we took down his buddy.

Every situation is different and if your life depends on it, you adapt. Whether you're a civilian or a police officer off duty, choose the option that best works for you, but keep retention and accessibility in mind. Always keep retention in the back of your mind and regardless of how you choose to carry your weapon concealed, be consistent in your training routine, and incorporate the way you carry your weapon within that training regimen for the purpose of ingrained memory.

Let's push forward! You figured out what method of carry works for you. You have practiced it. You have consistently included the deployment sequence within your training routine and you are confident that you would draw your firearm from your holster and deploy it, neutralizing a deadly threat if confronted with one. That's great, but we have a few crucial components that we must discuss which includes stance, the actual draw itself with a strong master grip, non-dominant hand support, and gripping the weapon while firing.

You have to remember that the way that you position yourself and execute the draw will determine how you grip and successfully fire the weapon during an engagement. If your draw is not firm and strong, you are committed to a weak grip once the weapon is out of your holster. That is not the situation you want to be in.

It's also worth mentioning that the majority of the accidental discharges and injuries happen while drawing and re-holstering the weapon. This is due to inexperience, lack of practice, complacency, improper ingrained memory, fight or flight, and adrenaline.

Even with the extremely experienced marksmen, practice is essential because skill levels deplete with time. You would be surprised how quickly performance decreases without practice in as little as a couple of weeks.

3.9
Take a Stance

Let's briefly touch on stance. Yes, Firearms 101, but bear with me because it is important. There are basically three types of stances commonly used: the Isosceles stance, the Weaver stance, and the Chapman stance (also known as the Modified Weaver stance). Some argue that the Isosceles and the Weaver stance is a little outdated, but I feel it's worth understanding. Also, many of these basic stances tend to be modified depending on the job function or personal experience of the marksman.

With the **Isosceles stance**, both feet should be placed a little further than shoulder width apart and parallel to each other with the knees slightly bent. The posture should be aggressively forward with both arms punched out at 90%, in order to absorb recoil. I have also seen this stance modified with the feet slightly off center, instead of parallel.

With the **Weaver stance** (named after the great Jack Weaver), the foot on your dominant side should be placed shoulder width apart and slightly back. The dominant arm should be locked out 90% and the support hand slightly bent and pulling back during the grip. **In other words, if you're right-hand dominant, your right foot should be slightly back, shoulder width apart, and again with an aggressive posture forward.**

The **Modified Weaver**, or **Chapman stance**, is a little more of an exaggerated Weaver and is considered to be a tactical or combat stance. Put yourself into the Isosceles stance. Then take one exaggerated step back with the dominant leg, locking it out 80-90% while keeping your support foot in place and "loaded" (the weight focused on the foot) with the knee bent.

In other words, if you are right-handed, bend your left knee, focusing your weight on your left foot, then take a healthy step back with your right foot while locking the leg 80-90%. Also, keep your strong and support arms the same as mentioned above with the Weaver stance. This stance squares off your body a little more than the traditional Weaver and will dramatically stabilize your footing so you can manage recoil and get back on target quicker, while maximizing the protection of your body armor. I have also seen this stance modified where the weight is distributed equally with both feet. Do what works for you!

Figure 3I   Isosceles Stance front view
Courtesy of Kurt Delia & Delia Tactical International, LLC

Figure 3J   Isosceles Stance angled view
Courtesy of Kurt Delia & Delia Tactical International, LLC

Figure 3K The more traditional Weaver Stance with the strong arm punched about 90% and the support hand slightly bent
Courtesy of Kurt Delia & Delia Tactical International, LLC

Figure 3L Weaver Stance with both arms punched out about 90%, front view
Courtesy of Kurt Delia & Delia Tactical International, LLC

Figure 3M The Modified Weaver or Tactical Stance as well as an example of point shooting using the chin-weapon-target strategy with both feet pointed towards the threat and arms punched out 90% for accuracy
Courtesy of Kurt Delia & Delia Tactical International, LLC

A slight modification I prefer with the Modified Weaver stance is punching both arms out 90% (almost like point shooting) as compared to bending the support arm. This will allow you to pivot with ease.

Now, a few things to keep in mind. The Isosceles stance does give you a complete field of vision as well as the ability to pivot in all directions. The downside is that your entire body is exposed, making you a bigger target to your adversary. Also, if you are wearing body armor, your vital organs will be more protected, but your foundation is not as stable because of how your feet are positioned.

Both variations of the Weaver stance do slightly minimize the profile of your body as a target, but you lose the ability to smoothly pivot, which is why I recommend punching out both arms at 90% while using the Modified Weaver, or Combat stance. Also, with the Weaver stance, you are more vulnerable if you are wearing body armor because such armor usually does not protect the side of the body since the stance requires angled positioning in respect to your threat.

Using these types of stances in a controlled environment like a range is ideal. However, you may be holding groceries while walking, you may be driving in a car, you may be running up a flight of stairs during an active killer situation, or you may have your toddler in your arms, among other scenarios. You are not always going to have time to get into that perfect stance. It is important to practice the basics so if the day should come and you have to engage a lethal threat, your actions are instinctual.

When you are at the range in a controlled environment, it is easy to do everything the way you are supposed to. The perfect stance, the perfect sight alignment, the perfect trigger pull with focused breathing. It's just dandy when you are not getting shot at.

When the shit hits the fan, time rarely stops for anybody unless you lose the gunfight or face God. Even then, I have a hunch that the clock keeps ticking. Practicing the fundamentals at the range or in tactical courses will give you the confidence, skills, and ingrained memory you need to successfully engage a lethal threat, no matter what the circumstances are.

But that being said, we do not always get a chance to be where we want to be or achieve that tactical advantage through positioning because these types of threats happen unexpectedly. This is why it is important to practice different scenarios and different circumstances while under the supervision of a trained instructor. It's also important to always go back to the basics and consider them your foundation to build upon. The classes are out there. Sign up for them and take them! This also is true for the grip. We don't always have an opportunity to get that perfect draw with that perfect grip, depending on the circumstances.

3.10
Drawing the Firearm and Grip

The Draw

So, your pre-draw grip, or master grip, as some call it, entails your dominant hand smoothly moving in the direction of your holster, firmly gripping from the back strap around the grip (handle). Your trigger finger should be slightly curved inward and over the outside of the holster where the trigger guard would normally be on the weapon. Your remaining three fingers should be firmly on the grip, including your pinky. Your thumb should be placed between your body/belt and the slide, so when you draw, it naturally falls into place. The web of your hand (skin between index finger and thumb) should be flush and as high as possible against the top of the back strap (top of the grip), also known as the "tang." Assuming you have negotiated the retention mechanisms, a smooth continuous draw with the elbows in should take place. Your non-dominant hand during the draw should already be at chest level, preferably with the thumb or palm on the chest. When your dominant hand brings the weapon into the firing position, your non-dominant hand will complete the grip depending on how you opt to grip your weapon. Remember, whether you are an on-duty police officer carrying a level 3 retention holster, off-duty, or a civilian carrying under your clothing, practice the draw. The type of clothing or holster you use will play a major role within the drawing process, and how you practice will save your life. One last point regarding the draw. Make sure you keep your elbows in, while smoothly thrusting the weapon forward with about 75% power, leaving you time to instinctually utilize all the fundamentals of marksmanship prior to engaging the threat. A proper grip will not only manage recoil, but ensure your weapon is on point with the target.

Figure 3N Master Grip while drawing with Appendix Carry
Courtesy of Kurt Delia & Delia Tactical International, LLC

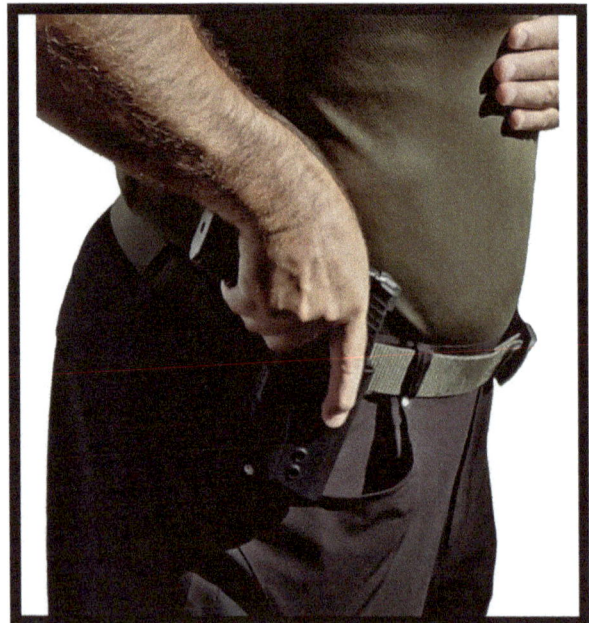

Figure 3O Obtaining a solid Master Grip prior to drawing is crucial
Courtesy of Kurt Delia & Delia Tactical International, LLC

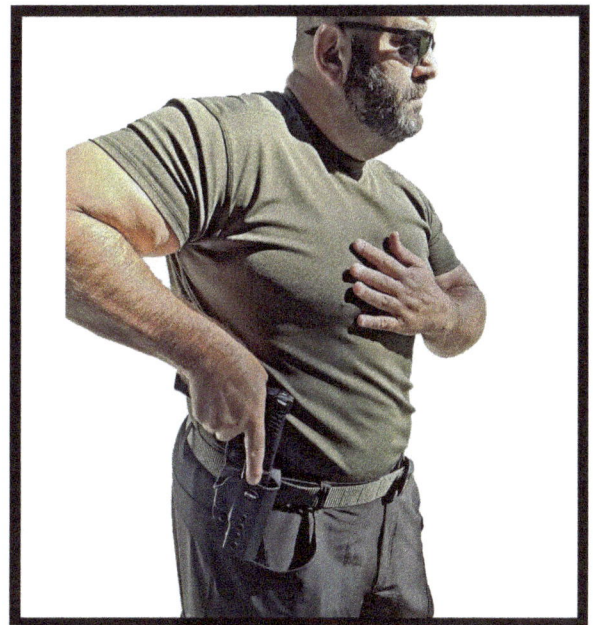

Figure 3P   Ensure a smooth continuous draw
Courtesy of Kurt Delia & Delia Tactical International, LLC

Figure 3Q   The support hand is near the chest and ready to complete the grip
Courtesy of Kurt Delia & Delia Tactical International, LLC

Figure 3R   A solid grip is completed with the support hand
Courtesy of Kurt Delia & Delia Tactical International, LLC

Figure 3S   Thrust the firearm forward with 75% power (and extended at about 90%)
Courtesy of Kurt Delia & Delia Tactical International, LLC

Figure 3T   Concealed carry draw with Master Grip
Courtesy of Kurt Delia & Delia Tactical International, LLC

Figure 3U   Drawing your firearm while carrying concealed takes practice but will eventually become fluid!
Courtesy of Kurt Delia & Delia Tactical International, LLC

Figure 3V Keep your eyes on the threat and your mindset with solid ingrained memory will lead the way
Courtesy of Kurt Delia & Delia Tactical International, LLC

Figure 3W Knowledge is your biggest weapon, but the element of surprise will be the aggressors greatest disadvantage!
Courtesy of Kurt Delia & Delia Tactical International, LLC

Get a Grip

We all have different experiences and come from different backgrounds or organizations. Some organizations encourage the "thumbs forward" grip whereas other organizations like the Israeli Defense Force, who seem to know a thing or two about urban combat, encourage the "knuckle over" grip, or what they call the combat grip. Believe it or not, this could bring up a couple heated discussions, but at the end of the day, you have to do what works for you. Your job function, background, organization, the size and shape of your hand and experience will often impact the grip that you use. Now, let's assume you have a proper draw, as previously described, as we touch on both of these grips.

Figure 3X Thumbs Forward Grip side view
Courtesy of Kurt Delia & Delia Tactical International, LLC

Figure 3Y Thumbs Forward grip top view
Courtesy of Kurt Delia & Delia Tactical International, LLC

Figure 3Z Thumbs Forward Grip top and front view
Courtesy of Kurt Delia & Delia Tactical International, LLC

Figure 3AA   **Thumbs Forward Grip angled view**
Courtesy of Kurt Delia & Delia Tactical International, LLC

With the thumbs forward grip (some call it the clamshell grip), the firearm is gripped with the dominant hand as the dominant thumb rests directly above the support hand's thumb which is parallel to the slide while pointed forward. The support hands remaining four fingers wrap around the top of the dominant hands three fingers under the trigger guard, subsequently closing the gap and completing the grip. Many argue this grip stabilizes the weapon and enhances the accuracy and speed during firing and seems to be the standard for many reputable organizations. While this may be true, everything comes with a price.

The knuckle over grip, however, entails the dominant hand completely gripping the grip (including the thumb) of the pistol while pressing the support hand's thumb directly on top of the dominant thumb, between the nail and the joint. During this grip, the dominant thumb is bending downward as if making a fist. Again, like with the thumbs forward grip, the support hands remaining four fingers are over the dominant hands remaining three fingers under the trigger guard. Please take a careful look at the pictures displaying both of these grips.

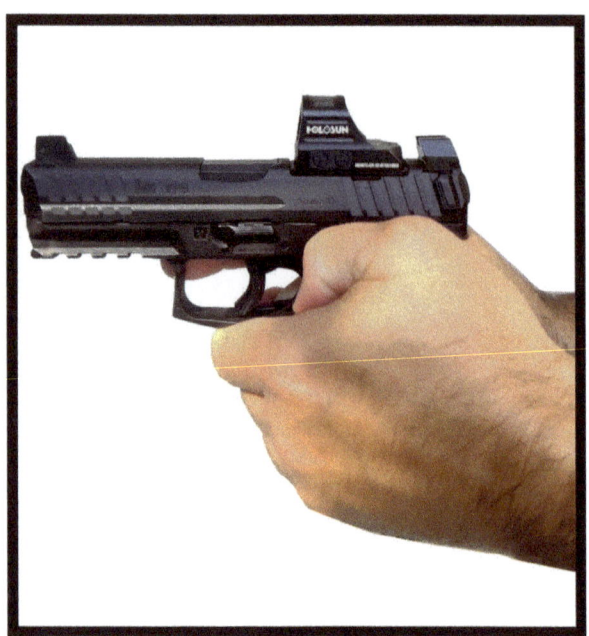

Figure 3AB Knuckle Over grip side view. The IDF calls this the Combat grip and for a very good reason!
Courtesy of Kurt Delia & Delia Tactical International, LLC

Figure 3AC Knuckle Over Grip angle view
Courtesy of Kurt Delia & Delia Tactical International, LLC

Figure AD Knuckle Over Grip front view
Courtesy of Kurt Delia & Delia Tactical International, LLC

Many police officers prefer the knuckle over grip (or combat grip) and for a very good reason. Working in an urban environment and finding yourself in a potential close-quarter combat situation requires you always to have control of your firearm, allowing you to not only fire with one hand, but also to utilize your non-dominant hand to move a citizen out of the way, fight or negotiate obstacles like a fence or a door while in pursuit of an offender.

The IDF prefers this grip for exactly this reason as do many law enforcement officers who work in urban America. It is sometimes stated that only inexperienced marksman or those who use revolvers use this outdated grip, which is not correct.

Figure AE Using the Knuckle Over Grip not only helps with retention, but allows you to use your support hand in close quarter combat situations
Courtesy of Kurt Delia & Delia Tactical International, LLC

The thumbs forward grip, on the contrary, requires you to move your thumb, destabilizing your control of the weapon, especially in a close quarter situation or shooting with one hand. Do what is best for you; it's not right for an organization or instructor to dictate otherwise.

Figure AF Which ever way you grip your firearm, this is how it looks from the dominant side!
Courtesy of Kurt Delia & Delia Tactical International, LLC

Regardless of how you opt to grip your weapon, you'll eventually have to fire it. In the next few segments, we are going to discuss target acquisition, sight alignment, point shooting, trigger pull, breathing, and a few tips and clues to enhance your performance while firing your pistol.

3.11
Target Acquisition, Sight Alignment and Point Shooting

Target Acquisition and Sight Alignment

Let's start with target acquisition, which is the ability to locate, identify and isolate your threat while understanding how to best utilize your sights. When I am talking about sights, I'm commonly referring to the standard iron sights that come with most pistols. Most police officers opt for the aftermarket options like tritium, which is a combat sight. It changes from white during the day to a glowing green at night for low light conditions with an intentional focus on the front sights.

SECTION THREE | Carrying the Burden   **101**

Moving on, it is also crucial that you are aware of other threats in your immediate area as well as innocent citizens in the line of fire. Keep in mind that an innocent citizen can be either in the back of the threat, behind a door or a wall, between you and the threat, or in the vicinity placing them in harm's way. Be aware of your surroundings and reposition yourself if necessary to keep innocent civilians safe and the lethal threat isolated with a tactical disadvantage while maintaining your cover as much as possible. Remember, cover will be an obstacle, like a wall or cement barricade that can stop a bullet as compared to concealment, which will only obscure you.

In theory, a traditional sight picture entails the front sight is on the target and rests in between the two rear sights and are lined up with each other. I am sure you are familiar with this, but I'd like to add a little more insight regarding a couple of different schools of thought.

One strategy is that your eyes should focus on the front sight, which is on the target with both the front sight and the target being clear. The front sight should be parallel, or lined up, with the rear sight. During this process, the rear sight should be slightly blurry prior to squeezing the trigger.

Another school of thought regarding sight alignment is a focus on a blurred threat or target and a clear sight picture (meaning a crystal-clear rear and front sight alignment) prior to squeezing the trigger. Also note that whichever way you opt to use your sights, the rear sight is used for the follow-up shots.

My recommendation regarding sight alignment should be a strong focus on the front sight and front sight only. **So, as a rule of thumb, align your front sight center "mass" on your threat, find and maintain your "wall," which we will get into ahead, take the shot, repeat if required, then introduce the rear sights if the threat is further away or with follow-up shots.**

While we are on the topic of sight alignment, it's worth mentioning that you should be aware of whether or not you are right or left-eye dominant. Some people shoot with both eyes open or just with their dominant eye open. Many things like illness, age, body type and other factors can play a role with how you utilize your eyes while firing your weapon. Adapt to your limitations, then practice with them. There are disadvantages and advantages for shooting with both eyes open or one closed. Many experienced officers keep both eyes open to be able to use their peripheral vision and maintain situational or threat awareness.

Red dot sights are a popular optic used by civilians, military, and police organizations worldwide. One big problem that many people have with red dot sights is finding the red dot during an engagement. The key to successfully utilizing this type of optic is practice and a consistent grip. Obviously, other marksmanship fundamentals are important, but having a consistent grip will make sure you find that red dot every time you need it instinctually. Practice will make it second nature.

Point Shooting

Let's briefly touch on point shooting. Some call it combat shooting and others would argue this description. I don't want to get caught up on the names. The names can change from time to time, depending on the instructor, their experience, or the time period they learned in.

Throughout history, this type of shooting was used when the sights on the firearms were not as advanced or the situation dictated a rapid deployment of their weapon. As such, point shooting was popular during World War II, among other wars of the recent past. I would imagine some of the more skilled gunslingers of the American West were proficient as well.

Historically, this type of shooting was widely taught by the military and law enforcement communities but became less popular due to the emergence of better sights and advanced optics. I feel that this is a strong skill to have and there are still classes available that teach this.

This method of shooting can be extremely effective up to about seven yards or 21 feet. Any more distance than that, you are going to want to have a good sight picture. We are not always going to have time or an ideal environment to get that perfect sight picture or that nice two-handed grip. From a practical standpoint, if time is a factor, it's not always a good idea to take your attention off the threat and focus on your sight alignment.

An effective shot in a lethal encounter does not always require the perfect placement of the round during the engagement in order to neutralize or stop a threat. Maybe the conditions are not ideal. Perhaps it's dark or we are somehow blinded by a bright light like a flashlight, gunfire, a streetlamp, or the sun. Maybe there are several immediate threats, and point shooting is our only option because being aware of our surroundings takes precedence.

One strategy for point shooting is the **"chin-weapon-target"** method. In other words, your weapon is up at chin level and aggressively punched forward with both arms locked out at 90% and a two-handed grip. Your weapon is in line with the target with a soft focus or confirmation on the front sight prior to squeezing the trigger. If possible, try to have both feet and the front of your hip bones naturally pointing towards the target while using the stances mentioned above. This will help with overall accuracy while stationery and pivoting. Repetition and a consistent training routine will ensure you are on target every time!

Figure 3AG Point shooting using the Chin-Weapon-Target strategy
Courtesy of Kurt Delia & Delia Tactical International, LLC

If you must fire with one hand, use the same strategy, but keep your support hand either on your side or palm down on your chest with the strong hand locked out at 90%. Also, remember that the weapon will be slightly off center from your chin towards your dominant side because you are not using your support hand. I feel that practicing one-handed point shooting is important because if you are in a situation that dictates one-handed shooting, you are likely either wounded, fighting, or time is not on your side.

Figure 3AH Point Shooting with one hand while using the natural flow of the body is a popular strategy because sometimes the threat isn't always in front of you
Courtesy of Kurt Delia & Delia Tactical International, LLC

Figure 3AI One-handed Point Shooting by locking the dominant arm with the dominant foot forward in order to manage recoil and stay on target. Keep your support hand on the side or chest.
Courtesy of Kurt Delia & Delia Tactical International, LLC

Every war has its own personality and requires adapting to a new enemy and environment. Communities change. Technology advances forward and people lose their instinct, including some of those that protect us if training is not prioritized.

3.12
Breathing while Shooting (Not Tactical) and Trigger Pull

Breathing while Shooting

Before we get into trigger pull, I'd like to touch on breathing. Obviously, in a lethal threat encounter, your heart is racing, and your breathing is likely rapid. The scene is chaotic, people might be screaming, and you're scared, rightfully so. Tactical breathing is key to lowering your heart rate in this type of situation for the reasons we discussed, but when we are talking about the fundamentals of marksmanship, we're talking about a different type of breathing that should be practiced in more controlled environments like the range.

Let's assume that you have your ideal grip, the meaty middle segment of your index finger on that "wall" of the trigger, and you breathe in, then out again. At this point, between breaths and during that pause after you exhale is when you complete the trigger pull by squeezing the trigger and then finding that wall again for a follow-up shot.

This is the moment when your body is in the most optimal position to fire the weapon, **from a fundamental perspective**. Breathing-in while you shoot may raise your round placement, and breathing out may lower it. Also, remember not to hold your breath. Now, amid a hot situation where you're tactically breathing in order to lower your heart rate, you may not always get a chance to fire between breaths, but like I said, it's just a fundamental of marksmanship. **Marksmanship basics to the side, if anything, just try to breathe normally!**

As mentioned above, the more time you spend away from practicing with your firearm, the more it is encouraged to return to the fundamentals of marksmanship in order to solidify your foundation, regardless of how much experience you have. When in doubt, always go back to the basics and rebuild from there!

So, we've touched on grip, stance, sight alignment, as well as point shooting. The last and—in my opinion the most important—attribute of marksmanship aside from grip is trigger pull. With the exception of some forms of shooting, in most circumstances we usually don't "pull" the trigger, we squeeze it.

Trigger Pull

We can't always control the circumstances of the situations we find ourselves in. Also, we may not always be able to control our stance, sight alignment, or even our breathing in an unexpected lethal encounter, but we can control our trigger pull, within reason. If you master your trigger pull, that's more than half the battle, regardless of whether or not you are point shooting, shooting from an awkward position, using specialized optics or sights, or your classic sight alignment strategy with factory sights.

Let's take a look at the optimal trigger pull in a controlled or range setting in respect to the basics of marksmanship, then we will discuss my recommendations for trigger pull in more of an exigent lethal threat circumstance. In all honesty, this also applies to every aspect of marksmanship discussed above, but as your skills progress, your practiced strategies from the range kick in if an unexpected lethal threat occurs.

You cannot pick the time and location where these threats will occur, but you can be prepared to apply a sufficient amount of baseline skill to stop the threat, even if the rounds aren't perfectly center mass in the chest. In other words, don't overthink it, and when the day should come that you must save your life, your training and ingrained memory will kick in.

Moving on, historically, many instructors recommended a consistent squeezing of the trigger without anticipating the shot, almost as a surprise, while holding true to the rest of the marksmanship fundamentals. Ideally, if the fundamentals are practiced in unison, this will help with accuracy and effective round placement. As mentioned earlier, the meaty segment of the middle of your index finger, or trigger finger, should be on the trigger and the trigger should be squeezed, not pulled or jerked, when firing the weapon.

I talked above about finding the "wall." Keep in mind that every weapon is different and knowing when the "slack" stops right before the trigger mechanism fires the weapon is called a wall. Many trigger mechanisms have some room, or slack, between where the trigger naturally rests until the trigger mechanism is fully engaged and fires the round. **Understanding where the wall is will allow you to reset the trigger mechanism for follow-up shots quickly and on target.**

Again, in respect to combat shooting, align your front sight center mass on your threat, find and maintain your "wall," take the shot, reset the trigger mechanism back to that wall, then repeat if required. Follow up with introducing the rear sights if the threat is further away for a more complete sight picture.

3.13

Malfunctions, Immediate Action and A Stab in the Dark

Malfunctions and Immediate Action

I discussed throughout this section the importance of retention and retention training under stress. Learning how to negotiate malfunctions with your weapon system under stress is equally as important. The common types of malfunctions comprehensively are **failure to fire, tip-up (when a round is lodged above the chamber), failure to extract the cartridge (stovepipe), failure to feed (numerous reasons), double-feed and failure to go in the slide lock.**

Initially, the exact cause of a malfunction is not always clear, especially to the untrained marksman. Regardless of the issue, it needs to be resolved quickly so you can get back into the fight.

There are **two remedial action drills** that will clear the majority of the pistol malfunctions that are more common such as hearing a click or seeing a double feed of rounds or cartridges.

If you hear a click, chances are that the ammunition is bad, the magazine is faulty or there was a malfunction with the firing pin (which is terrifying), to mention a couple.

In this situation, keep the weapon pointed towards the target while keeping the finger on the trigger guard. Then, with the support hand, tap the bottom of the magazine baseplate upward and with the weapon still pointed towards your threat, rack the slide. Tap, rack, then re-engage! This is simple, and it works.

Now, if you see a stovepipe malfunction or a round lodged against the top of the chamber (tip-up), you will want to lock the slide to the rear keeping the weapon pointed towards your threat. Then strip the magazine to the ground, rack the slide once or twice, reinsert the fresh magazine, and then chamber a round to get back on target. Many police academies teach this method, but what if you only have one magazine with you or limited ammunition? You don't want to strip your only magazine to the ground and take your eyes off your threat. This is dangerous. The simple answer is to carry more magazines!

Police officers who are within the patrol division with most organizations have several magazines and since most engagements last under 15 seconds, they would probably have enough ammunition to stay in the fight.

These two drills will clear the majority of the malfunctions, but a lot of things could go wrong. Bad ammunition, inclement weather hampering the performance of the firearm or ammunition, a faulty trigger mechanism, or perhaps a faulty magazine spring. The list can go on and on, but you can practice for the more common malfunctions. Explore the use of "dummy rounds" which will allow you to practice negotiating different types of malfunctions at the range and do so under the supervision of a trained professional.

Obviously, if you see the slide locked to the rear, you're likely just empty, so simply reload a fresh magazine. Many people assume there is a malfunction when the weapon is just in slide lock. Understand your weapon and master it.

Remember, make sure you take the proper tactical classes in the field to practice these immediate action drills under the supervision of a trained instructor. Dealing with malfunctions needs to be practiced because when fear kicks in, not understanding how to instinctually negotiate a malfunctioning weapon can be deadly. As a new officer, I used to have nightmares and anxiety dreams about weapon malfunctions on a regular basis. What helped me was practice and confidence in my weapon system!

Speaking of anxiety, I would like to discuss one more concept that I feel is not only crucial to understand but will help transition us into the Use of Force discussion ahead. Sure, it is a little premature, but it will no doubt put your mind in the right place because this next discussion, especially that of deploying deadly force, is intense.

The Tueller Drill | A Stab in the Dark

In 1983, police instructor Dennis Tueller found himself teaching new recruits whilst attempting to explain the components of the reactionary gap (the time delay between seeing the threat and responding to it) during a knife engagement. The challenge was to determine the best distance that allows the officer to visually comprehend the threat and then react to it with his firearm. Since then, American law enforcement adopted this drill as the "21-foot rule," which is, according to Dennis, grossly wrong. Many factors must be determined in terms of deploying deadly force during a knife engagement. Such factors include distance to the attacker, the officer's experience, the officer's ability to draw under stress, the speed of the attacker, obstacles, and the totality of the circumstances, to mention a few. The Tueller Drill determined that twenty-one feet does not allow enough time for the officer to respond and that the officer should have his firearm drawn well before that distance. Furthermore, during his experiments with the recruits, it only took 1.5 seconds for the knife attacker to successfully reach the officer.

Figure AJ NEVER underestimate the lethality of a knife!
Courtesy of Dr. Ron Martinelli

Figure AK Good cover and creating distance can give you enough time to engage and neutralize the threat!
Courtesy of Dr. Ron Martinelli

As you will learn ahead, the totality of the circumstances is crucial when deploying deadly force during a lethal engagement, whether the attacker has a firearm, or a knife, which in many cases can be more lethal. The bottom line is that although twenty-one feet is not enough distance that will allow enough time to respond to a knife attack, every circumstance is different and requires a different course of action. Assessing the threat, creating distance, using available cover, and then making the decision to act in order to stop the threat could be the difference between life and death. As we move forward into the use of force discussion as well as an overview of the OODA Loop strategy towards the end of the section, keep this conversation in mind. One last point regarding knives. According to forensic criminologist Dr. Ron Martinelli of Martinelli & Associates (mentioned ahead), throwing knives are extremely lethal and surprisingly effective. He had the opportunity to conduct an experiment with knife throwing expert Mathew Dunn and found that they can **"access and deliver a 10" lethal missile traveling 30 mph from thirteen feet away with point of delivery center-mass hit on target in only 0.29 of a second!"** Furthermore, at 30 mph, that knife is traveling at 45 feet per second. It takes .56 seconds for an officer to comprehend a threat and according to Dr. Martinelli, about .56-.58 seconds to react. That old saying "never bring a knife to a gunfight" might just be wrong.

Hopefully, these past few segments have given you a different perspective as well as a stronger foundation for you to evolve as a responsibly armed citizen in the new world. It is solely a foundation that can only be mastered through the proper training, practice, and experience.

I had an opportunity to speak with Dr. Ron Martinelli, an accomplished author, forensic criminologist, and the owner of Martinelli & Associates, Justice & Forensic Consultants, LLC. Aside from his very impressive background, he was also personable, straightforward, and passionate about the truth. The firm's expertise entails several components, including firearms ballistics, criminal investigation, law enforcement practices, crime scene and forensic construction and, of course, the use of force. Being the gold standard regarding every aspect of deadly force, Dr. Martinelli asked firearms guru and cohort Larry Nichols if he would conduct a peer review of the firearms and deadly force segment of this book and he humbly accepted. Larry is an author, self-defense expert, forensic expert, and the Director of Firearms Training at the Officer Safety Institute's firearms training program where he is a master of firearms and the use of force. He is also a decorated

Marine who served in Vietnam, where his warriorship journey began, and he currently has over 30 years of experience as a professional law enforcement firearms instructor! I appreciate the precious time sacrificed by these men to conduct their review of my work. With that, let us continue into the dynamic discussion on the use of force!

Use of Force

Disclaimer: As an armed citizen, you are responsible for understanding the local, state, and federal laws in all aspects regarding firearms, including using deadly force in self-defense, that specifically pertains to where you live, work at, or travel to. You are expected to abide by these laws that are subject to change. This book, its content, the author, and his advisors only provide a platform for discussion of the subject matter. This discussion does by no means provide an absolute circumstance where deadly force should be used as all circumstances are different, requiring a different reasonable course of action.

3.14
Humble Beginnings

Throughout history, law enforcement has undergone drastic changes in every respect regarding how they police, especially when it comes to the use of force. When I say use of force, I am not only referring to deadly force. I am also referring to every aspect of force from the officer's presence to verbal commands as well as the "less lethal" options, like **Oleoresin Capsicum** (known as OC or pepper spray), a baton, or a CEW device (Conducted Energy Weapon) such as a Taser, to name a few. Before we discuss the use of deadly force from a civilian perspective, it's important to understand how these policies evolved and why from the LE side. Law enforcement's use of force policies, whether they were justified or not, has brought us to this point in time due to social outcry for change and more officer accountability. Change can be a positive thing but, in this case, the changes within law enforcement have drastically affected our safety and well-being, as discussed in Section 1 and throughout this book.

One wrong, split-second decision by an officer can not only affect the life of the citizen he is engaging with, but also his life, his family's life, and the community that he serves. The training is grossly substandard considering the level of responsibility, ever-increasing accountability, and power that a police officer has. Unfortunately, as the use of force policies has evolved (if you can call it that), the training required to keep the officer in tune with the use of force policies du jour isn't enough.

During the turn of the last century, "use of force continuums" were created in order to offer an appropriate force option in response to a subject's actions. Currently, most local, state, and federal law enforcement organizations, including the military, have very similar use of force policies, usually displayed within a detailed graph. The graph systematically dictates what actions and weapons, if any, the officer is allowed to utilize, depending on the circumstances and the actions of the subject. Let's break down the general outline of an example of a use of force continuum, and then we'll discuss some of the recent changes that have taken place.

Believe it or not, officer presence comes in number one for most use of force modules. Remember Section 2 when we were talking about posture? In most situations, a confident, well-spoken officer with a sharp uniform will be enough to command respect and diffuse a situation. Next, we have verbal commands. Giving the subject a clear, concise direction, and course of action is important, depending on the circumstance.

Moving on, we have soft control followed by hard control techniques. Soft control refers to tactics like pressure points and joint manipulation, usually while attempting to administer handcuffs to a subject. Hard control tactics bring the force options to another level, utilizing options like punching, kicking, stuns, and pepper spray.

The last two options are "Less Lethal" weapon options and, of course, deadly force. Less lethal options can entail weapons like a baton, pepper spray, the CEW device, or even police dogs. These weapons are, in theory, less lethal. Deploying these weapon systems irresponsibly, however, can be deadly. For example, the baton, in any variation, retractable or not, should be deployed on the torso or limbs of the body, avoiding the head, unless deadly force is appropriate. A head strike with a baton can be lethal and can be considered deadly force.

The final form of force and last resort is deadly force. Deadly force can be deployed with a firearm or any other means to stop the threat due to the circumstances. When an officer is in a deadly force situation, it is utilized either after all other force options have failed (hence, the more traditional continuum) or the lethal threat is immediate and exigent to the officer or community and likely to cause death or great bodily injury. We will discuss this in more detail ahead.

The use of force continuum was due for a few changes, but let's throw in a little bit of social outcry, incompetent politicians and partisan media, and we have **The National Consensus Policy and Discussion Paper on Use of Force.** The law enforcement community felt they had to be progressive, and yes, the long-utilized continuums did seem outdated.

The paper was submitted by the International Association for Chiefs of Police in 2017 and then modified again in 2020 after 11 police organizations came together to create this paper. The paper, with all of its glory, was suggested to be not a requirement but a guideline for law enforcement organizations worldwide regarding the use of force for the current day law enforcement officer. I'm sure the 16-page document wasn't easy for 11 organizations to agree upon, knowing it would be the suggested foundation for most modern use of force modules globally, influenced by the current-day social domain.

I would like to discuss a few things that stand out in my mind regarding this paper. It seems to me that it's a direct reflection of the civil unrest that subsequently paved the path for a document like this to exist. It also seems to me that officer accountability is the primary focus, the well-being of the offender comes in second place and officer safety comes in last, which is no surprise. Of course, this was merely my opinion after reading the content-rich paper several times, and it was clear to me that posterior protection was front and center.

I do understand the complexity of the topic and a balance between officer safety and community engagement. Deploying any type of force as a police officer these days is highly scrutinized, and this paper is a clear reflection of this.

In this paper, the topic of de-escalation stood out to me the most. Typically, de-escalation entails enhanced verbal tactics or actions taken by the officer in order to diffuse a situation, which is always a great skill to have. Many people assume police officers are quiet, cynical relics stuck in time. The truth is that most of them are chatterboxes and seem to have the natural gift of gab, which is always helpful on the street. Not all officers have this ability and teaching them to speak to a subject in a calm, non- aggressive tone can cool down tense circumstances at times, especially when emotions are elevated.

The paper also suggested that "tactical re-positioning" should be a de-escalation tactic as well in certain situations. By this they mean physically backing off, which I found disturbing. Yes, there are times that common sense should prevail, but we are not social workers. We are the police who should do something called policing.

It was also suggested that the officer gives verbal commands prior to deploying deadly force if time permits. I will not get into detail, but I can reassure you that most officers verbalize the commands to the bad guy if time permits, usually mixed in with a little profanity because tensions are high. Hopefully, law enforcement organizations will read through this document and use some discretion when forming their own use of force modifications based on the paper.

Speaking of reasonability, the paper suggests that "reasonable force" should be used "when no reasonably effective alternative appears to exist." Again, this is concerning to me, because most of the time, the officer is fighting for his life and doesn't have time to go down a checklist or look into other options under exigent circumstances, deadly or not. Also, any use of force modifications should be reflective within the training of the organization, which seems to be hit or miss. In the past, for an officer to use deadly force, he was in imminent risk of death or great bodily harm. Now, according to the paper, it should be immediate. Again, every situation is different, and officers are trained observers. They see things that most humans do not and, sometimes, they are forced to respond within seconds. We will get into this more in Section 4 when we talk about situational and threat awareness.

The paper restricts the use of choke holds and vascular restraints, unless deadly force is justified. Analyzing the **"totality of the circumstances"** is important, and if the officer feels the need to use deadly force with his hands, things are going very, very wrong. Although if this was recorded by video, an officer choking a citizen to death, regardless of the circumstances, it wouldn't look very good and likely would be on the news that evening, stirring up yet another riot stemming from bad journalism.

Now, I have a few thoughts regarding choke holds. Just recently, I spoke with Dr. Martinelli, who feels that choke hold options such as the Carotid Restraint Control hold in certain circumstances makes sense. In a control hold like this, blood flow is temporarily restricted until unconsciousness. Under certain circumstances and the proper training, it can be a viable option. With most police departments under scrutiny and very limited funding for training, mistakes can happen, especially under a violent and stressful encounter. Now as a civilian, with the proper instruction, having this tool in the use of force toolbox is a great option, but under stress, a lot can go wrong.

This is about education. Educating the officer, the civilian legally carrying a firearm, the journalist, and yes, even the wise educators in academia who have strongly influenced their students with extreme anti-police stances, limiting force options by law enforcement that can save lives. Perspective is everything, and knowledge is power. Knowledge also takes the power away from those pulling the strings of chaos, yanking the rug from underneath them.

It's easy to judge from the outside but put yourself in the shoes of the officer and I can promise that you may have a very different perspective. Recently, some activists and journalists have been allowed to train with officers, putting them in tense situations, some of which require a simulated deadly force response within seconds. I think this is brilliant as it's changed the opinions of many.

The paper does suggest that it is the officer's duty to intervene if excessive force is being used. I do agree within reason, depending on the situation. Perhaps the officer, who is in the middle of a hand-to-hand engagement, just chased the subject on foot for five blocks and the bad guy is under the influence of a narcotic, causing the officer to use more force due to the strength of the suspect. The arriving officers may see the tail end of the encounter and jump before it is safe to do so. Every situation is different and should be looked at with a "reasonable" set of eyes.

The use of force policies utilized by law enforcement is extensive and varies from Department to Department, but I wanted to give you a bird's-eye view because many civilian use of force parameters parallel those used by the police, especially when it comes to deadly force.

Let's take a look at the modern-day, recommended criteria for an officer's use of force according to **The National Consensus Policy and Discussion Paper on Use of Force** as of 2020. According to this paper, it states, *"An officer is authorized to use deadly force when it is objectively reasonable under the totality of the circumstances. Use of deadly force is justified when one or both of the following apply: To protect the officer or others from what is reasonably believed to be an immediate threat of death or serious bodily injury and/or to prevent the escape of a fleeing subject when the officer has probable cause to believe that the person has committed, or intends to commit a felony involving serious bodily injury or death, and the officer reasonably believes that there is an imminent risk of serious bodily injury or death to the officer or another if the subject is not immediately apprehended."*

The terminology, the use of force modules, and the policies are dependent upon the state, the jurisdiction, and the organization the officer works for. Most modules are fairly close in nature; remember, the consensus paper was only intended to be a guideline.

Throughout this section, I will mention the word "reasonable" a lot. When it comes to deadly force, several factors will be looked upon to determine if deadly force was justified whether you are a civilian or a police officer. Determining what a "reasonable officer" or "reasonable person" would do in a similar circumstance is heavily pondered and would be a more prominent factor that would justify the use of any force, including deadly force. We will dive into this and other factors ahead as we transition into a civilian's use of deadly force in **Segment A**.

I don't want to jump ahead into topics discussed in segment C yet, but there is a crucial attribute that I must discuss while we are discussing the deployment of deadly force. This is that you have two main actors in this circus called survival. No, it is not the clowns who made it tougher for the law-abiding citizens to exist in peace. These two main actors are the *aggressor* and the *victim*. Remember that the bad guy is going to lie his way to victimhood, and the system is designed to help him do just that. Know your rights, understand your local and state gun laws, and be the first to call the police after an incident occurs. We will get into this in Segment C in more detail, but I feel that this is important to mention before we dive into Segment A below.

Another important factor to understand prior to deploying deadly force that I feel is imperative is, once again, an aspect of situational awareness. Many times, deadly force encounters are recorded by video but don't always clarify the totality of the circumstances of the incident. We all know what happens if the media gets a hold of a video involving a deadly force encounter when all the important facts aren't obvious.

That aside, police officers in the academy are taught to slow down in order to observe the entire situation and figure out what's really going on. These police officers eventually become trained observers whose observational skills can be the difference between life and death of themselves, their fellow officers, and the community they serve.

For an armed civilian with good intentions, I feel the risks are greater if these observational skills are not learned. Section 4 dives deeper into threat and situational awareness, but it's important to understand now that things aren't always what they seem. Seeing a scraggly, bearded, underdressed man running out of a bank holding a firearm may be an undercover officer in pursuit of an armed offender. Shooting him may not work out well for anybody except the bad guy he was chasing. Also, many police officers work "side jobs" as security, finding themselves in situations that can put them at risk, and it's not always obvious they are off-duty police officers. As we mentioned earlier, bad guys lie. Be aware of the entire circumstance, use and listen to verbal commands, and pay attention to detail before intervening in any situation.

As we dive into Segment A, which focuses on a civilian's privilege to utilize deadly force under special circumstances, keep in mind that deadly force, in any manner of deployment, should be the last resort and avoided if possible. Civilians usually do not have "less lethal" weapon options, so the primary topic of discussion will be that of deadly force. I am not an attorney, but I have two decades of real-world experience in enforcing the legal system and utilizing use of force modules as a law enforcement officer on some of the toughest streets of urban America.

This section was reviewed by specialized attorneys, police firearm instructors, as well as a handful of civilian firearms instructors in order to collaborate with my experience and my perspective within this ever-evolving place we still call America. As we begin our discussion on deadly force, keep in mind that gun laws differ from state to state, and then we will dig deep into this discussion that few authors have put in print, so let's jump off this cliff of "anathema" together.

Use of Deadly Force: Segment A

As we discussed above, every law enforcement organization has its own policy regarding the use of force, but (within reason) they are very similar in nature. Regarding deadly force, the elements required in order to deploy such force are comparatively similar within the law enforcement and armed civilian community in the United States. This concurrence respectively leaks into the realm regarding a civilian's use of deadly force, but there are many more factors to consider. As a civilian, you do not have a union to defend you. Even if you are cleared of criminal charges, civil liability may be your next hurdle, regardless of whether or not you were justified. Hence, ensure you have the proper self-defense protection in place. Also, every state has different gun laws that dictate when, where, and even how deadly force can be deployed, which we get into more in Segment B.

As we discussed in Section 2, training is the one thing that will get us home that we don't seem to have time for. Throughout this book, I stress the importance of taking tactical courses as part of your "Warrior Journey." Warriors should master their firearm with the hopes that the day never comes that they must use it. **Knowledge is power, but restraint is our humanity—that is, after we stop the lethal threat.** Training to survive a deadly force encounter is the ultimate goal but this is half the battle, literally. What about knowing **when** to use deadly force or understanding your local gun laws? Not understanding this may get you home for a short period of time to kiss your smiling kids just to hug them goodbye before you go to prison for murder. It can and it has happened to both civilians and police officers.

Law enforcement's in-service training is minimal, and their recommended annual use of force training that many departments have barely meets industry standards or the demand of constantly changing threat levels they encounter on a daily basis. To me, this is ludicrous considering the level of responsibility they have as well as the changing use of force policies of the modern era.

As a civilian, not understanding when you are "privileged" to use deadly force is dangerous and irresponsible. Using deadly force is a gray area in most situations. What makes this reality hazy are the numerous gun laws that are different from state to state as well as a number of other factors that we will discuss ahead. With that being said, we're going to push forward, but you need to remember that deadly force is the last resort.

When it comes to a **civilian's** use of deadly force, I prefer to take a more cautious stance in terms of when it's deployed. I am attempting to strike a balance, understanding that most states have different deadly force guidelines. With this being the case, finding that middle ground is important. For example, as mentioned earlier, the fear of an aggressor inflicting immediate death or great bodily harm upon you and then having the means to deliver or act upon this threat seems very familiar at its core. Sure, some of the terminology may differ from state to state, but at the end of the day, the foundation is present. With that foundation comes the concession of the law-abiding, armed citizen or police to respond.

Civilian firearms instructors have set guidelines in respect to deadly force that are concurrent with their state's laws. In Segment C of this section, we dive into the post-shooting recommendations that you should know, but it is worth mentioning a very profound fact now about what happens during the post shooting investigation: The police do the investigation! The same officers that investigate your actions after your deadly force encounter likely will not only review state and local laws in detail, but they may also be influenced by their own deadly force policy or that of the consensus paper we discussed above that their organization, may have adopted.

The consensus paper, whether I agree with the content or not, is cautious. It's very cautious, and from a civilian's perspective in terms of deploying deadly force, I think it's worth becoming familiar with considering that many states mirror these standards within their state laws. The rules of engagement that civilians must abide by are not very different from that of law enforcement and being that many law enforcement organizations across America are using this consensus paper as a guideline, it makes sense. With that being said, let's review a few important definitions directly from the National Consensus Policy and Discussion Paper on Use of Force.

According to this paper, **DEADLY FORCE** is defined as "Any use of force that creates a substantial risk of causing death or serious bodily injury."

It goes on to say that, **OBJECTIVELY REASONABLE** is defined as "The determination that the necessity for using force and the level of force used is based upon the officer's evaluation of the situation in light of the totality of the circumstances known to the officer at the time the force is used and upon what a reasonably prudent officer would use under the same or similar situations."

Now, the last summarized snippet from this paper I would like to quote is in reference to the **USE OF DEADLY FORCE**. It goes on to say that an officer is authorized to use deadly force when it is objectively reasonable under the totality of the circumstances. Furthermore, use of deadly force is justified when it is to protect the officer or others from what is reasonably believed to be an immediate threat of death or serious bodily injury.

As I have researched the use of deadly force from the more left-leaning states to the right, the line down the middle was well within the boundaries of the above definitions. Here, I chose to cite the use of such force in self-defense in California, Texas, and Illinois. Let's take a look ahead. **Keep in mind that these laws are subject to change and seeking advice from an attorney is highly advised.** The structure and format of these laws are kept original so you can literally read them without interpretation.

Looking at **California**, a historically left-leaning state, you are justified in using deadly force in self-defense when the following occurs:

A. *You reasonably believed that you, or someone else, was in imminent danger of being killed, suffering great bodily injury, or being the victim of a forcible and atrocious crime, and*

B. *You reasonably believed that you needed to use deadly force to prevent the danger from happening, and*

C. *You used no more force than was reasonably necessary to keep the harm from occurring.*

In **Texas**, as of 2023, the following Texas Penal Code Section 9.32 applies for The Use of Deadly Force in Defense of Person, and I quote:

a) A person is justified in using deadly force against another:

(1) if the actor would be justified in using force against the other under Section 9.31; and

(2) when and to the degree the actor reasonably believes the deadly force is immediately necessary:

(A) to protect the actor against the other's use or attempted use of unlawful deadly force;

(B) to prevent the other's imminent commission of aggravated kidnapping, murder, sexual assault, aggravated sexual assault, robbery, or aggravated robbery.

The last state we will take a look at is **Illinois** under **720 ILCS 5/7-1.**

Sec. 7-1. Use of force in defense of a person.

(a) A person is justified in the use of force against another when and to the extent that he reasonably believes that such conduct is necessary to defend himself or another against such other's imminent use of unlawful force.

However, he is justified in the use of force which is intended or likely to cause death or great bodily harm only if he reasonably believes that such force is necessary to prevent imminent death or great bodily harm to himself or another, or the commission of a forcible felony.

(b) In no case shall any act involving the use of force justified under this Section give rise to any claim or liability brought by or on behalf of any person acting within the definition of "aggressor" set forth in Section 7-4 of this Article, or the estate, spouse, or other family member of such a person, against the person or estate of the person using such justified force, unless the use of force involves willful or wanton misconduct.

I really do not want you, my reader, to go into paralysis by reading too many quoted legal statutes, but I wanted to prove my point right from the source. Take note that the keywords that are emphasized in each state, including the consensus paper, are **reasonable and necessary**.

Moving on, the core fundamentals of using deadly force are similar in nature but different enough in that it is imperative that you make sure you understand in detail a state's specific use of force laws before entering, traveling to, or residing there.

Also, another important point to remember is that this segment is designed to give you the knowledge to build upon and is by no means an absolute in terms of when deadly force should be deployed because every situation is unique, involving multiple factors. Furthermore, with the space evolving as rapidly as it is, changes can happen quickly from gun legislation to when such force is justified. Do your research.

Also, remember that although you may not always have a firearm to defend yourself with under lethal circumstances, the same rules apply. You may be just traveling without your firearm or in a gun-free zone yet still find yourself in a situation that may require a deadly force response. Keep that in mind as we push forward, especially in Section 4.

Yes, there may be clear circumstances where deadly force may be deployed, but the majority of the situations you may find yourself in are very cloudy with lots of moving parts. Speaking of cloudy, provocation is absolutely frowned upon and will be considered during the post-shooting investigation or trial in respect to your deployment of deadly force. Defending yourself against an armed aggressor while you are stopped at a red light is much different then following him to start a fight and possibly a firefight if he is armed. Do not look for a fight, because even if it leads up to a deadly force situation that may normally fall in your favor, the fact that you provoked it may change the outcome legally and civilly.

The first major component in deploying such force is fear, as long as other elements—which can vary—are present and unprovoked. With this **fear of immediate death or great bodily injury comes the "privilege" of using deadly force in order to stop the deadly threat.** Remember, your goal is not to kill the active killer, for example. Your goal would be to "stop the threat," because killing someone is a crime after the threat has ceased. If the threat stops and becomes active again, then you treat it as such. Stopping someone from killing you is self-defense and your survival. Killing someone after the threat is no longer present is called murder. There is a difference, and you must know it!

The next major component is regarding the **delivery system**. Does the aggressor have the immediate capability and means to act upon, cause, or deliver the deadly threat at that moment in time? This talking point is important, so pay attention closely.

Finally, allow me to discuss what is called the "disparity of force" or the victim-subject factors, and what I like to refer to as the **"X" factors**. These are the factors like age, size, health, disability, or even environmental factors such as location that may influence not only the deployment of deadly force, but the post-shooting investigation conducted by law enforcement, charges, or even your self-defense trial if it gets to that point. We will discuss some examples of this further ahead.

Now, let's back up a little and look at these deadly force components from a scenario perspective. A man standing on your front lawn yelling his threatening intentions while pointing a rifle towards your window while your children are playing in your living room certainly constitutes the fear of immediate death or great bodily injury to you and your family. However, if that same man is holding a knife as you and your family are safely within your dwelling, calling the police makes sense. What changed? Well, with the rifle, he had the **means to act upon and deliver the threat because he can fire into the window or residence, causing death or great bodily injury.** With the knife, his delivery system is NOT likely to cause immediate death or great bodily harm in this specific circumstance.

Let's spin this same scenario. While you are inside of your house on the phone with the 911 dispatcher telling them a disturbed man is on your front lawn swinging a butcher knife into thin air, your oblivious teenage daughter pulls up into the driveway with her music blasting. Before you could warn her to stay in her car, the aggressor then starts rapidly walking towards your firstborn child as she exits the vehicle.

In this case, the lethal threat becomes active again, and he has the means to deliver this deadly threat to your daughter. You exit your home with your firearm, and from 20 feet away, while the aggressor is closing in on your child, you neutralize the threat, saving her life.

With this modified scenario, you have to realize that the circumstances changed with your daughter coming home. This unexpected variable affected the aggressor's delivery system, giving him the ability to inflict immediate death or great bodily harm upon your child with the knife as she exited the vehicle.

Now, let's further discuss the "X" factors which are, but not limited to, age, size, health, disability, or environmental factors. As I previously mentioned, these factors can impact the investigation conducted by law enforcement, the charges, if any, brought against you or the aggressor, and even the outcome of your trial if it gets to that point. Deploying such force is hazy enough as it is, but the "disparity of force," or subject-offender factors (X- factors) can turn the incident into a dust storm, as the cases we discuss towards the end of Segment B will humbly prove.

Let's start with age. The vulnerable age of a child or frail senior citizen is an X-factor. A large, unarmed, muscle-bound man punching a toddler or a frail 85-year-old woman can be deadly on the first strike. If that same 85-year-old woman, who happens to carry a firearm concealed, is able to deploy it, as the unarmed aggressor is charging towards her, the X-factor would likely impact all aspects of the post-shooting process. Under the same exact circumstance, if the victim was a younger man, who happens to be a cancer patient, or who just had back surgery, again, the X-factor may also impact the investigation or charges, which is exactly why documenting your injuries, illness, overall health, or limitations is important. Remember, every set of conditions is different and is looked upon from the perspective of what a reasonable person would do under the same set of circumstances, while closely analyzing if the lethal threat was immediate and active.

That scenario with the man with the rifle in front of the house was immediate, however, with a knife, it was not immediate until the daughter pulled up. The logic of these dynamics must be clearly understood. The circumstances became immediate, or exigent, and necessary at that point as the aggressor's delivery systems, actions, and proximity to the potential victim changed.

Deploying deadly force in an attempt to preserve life and prevent bodily injury to you or others has a lot of moving parts in an ecosystem that is constantly changing. Regardless of the circumstance, the active threat must be immediate, the circumstances must be exigent, and your response to the threat should be minimal, using only the force necessary to stop it in its entirety. Yep. It's a mouthful and understanding this is your lifeline!

These are the same questions that any investigator, state's attorney, or a member of a jury would ask if you find yourself arrested or perhaps in a self-defense murder trial: If a reasonable person was in the same situation as you, would they be in fear of death or great bodily injury and respond the same way as you did?

Let's do a quick recap of the components we discussed in respect to deploying deadly force in self-defense. Again, keep in mind that all states and jurisdictions have their own laws that you must be aware of, depending on where you carry your firearm or respond to a deadly threat.

- First of all, you or others around you must be in immediate danger of death or great bodily injury under exigent (urgent) circumstances.
- Second, does the aggressor have the immediate capability and means to act upon, cause, or deliver the deadly threat at that moment in time?
- Third, you must thoroughly understand the dynamics and limitations of the "disparity of force" (victim-subject factors), or what I call the X- factors.
- Finally, your actions should be reasonable, necessary, and unprovoked assuming that a reasonable person in the same circumstance would respond the same way as you did.

If you have satisfied the requirements that justify such force, it is suggested that you:

1. Achieve target acquisition (assuming you are using a firearm).
2. Isolate target, maintain situational awareness, assess further threats.
3. If time permits, use verbal commands to give the aggressor another chance to stop.
4. Deploy deadly force only UNTIL THE THREAT IS STOPPED.
5. Commence tactical breathing.
6. Notify the police and request an ambulance if injury occurs and assist any other victims, surrender your weapon to law enforcement and cooperate with their investigation. Again, Segment C discusses this step further.

As a reminder, we will be discussing post-shooting recommendations which will include interactions with the police from the moment they are called until they arrive. Furthermore, Section 4 will dig deeper into situational awareness. Feel free to jump ahead as needed. Before we dive into Segment B, I feel it is important to discuss a widely used warfare maneuver strategy that anybody in a deadly engagement should understand, regardless of whether they are armed or unarmed. This is called the OODA Loop.

The OODA Loop: A tactical advantage you must know!

This strategy was created by U.S. Air Force Colonel and fighter pilot John Boyd in the mid-1950s for the purpose of systematically enhancing the decision-making process during air combat under high stress engagements. Just like many topics in this book I have discussed, this strategy, also known as "Boyd's Cycle," is complex, however, I feel there are some key takeaways here that will enhance your performance during a deadly engagement. As the military learned, air combat was not the only application for the strategy. As time proved, every aspect of military operations benefited from the strategy including the wars of the recent past.

OODA stands for **O**BSERVE, **O**RIENT, **D**ECIDE, and **A**CT. The Loop aspect of it is exactly that: a closed cycle that entails specific steps with the goal of forcing your adversary to get stuck within the loop, allowing you to overcome him, and win. In other words, your goal is to disrupt your adversary's loop, exploiting his reactionary gap (about a half second) and forcing him to reset it by maintaining aggressive, decisive, and intentional actions until victory is achieved. By repositioning, one can force their adversary to reassess this change (resetting his loop), allowing an opportunity to strike, which will, once again, reset his loop. This strategy has been widely used by police organizations, martial artists and even in business. I feel that not only should law enforcement master this strategy, but so should armed civilians. This includes organizations ensuring this strategy is within their TAARS plans in terms of responding to and surviving a targeted attack.

So, the first step is to "observe." It is imperative to be aware of your surroundings, assess the pertinent data and determine any ongoing threats. Section 4 dives into situational and threat awareness which will help give you the tools to do this more effectively. The second step is to "orient" yourself based upon the observed data. You want to position yourself (and reposition) in a tactical location in respect to your adversary. This can be cover, an elevated position or anywhere that will create confusion, forcing him to react and reset his loop. The third step is to "decide" what you are going to do, and the last step is to "act." By taking action, you are changing the dynamic of the area of operation, disorienting your foe and giving you some control within an unpredictable, fast-paced environment.

The OODA Loop is a battle-tested strategy that has stood the test of time and with practice, it can become an amazing tool that will place your adversary at a clear tactical disadvantage!

It is also worth mentioning one more concept regarding human threat response. This is Hicks Law. Hicks Law suggests that humans can only respond to one stimulus at a time, depending on the number of choices they have. The more options they must decide upon or the more obstacles they must negotiate, the longer it takes them to respond successfully. This could be a knife attack or perhaps even looking at multiple items on the menu in a restaurant. This is why training, policy and mindset are so important.

As we press on regarding deadly force ahead, keep the OODA Loop and Hicks Law in the back of your mind. How would you utilize this tactic to throw an attacker off-balance enough to position yourself to neutralize or survive the deadly threat or targeted attack?

In retrospect, there are many factors that must be considered prior to deploying deadly force in self-defense situations, including tactics and strategies, as discussed above. Very few lawyers, state laws, and civilian or police firearm instructors are conclusive regarding when to use deadly force because the goalpost is always changing in this very controversial arena. Every situation is unique and the lives of everyone involved will be affected one way or the other.

The one thing we know for sure is that if you deploy deadly force, under any condition, you will be scrutinized by the police, the state's attorney, the media, the aggressor's family, and those systematically attacking the Second Amendment.

Perspective is important and knowledge is the real power! Let's move into Segment B!

Use of Deadly Force: Segment B

As we have jumped into the abyss together, we have yet to hit the ground whilst we navigate through this very foggy topic of deadly force. I would like to start off by discussing a few controversial principles that I feel are necessary to be familiar with, and then we will dive into some scenarios in order to help you understand the mechanics of deploying such force. This segment will finish up with a few uncomfortable cases from which I feel we can all gain insight.

Let's start off discussing Castle Doctrine, Duty to Retreat, and Stand Your Ground Laws. As I have preached like a pastor on a Sunday, every state has its own gun legislation, but I feel that regardless of the state you live in or travel to, you should be familiar with the fundamentals of these principles. Sometimes these laws are overridden by higher courts and other times these decisions stand.

Some states have Castle Doctrine or Stand Your Ground Laws. Perhaps the state you live in requires you to make every *"reasonable"* effort to retreat prior to deploying deadly force, which is Duty to Retreat. This is not always easy when your children are upstairs sleeping as an armed home invader is kicking in the front door; however, what would a *"reasonable person"* do in your same circumstance? Is the intruder alone or does he have his partner in crime waiting at the back door?

Obtaining your firearm and opening the door to deploy deadly force may be looked upon differently as compared to the aggressor kicking or attempting to kick in the door regardless of whether or not your state has a Castle Doctrine or Stand Your Ground Law. Remember, the totality of the circumstances will be examined with a magnifying glass, and your split-second decision that you made with angst will change your life forever, especially if you are in the midst of a politically charged State's Attorney.

This is why it's imperative for you to consult with an attorney and a knowledgeable firearms instructor within your state in order to make sure that you're up to date with the latest and greatest. Protect yourself. As I've said, the devil is in the details, but at the end of the day, it's important to keep the elements needed in order to deploy deadly force in mind as we have extensively discussed.

Let's start with Castle Doctrine. Castle Doctrine essentially implies that one may use deadly force to protect their home (their castle) from invaders without being required to retreat. Some states, that are strong advocates for Castle Doctrine, do extend this to other locations like church, work, place of worship, or even your vehicle. Out of hypervigilance and for the intents and purposes of this discussion, when I reference Castle Doctrine, it will apply to an abode because the home is where it is the most widely understood to encompass.

Yes, regardless of the state or its gun laws, if you should find yourself in a situation that may require deadly force, keep these elements in mind while deploying the minimal force necessary to stop the threat.

As of 2023, about 45 states support some variation of Castle Doctrine. Does this mean that if you live in the remaining five states that do not have or strongly support this law that you should allow an armed aggressor to kick in your front door at three in the morning? I would say no, and good luck finding a jury that would support the state's attorney's case should she have the gall to prosecute the fine citizen for protecting his family from home invaders.

Castle Doctrine, like Stand Your Ground laws, can at times be used as a defense and offers some legal protection to the citizen while protecting his abode, depending on whether or not he was within the boundaries of the state law. Again, this depends on the state, and as always, I would take a careful stance when deploying such force in any circumstance, even if the state offers a little more wiggle room in terms of deploying deadly force. I say this because fatal mistakes happen.

Many innocent people have been accidentally or unnecessarily killed or injured due to the armed citizen's inability to validate the lethal threat as being such. If these mistakes happen in states with a strong Castle Doctrine stance, it tends to protect the armed citizen who unreasonably deployed deadly force.

What boundaries, do you ask? Well, generally speaking, the aggressor must have or is in the process of attempting to gain entry while you or other residents are inside. In other words, deploying deadly force on that man on your front lawn who is armed with a butcher knife does not seem reasonable, as the threat is not immediate to those inside at that specific instance. The moment he starts kicking in the front door, he is putting himself in a position to have deadly force deployed upon him if you or your family are inside. While he is just on the front porch, it would make sense to call the police with a detailed description if nobody is in immediate threat of death or great bodily injury as his delivery system is weak, being that he has a knife in respect to your current proximity. If he becomes an aggressor and was armed with a firearm, then this would change the circumstance.

Now, let's say you just pulled up in front of your home, which is empty, and this same man, armed or not, is violently attempting to gain entry. What then? Does Castle Doctrine apply? I would have to say no, and even if you live in a state where it does, tread lightly. Of course, as always, be prepared to defend yourself, but call the police and give an accurate description of him in case he departs prior to them arriving. They will likely catch him, and when they do, you will be able to identify him as being the one who committed the burglary.

Of course, the dynamic of the situation can change if that same teenage daughter is in her room, and you went to the store to pick up a few groceries. As you pull up in your vehicle this time, you see the same man kicking in the front door. Or, perhaps, he just walked in the unlocked door and there is not a weapon visible. Verbal commands, or a less lethal or general force may be a cautious option, depending on the totality of the circumstances. When your loved ones are potentially in harm's way, action is imperative, regardless. A little communication can go a long way sometimes. Maybe after a few drinks after work, he just walked into the wrong residence as he may be a new resident in the community and the townhouses are identical from the front.

Years ago, when I first moved into that high rise condo that I mentioned earlier in Section 2, I accidentally walked into the wrong apartment unit which was also a corner unit adjacent to mine. The building was a maze, and I clearly was distracted with my mobile device as I was looking forward to walking my dog and drinking a cold beer after a long, hot day at work. I opened the door and saw my new (and wonderful) 87-year-old, partially blind neighbor in her nightgown and in her kitchen. I froze and slowly backed up, making a hasty and stealthy exit, locking the door on the way out. It was awkward when I saw her in the elevator the next day. She smiled and said that I should have stayed for coffee. Feeling the blood rush to my face in embarrassment, I just laughed and apologized for the mistake. She was not as blind—nor was I as sneaky—as I had thought, and we eventually became very good friends.

Accidents happen because we are all human and at times distracted. Looking back, I am glad she wasn't armed. I can't even imagine, but these things happen more often than you think.

Getting back on point, you need to understand that in most states, if the threat is no longer immediate, deadly force is not supported, depending on the totality of the circumstances. Even in states with strong Castle Doctrine laws, you may have to convince a jury that the retreating man, after he exited your home, was still a lethal threat at the time you shot him in the back of the head. Good luck with that.

In other words, if an aggressor makes entry and then turns around and retreats after seeing that rifle in your hand, the threat is no longer active. Now, I can absolutely understand the rage towards a man who just kicked in your door at three in the morning, terrified your entire family, interrupted that rare moment of intimacy with your spouse, and dropped his pistol in front of your three-year-old toddler who picks up everything he sees before deciding to retreat.

Many folks, especially those with a military or police background, are aggressive under stressful, lethal encounters, as they should be; however, as I have said in the past, restraint is our humanity. In that scenario, restraint may also dictate your freedom. As a civilian, if time permits, just call the police, giving them a detailed description of the offender. Take a few deep breaths and remember, the bad guy wasn't the only person who dodged a bullet that night.

Some states may still allow the use of deadly force but take the conservative approach regarding such force. Also remember that other means of force, like less lethal, are always an option if the threat is not deadly but still nonetheless a threat.

Use some common sense, understand your state law, and if it escalates into a deadly force situation, your training and instinct will take the lead. Always start by calling the police, if time permits, but when loved ones are in harm's way, you may not always have the time as the lethal threat is immediate under exigent circumstances.

Now, let's discuss the fundamentals regarding Stand Your Ground laws. Remember that Stand Your Ground laws, like Castle Doctrine, can differ from state to state. With that being said, I will take my cautious approach to this discussion that falls in line with when I feel the possibility of deadly force should be deployed.

Generally speaking, Stand Your Ground allows a citizen the right to use force, including deadly force in self-defense, without the "Duty to Retreat" (although some states do require this) in order to prevent death or great bodily injury, so as long as the good citizen has the legal right to be at the location and the circumstance is unprovoked. Now, some states that heavily support Stand Your Ground laws do have enough wiggle room for deadly force to be deployed in circumstances that seem to push the confines of morality. As we navigate ahead, keep these deadly force elements in mind, which are minimal, reasonable, and a last resort. This will not only preserve life, but it will also save you the mental, emotional, and financial turmoil that can and will happen after the shooting. It will also help ensure that when such force is deployed, it is deployed to terminate a genuine active lethal threat.

Other states, on the contrary, require the armed citizen to make every attempt to "retreat" from the encounter before deploying deadly force, unless you are in your home. This is called Duty to Retreat. It's important to know also that most states that support Castle Doctrine do not require or expect a citizen to retreat from their own home. Duty to Retreat generally requires the citizen to safely make an attempt to flee from the aggressor or the dangerous circumstance before using deadly force outside of the home.

For example, if you are at a red light and an armed aggressor attempts to open your car door and you safely drive off only to suddenly stop 50 feet away, exit your vehicle, and deploy deadly force with a firearm, you will have a tough time convincing a jury your use of force was justified.

In all honesty, even in a strong Stand Your Ground state, the police, a jury, or State's Attorney in your self-defense trial or investigation may scratch their head a little as you would have to justify why you stopped after you safely drove off. Was there a train in front of you? Were you in the middle of a traffic jam? Did it happen in a dead end and the aggressor is closing in on you? Or, did you need enough time to obtain your firearm from the glovebox, then decide to stop and engage the now non-aggressor who is walking in the opposite direction? I say non-aggressor because at that point, you just became the aggressor, at least from the civilian perspective.

Obviously, the latter is ill-advised, but it's an example of how things can take a wrong turn, leaving the good citizen a weak defense should it go to trial criminally or civilly.

In that same circumstance, as you're driving off, if a train prevents you from fleeing and the aggressor is running towards you with his weapon at the ready, then this aggressor is placing himself in a position to have deadly force deployed upon him. Again, as a reminder, get into the habit of using verbal commands which may in itself divert an incident! It gives the aggressor a chance to stand down and the commands may be heard by witnesses, which will benefit you. A witness may not see the event unfold, but they may very well hear your attempt via verbal commands to prevent the engagement.

The totality of the circumstances will be looked upon with that same question: What would a reasonable person do in the same circumstance? Eventually, the truth will come out, one way or the other, as it should.

That's a lot to think about when "fight or flight" kicks in or your family is with you. This responsibility of retreat, in my opinion, should not fall on the lap of the law-abiding citizen during a lethal encounter, although a little common sense should be used as every situation is different. This to the side, just because you can shoot doesn't always mean that you should.

Firing one round that successfully stopped the threat will be looked at by a State's Attorney or jury differently than firing ten times after the threat was already stopped. Sure, the Acute Stress Response was in full swing, but those attempting to put you in prison and throw away the key will use every aspect of your actions, including your recollection of the event that occurred under stress and fear against you. This is exactly why you DO NOT TALK TO THE POLICE until your attorney advises you to and has a chance to speak with you. I love law enforcement, as most of my life has been dedicated to it. I can truthfully say that most police officers have good intentions, even while interviewing the good citizen after a shooting or deadly force event, but the best way to protect yourself is to say nothing until advised to do so. What you should do is comply with all commands of the responding officers, as Segment C will discuss.

Yes, you just survived the deadly force encounter, but you have to remember about what we talked about in Section 2. The way that you interpret the events immediately after the encounter will be different in a couple days once the dust settles emotionally, mentally, and physically. We will also further discuss my post shooting recommendations in Segment C.

The bad guy had the luxury of picking his victim, the location, and time of his crime. You, on the other hand, did not choose the time or place of this engagement. Your split-second decision will be aggressively probed as you and your family's freedom, emotional well-being, health, and financial survival is at great risk.

As we are nearing the end of Section 3, we are going to briefly touch on a handful of interesting cases that I feel are uncomfortable but crucial to discuss because of the unusual circumstances. I am confident there are some key takeaways that you may benefit from.

These cases are: The Kevin Monahan shooting in Upstate New York, the Andrew Lester shooting in Kansas City, Missouri, and the John Hurley shooting in Arvada, Colorado. Now, as of early 2024, a couple of the cases we are going to discuss are still awaiting or have just completed proceedings, which requires me to tread lightly. The final dispositions of these cases are important, especially for those involved, but for the rest of you, the lessons learned are invaluable regardless of which way the scales of justice lean. Respectfully, you must ask yourself if you were in the same position, what would you have done?

Let's start with the Kevin Monahan shooting case. On April 15th, 2023, just before 10:00 p.m., in the rural town of Hebron, New York, two cars and one motorcycle accidentally pulled into the driveway of the residence of Kevin Monahan. In one of the cars was a passenger named Kaylin Gillis. The group, who were looking for a friend's house, realized they accidentally pulled into the wrong driveway and immediately backed up and attempted to exit. It was alleged by law enforcement that at that point Monahan exited his residence and fired two times from his shotgun, striking 20-year-old Kaylin in the neck. She succumbed to her injuries and died a short time later at another location.

The police eventually arrived at the scene and, out of precaution due to the tactical disadvantage, officers did not approach the porch but attempted to verbally convince Monahan to exit his home peacefully, but he did not initially comply. After about an hour and under the advice of his attorney, Monahan exited his home, was taken into custody, and subsequently charged with Second Degree Murder. His dialogue with police was minimal, although, at one point he did blame hunters and asked officers to leave so he can go back to sleep. Monahan apparently had a reputation for being confrontational and supposedly was frustrated with the numerous folks who accidentally had been pulling into his driveway in the past.

Let's dig a little deeper into this case with the few facts we do know, and then you decide if Monahan was in a strong position to deploy such force. Twelve jurors attempted to put themselves in Monahan's shoes and tried to figure out if his actions were reasonable. This case is extremely disturbing because many of us have young children. Sometimes these kids, like we all do, make mistakes. Perhaps a delivery driver would have made the same mistake as well whilst attempting to deliver a pizza or a package. How would the circumstances have changed if the delivery driver was armed?

Prior to the shooting, the occupants never exited their vehicles, nor did they engage with Monahan verbally or physically in any manner. One must determine if the immediate threat of death or great bodily injury to Monahan was present, but this did not seem to be the case based upon the known facts.

Second, due to the fact that Kaylin and the other citizens were within their vehicles and were in the process of departing the property, not only is any perceived threat no longer active, but the delivery system of any threat was also not present or no longer present. Again, this is due to the fact that they had departed, as well as the proximity and distance between both parties. In terms of victim-subject factors, there are not any based upon the facts as I understand them.

I would like to take this moment to remind you that throughout this book we have discussed how mindset is extremely important and is a key ingredient in surviving a deadly force encounter. By the same token, the wrong mindset can poison your logic. Anger is a powerful emotion and could easily lead you down the wrong path. The circumstances are tragic, as a beautiful young lady lost her life and Monahan who was found guilty was sentenced to 25 years to life.

Let's now discuss the Andrew Lester shooting of a 16-year-old African-American male on April 13th, 2023, in Kansas City, Missouri, based upon the facts as we currently know them. Again, this is another recent incident that has yet to make it to the criminal trial as of early 2024. The teen was asked to pick up his younger twin siblings at a specific address and mistook one street for another similar sounding street and ended up at the home of Andrew Lester, an 84-year-old white male at approximately 9:40 in the evening. Lester, who was sleeping, heard the doorbell and retrieved his pistol, then relocated to and opened the interior door. The teen was outside of the house standing on the other side of the storm door upon which Lester fired one shot, hitting him in the head, then firing a second shot, striking him in the arm. Lester then allegedly yelled, "Don't come here ever again," and the victim fled the scene severely wounded, attempting to get help. Luckily, he survived, otherwise, we may have had a very different story as it would have been one-sided and a tough case to investigate or prosecute.

The police were subsequently dispatched to a call of a shooting near the residence and spoke to Andrew Lester, who related that the person he shot at put his hand on the door handle and felt that he was trying to break in. Lester further related that he was "scared to death" of the teen's size, who happened to be about 5'8" and 140 pounds at the time of the shooting. The next day, Lester was taken into custody and interviewed by the Kansas City Police Department.

He was released that day, which was April 14th, but was eventually charged on the 17th with First-Degree Assault and Armed Criminal Action due to the public outcry. I can only speculate why Lester was released and charged a few days later, but you must remember that these investigations are complicated with lots of different moving parts. Perhaps the investigators were waiting to complete their interviews so they could get all the facts, as they should. I am not sure if the victim was available at that point due to his injury, but conducting a thorough investigation before charging makes sense. Based upon the age or health of Andrew Lester, releasing him until further information was learned about the shooting also made sense to me. The Clay County DA did state that there may be a racial component which can affect the charges, if that is the case.

While I was researching this case, I reviewed several interviews with this young man and was impressed with his maturity, his positive outlook on life, and his honesty about his struggles since the shooting. I truly wish him a speedy recovery and an amazing life. I feel his story really puts perspective into what happens on the receiving end of a firearm and provides context regarding the ramifications of deploying deadly force on a human being.

Carrying a firearm is an awesome responsibility. Deploying deadly force is detrimental to everyone involved, and this case is a powerful testament to that. This could have been any of our children knocking on that door or pulling up into that driveway in upstate New York.

This shooting, like the Monahan case, is a strong example of how things can go drastically wrong. What if it was Halloween and a group of young children were at the door trick or treating? Or, that over-worked delivery guy with three kids just trying to keep the lights on at home, working 12-hour shifts?

Comparing Lester's actions to the elements that I feel are needed to deploy deadly force, we have to ask the question: Was Lester in fear of immediate death or great bodily injury under exigent circumstances? Sure, it was late, the doorbell rang, and Lester, who may have been rattled and woken out of a sound sleep, saw an unknown person at his front door. I do not know the history of the area, its crime stats, nor if he was ever a victim of a crime like a burglary or such.

Regardless, the boy was not armed, he was not attempting to make entry into the residence and was not threatening physically or verbally in any manner. Both perspectives will certainly come out during the trial, but it's important to pay attention to the facts.

Second, did the teen have the means to deliver the threat of death or great bodily harm? Well, Lester and the boy, who was unarmed, were separated by a closed glass storm door.

I can only speculate, and I will do so with caution, as the trial has not started, and many facts are still publicly unknown. It was dark and late at night. Lester was woken and likely startled. He was, at the time of the shooting, 84 years old with possible health issues. If Lester and the teen were within reasonable proximity to each other and if the young man, who was unarmed, had attacked Lester, then the X-factors like age, build, health, etc. would possibly support the justification of deploying deadly force. **This, however, is clearly not the case.**

Whatever factors led Andrew Lester to pull the trigger that night, it affected everyone involved. My job is not to pass judgment but to state the known facts so you, my reader, can walk away with the proper knowledge.

That's what the court system is there for—when it works. To those of us on the sidelines, this is a clear reminder of how much responsibility goes into carrying a firearm, and one wrong decision can change your life and the life of others forever.

We live in different times, and I feel it's imperative for armed civilians to be patient, tolerant, responsible and cautious when deploying deadly force. We all have baggage. Some of us have tough days or emotional challenges due to life circumstances. When you strap a gun to your side, that baggage needs to be put on the shelf.

Throughout Segment B, I wanted to create a solid foundation that takes a cautious approach while deploying deadly force with a firearm or any other means in order to prevent death or great bodily injury. I also wanted to stress that this type of response often happens under unusual circumstances. Sure, the use of such force is already extremely cloudy as it is, but these unusual circumstances influenced by the environment and elevated emotions can create the perfect storm for mistakes to happen.

Now, let's discuss this last case, which is the John Hurley shooting. Like the other cases, everything about it is disturbing, but we have a few moving parts that hit home for all of us in every imaginable way.

On June 21, 2021, the Arvada Police Department in Colorado received a call of a suspicious person at the Olde Town shopping center. Officer Gordon Beesley arrived on scene shortly after, exited his police vehicle, and began to investigate the incident on foot.

The aggressor, whose name is not worth the ink, observed the officer, exited his vehicle with a shotgun, and began to charge at the officer while shouting. Officer Beesley quickly turned around and was shot twice, subsequently dying from his wounds. This was an ambush, and the aggressor, who had a deep hatred towards the police, knew exactly what he was going to do that day. The aggressor then fired multiple shots into the nearby police vehicle and up into the air before returning to his own truck. He then exchanged the shotgun for an AR-15, likely with the intent to commit more carnage.

During this time, armed civilian John Hurley was in the vicinity and heard the gunfire. Without hesitation, the 40-year-old bravely responded while armed with his semi-automatic pistol. Using cover, John engaged the aggressor and neutralized him, saving countless other lives. Arvada officers, who had a description of the aggressor, responded within minutes and observed John holding the rifle that belonged to the aggressor, believing he was a second shooter.

As a result of John holding an AR-15 and the officers arriving at a chaotic scene of an active shooting call with an officer down, the fog of war can happen, and it did. One of the responding officers deployed his weapon system and shot John Hurley, subsequently killing him. Two heroes died that day, and there is a lot we can all learn from it. Distancing the aggressor from his weapon system makes sense, but as a civilian, you need to be very careful, and to date, the reason why John was holding the rifle is unclear. Perhaps he was clearing it or feared the attacker was still alive and still had control of his rifle, potentially causing more harm.

That responding officer that fired upon John saw what he saw and took action. In his mind, he felt the public was in danger of immediate death or great bodily injury. As a result, the officer deployed deadly force, and was justified, according to the findings from the internal investigations that followed. These things regretfully happen, and no matter which way you look at it, it is horrible. Moreover, any officer in that position would have likely made the same decision.

With that being said, we're going to break this down based upon the publicly available facts as I understand them. Prior to this incident happening, according to the Arvada Police Department, the aggressor's brother called the police in the early afternoon, requesting a welfare check. Officer Beesley and another officer responded attempting to make contact with the subject (soon to be aggressor) without success. Within 10 minutes, the suspicious person call at the shopping center was dispatched and officer Beesley responded. As I mentioned above, the aggressor ambushed Officer Beesley, subsequently murdering him. John Hurley responded to the gunfire and swiftly neutralized the aggressor, who died from his wounds. One of the responding officers who was on scene shortly after the shooting observed

John Hurley holding an AR-15 and his pistol, upon which the officer deployed deadly force, fatally shooting the good citizen.

I had the opportunity to watch some of the footage from this incident. When John Hurley decided to engage the aggressor, he utilized a brick wall for cover and then when he had the opportunity, he deployed deadly force, terminating the murderer. His actions were aggressive and decisive. He seemed to have exceptional situational awareness and was extremely calm considering an officer was mortally wounded to his left. It was obvious he was not only trained, but mentally prepared.

In terms of deadly force, the aggressor already shot a police officer, had every intention to continue his murder spree based upon his actions, and was clearly a threat because he still had the rifle in his hand when John deployed deadly force. John was well within the boundaries.

In terms of the responding officer who deployed deadly force upon John, this is where it gets a little sticky. The officers were not wearing body cameras from what I understand, and most of the released footage that I observed was obscured by trees.

Considering the totality of the circumstances, a reasonable person, or officer, arriving on scene would assume that John was a threat, as he was holding a rifle in his hand within proximity of a wounded officer and an unknown male, later learned to be the actual killer. Also, jeopardizing the officer's element of surprise in a hostile, high stress environment could be lethal for the officer or the community. Hence, it makes sense that the officer immediately deployed deadly force which unfortunately killed the hero citizen.

I can only imagine what was going through John's head while responding. Seeing a police officer mortally wounded and taking the life of another human being under immense stress had to have been traumatizing.

On that dreadful day, John made the thin blue line a little thicker, and the world lost two warriors. Additionally, John Hurley missed his calling as a cop.

Some Last Thoughts

As I have discussed throughout this book, targeted violence in all forms has strained the very soul of America. Terrorist cells that hide within the shadows of society on our very soil have been paying close attention. Regardless of who pulls the trigger, swings the knife, or drives the vehicle into a crowd, if the lethal threat is active, then you have to make a decision as an armed citizen.

On that note, let me remind you that police officers have a very dangerous job. As I have discussed previously in this book, the situations that these warriors in blue find themselves in can be lethal and can happen in seconds. Sometimes they find themselves on the losing end of the battle. If you have the displeasure of watching that happen and you are armed, you're going to have to make a decision that will affect your life and the officer's survival. There are numerous circumstances that can put an officer in this type of situation. It does not always have to be with the firearm. It can be with a knife, a taser, an object like a baseball bat, or even the aggressor's bare hands. Whatever the lethal threat that will likely cause death, great bodily injury to the officer, or even the officer getting disarmed, seconds count.

Earlier we mentioned some recent examples of citizens assisting police officers on the brink of death. If you find yourself in this situation, and you decide to deploy deadly force to save the officer's life, make sure you identify the threat (target acquisition), isolate the threat, maintain situational awareness, and if time permits, use verbal commands, then deploy deadly force until the threat is stopped. Also, it is worth mentioning that notifying the police dispatcher directly from the officer's radio will expedite backup units! Just remember, as Segment C stresses ahead, make sure your firearm is not in your hand when responding officers arrive!

So, Segment B took a nosedive into the nuts and bolts of deploying deadly force based upon my cumulative interpretation that parallels most of the recommended guidelines used by law enforcement and states across the nation that civilians are also expected to abide by.

I have attempted to create a foundation for you to grow that places you in a better position in order to protect yourself physically, mentally, emotionally, and legally. Deploying such force should never come lightly because it affects everyone involved. Again, every state is different, so I can't stress enough how important it is to understand your state and local laws in order to ensure that if you are faced with the decision to deploy deadly force, that you will have the knowledge that you need to survive the moment as well as the aftermath. Let's continue into Segment C!

Use of Deadly Force: Segment C

Regardless of what circumstances brought you to the place where you felt in your heart that deadly force was the appropriate action, it happened. Sure, in a perfect world, we would like to be the first person to call 911, but a few things have to happen first. Remember that every situation is different and will require a different course of action. The one thing we do know is that the police will arrive eventually, ready to engage anybody they perceive as a threat. If you are a civilian, an off-duty officer, or an undercover officer in plain clothes, you are at the mercy of the responding officers and you need to understand that you are a threat upon their arrival. Even more frightening, perhaps a lethal threat is still ongoing and the responding police arrive in the middle of it. It's a high stress, chaotic situation that these responding officers are dropping into with lots of unknowns.

I've heard some reputable instructors and organizations recommend to their students that when they hear the "Calvary" come or police sirens, that's the best time to re-holster. As the John Hurley shooting proved, you <u>do not want to have ANY weapon in your hand</u> when the police arrive, and the only thing you should assume is that if the police are not already there, they will be within minutes. In their minds, everybody is a threat upon their initial arrival. **The one thing that I can conclusively recommend is that after you holster your weapon, interlock your hands on top of your head and leave them there until further instructions from the responding officers and advise them that you want an attorney present should you be taken into custody.**

When they do arrive, let them know that you are armed and allow them to secure your weapon and stabilize the scene. You may end up in handcuffs, which is okay because it's temporary. Depending on the situation, you may even get arrested, which is also OK. We will discuss how to communicate with them in the pages ahead.

Let's back up a little. Prior to the police arriving and immediately after the shooting, the first thing you need to do is **assess if there are any more threats** in front of you or around you before **holstering and concealing your weapon**, which you should do as quickly as possible. It's a judgment call that you have to make and I can't make it for you, but considering that situational and threat awareness can be blurry after an engagement, placing your weapon on the ground could be dangerous.

Is the bad guy still a threat? Did he temporarily pass out just to regain consciousness and regain control of his weapon? If you are wounded, will you pass out while your weapon and your crying newborn baby is lying next to you? Are there more lethal threats in the vicinity?

Once you have realized that the immediate area is clear of all threats, **you need to start tactical breathing** to bring down your heart rate so you can think clearly, slow the bleeding if you are wounded, and clearly hear the commands when the police arrive should you be experiencing auditory exclusion. You also want to be able to effectively call 911, which we will get into ahead as well. Then, you need to assess injuries to yourself and others around you and perform field triage if necessary.

Depending on where this encounter happened, chances are that somebody already called the police; however, call anyway. Some self-defense attorneys recommend saying absolutely nothing to the 911 operator or the responding police. I have a few thoughts on both, including my personal recommendations. As always, consult with your attorney with what steps he recommends, considering he will be the one who represents you.

Now, we're going to discuss what to tell the 911 operator and how to navigate through your initial interaction with the police upon their arrival.

All 911 calls are recorded. As such, it can be used as evidence against you in court, during the investigation, or subsequent to charges filed by the state. As we discussed in Section 2, the reality of what happened as compared to how you perceive your actions can be very different and distorted. You will have a clearer recollection of the incident in a couple of days after a good night's sleep; in the meantime, you are going to have to notify the police while on scene. I know it's common sense, but I feel compelled to reiterate this little detail. No, we can't go home, take a nap, order a pizza, and then decide to call the police. Yes, folks, it has happened, and even though you may have been well within your rights to deploy deadly force, leaving the scene is a crime.

Now, you made the responsible decision to call the police. **Tell the 911 operator that you just deployed deadly force, your location, what your** description is, what the aggressor's description is, and request Emergency Medical Services (EMS) if there are injuries sustained.

I would recommend requesting EMS regardless because you never know if anybody was inadvertently hit by gunfire during the engagement. Dr. Martinelli also suggests in addition that you should say, "I thought he (the attacker) was going to kill me and felt that it was necessary to use deadly force."

Other than the recommended info above, be vague, remember to breathe, and interlock your hands on top of your head immediately after your call if you're the one that made it. You will have a chance to tell your story but save the details as you remember them for your attorney. Your recollection of the event WILL NOT BE ACCURATE even if it just happened, so use caution with what you say to the dispatcher, the responding police, or the investigators.

Now, the police finally arrived on scene and your hands are interlocked behind your head. You tell them you are armed and where your weapon is as they scream at you to drop to your knees and they cautiously approach in order to handcuff you.

The scene is finally secure, and you can't wait to tell your story, right? Wrong! The police have good intentions and want to ensure that all the facts are properly understood and applied to the laws of the land. Whilst their intentions are clearly noble, there are a few things you need to remember.

Again, your recollection of the events may be distorted and contradict video footage or eyewitness accounts of what actually happened. YOU WILL NOT remember how many shots you fired off the top of your head, so do not attempt to guess. If you think you fired four shots and you fired 12, it won't look good, regardless of how justified you were to deploy deadly force. It may even contradict the 911 call that you made a few minutes earlier telling them way more than you should have. Finally, you need to understand that most police officers wear body cameras which can and will be used as evidence.

In terms of your verbal interaction with the police during the initial interview on scene, I recommend the following:

- Be respectful and courteous
- Tell them your name

- Point out the witnesses
- Point out other evidence like shell casings, surveillance cameras, or any physical evidence that you feel the police should know. This does not include a verbal statement without your attorney present.
- Politely request to call your self-defense or concealed carry protection coverage hotline or attorney. If you don't know the number offhand or your phone is confiscated, call your family so they can make the notifications for you. Keep this information easily accessible in your home, wallet, or purse, just in case.
- Do not give any further information until your attorney arrives. Claiming self-defense immediately after the incident isn't always a good idea. Let your attorney decide if this is the best course of action moving forward.
- Dr. Martinelli further recommends relating to the officers that you are stressed, that you want to cooperate and that you wish to assert your 4th Amendment rights, whilst not offering permission to search your home or vehicle.

As I said above, the purpose of the investigation is to figure out what happened. The police, although they may have good intentions, may inadvertently hurt you should charges be filed. The truth isn't going anywhere, and there's a time and place to tell it, so breathe. Give yourself time for your acute stress response to normalize and allow your attorney to do his job. As for your weapon, it is evidence, so don't expect to get that back anytime soon.

When you do make it home, you're going to be "tired but wired." Your mind will be racing while replaying the incident over and over in your head, but you have to realize that time is now your friend, finally. Do a little exercise, go for a brisk walk, or run in order to release the remaining adrenaline. I don't think your spouse would complain. Then have a good meal and get some sleep. In a couple of days, your recollection of the events will be much clearer so you and your attorney can create a timeline of the engagement.

Most importantly, consider speaking to a therapist. Not only will you have emotional stress regarding the engagement itself, but the battle may also have just begun, financially, civilly, or criminally. Yes, your training was on point as you neutralized the threat. You also ensured that you had the proper legal consultation should such an event occur, but please take care of your emotional well-being by getting the proper therapy or counseling because, as I have said, cortisol is the silent killer.

So, here we are as we depart this cloud of enigma called deadly force... or have we really? By now, you should have more of an understanding of when deploying deadly force is a viable option under certain circumstances. Very few circumstances are proof positive and conclusive whilst deploying such force. The goalposts are always changing, so remain diligent and understand the gun laws that pertain to the state that you reside in or travel to. In the beginning of the use of force section, we jumped into this abyss together while flying through circumstances and situations where deploying deadly force may be plausible. Not every threat dictates the deployment of deadly force, so less lethal options should always be explored and practiced. With that being said, the foggy legality of carrying a firearm is an ongoing, never-ending journey. Let's move on to Section 4.

SECTION FOUR

TAARS

Threat Awareness, Assessment, Response and Survival

4.1
Bleed on Paper

Hemingway once said, **"There is nothing to writing. All you do is sit down at a typewriter and bleed."** Other than a little journalism and a lot of police reports, I never considered myself such an author. I still don't. The one thing, however, that this book has made me do was "bleed on paper," along with a couple tears, a few rants, and a lot of long walks. Selfishly, I say this as many have lost their loved ones as a result of these heinous acts. These are mothers, fathers, daughters and sons of those who are still asking why. Section 4 humbly brought me back to the reasons why I wrote this book in the first place.

I have to admit, in order for me to have finished this book, I had to become, once again, callous. While on this journey to authorship, over 20,000 Americans were shot or wounded as a result of targeted violence. The numerous case studies, officer body camera analysis, and countless hours of research in order to support my perspectives ripped off the scabs that seemed to have sustained me up until this point.

As I've said, this is not the book I wanted to write, and to be quite honest with you, it's still not. This has been an uncomfortable process for me, but the blood spilled by the victims of such havoc has inspired me to push forward. This reality should be painful for all of us because if it has not affected you yet, it will soon enough. Maybe then at that point, the world will start moving in the right direction. This violence will end one way or the other, but it cannot continue the way it has been. Unfortunately, humans make changes only when they have to and with so many moving parts within this equation, the solution needs to be systematic with short to long-term solutions. Our safety is everyone's problem and the first step is to place politics to the side, roll up the sleeves, and get to work.

The country has continued to become more violent; the lawmakers have virtually done nothing to successfully address the fundamental root of the problem, and Americans continue to be murdered in a land that is said to be free at the hands of their own citizens. Our adversaries have not even begun to join the slaughter, but they are paying close attention. Not if, but when they do, this active killer epidemic will not even be close to the devastation that our nation's enemies are capable of from afar, or the Trojan Horse from the southern border. Our enemies' biggest fear is our ability to unite, regardless of our differences, and for this reason they are careful.

Targeted violence in America has no quick solution. The one thing I know is that in order for a flower to grow, the soil must be primed, the seed needs to be placed into the earth, and with the proper water and sun, it will grow one way or the other. It can grow into a beautiful flower or perhaps turn into a weed. Nurturing is everything, and humans are no different. The long-term solution needs to be multifaceted, but raising our children with the value system that reflects the society we want to live in, regardless of racial, religious, or political factors, seems to be a great place to start!

This does not mean we sacrifice our children and loved ones in the process. While we are trying to figure out a long-term solution, these acts of terror can and must be prevented, and if necessary, the offenders neutralized during an attack. The good news is that even though the road is bumpy, we are still moving, which means there's hope. Our optimism and resilience are what makes us human. It's our differences that make us American! No matter what our flag is, we all want to live a healthy, happy, and peaceful life.

As I have said, humans have been built for conflict. Not everybody carries a weapon or is trained to respond to a lethal threat during a targeted attack. Some run and others fight. Sometimes, we are caught off guard and fall prey to the element of surprise while at work, church, home, school, in a hospital ER room, a theater, or perhaps at a parade. The world is a bad guy's oyster, and as I discussed in Section 1's epic rant, society's twisted value system, unchecked social media, exposure to violent video games and movies, partisan media outlets, and incompetent politicians make it easy for these predators to flourish, then replicate. Evil has no limits, and we should do everything in our power to stop it at its core.

From a warrior's perspective, we have reviewed a lot of content that will put you at a clear advantage should you find yourself in the midst of a lethal threat, but what about the rest of the 90% of society? We cannot always be there next to our loved ones to ensure their safety, but we can make sure they are prepared, observant, and ready to respond and survive an attack, no matter where they are. It's also imperative that organizations have the proper protocols in place to identify and mitigate potential attackers within their organization as well as have a viable response and survival plan should an attack occur internally or externally.

Section 4 incorporates the content discussed throughout this book yet focuses on new skills, critical knowledge, and perspectives that will ensure that you, your loved ones, or your organization are prepared to detect, respond to, survive, and even engage an attacker. As I have hinted throughout this book, we also will discuss what I feel is the underbelly of the targeted violence epidemic in America.

We will fearlessly leap into the art of threat and situational awareness, dissect two NTAC studies that I feel are essential to the scope of this book, and then finish with an overview of my six-step Hybrid Threat Assessment and Response Guideline (integrated within the TAARS model) for targeted violence that every organization should understand.

I respectively call Section 4 **TAARS, or Threat Awareness, Assessment, Response and Survival. TAARS** is not only a model that cumulatively enhances your posture in every aspect to targeted violence, but it also offers a viable blueprint that every citizen and organization should be familiar with. Regardless of what organization you work at, attend, or are part of, this model (as does my guideline) will ensure that you, your loved ones, or those entrusted with their safety are on the right path.

We are on the home stretch, so let's push forward!

4.2
The Art of Situational and Threat Awareness

We may have the skill set to react and terminate the threat, but with our family members or co-workers right next to us, poor strategic positioning, being unarmed or in a gun-free zone, or just getting caught off guard, we need to adapt, survive, and be able to stop the lethal threat if given the opportunity by any means necessary. Being aware of your surroundings, detecting potential threats, and taking the appropriate physical environmental precautions which may help to avoid the encounter from even happening needs to take priority. Not everybody agrees with the concept of situational and threat awareness, and even more frightening, some of these trainers teach law enforcement and civilians almost the opposite. I think every skill set we could learn is important, but the notion of disregarding the art of situational and threat awareness is half-witted. Don't walk through life fearful of everything, but don't buy that "snake oil" either.

Let's face it, most people will instinctively protect their family first, as they should, but you must remember that the best way to protect your family is to quickly neutralize the aggressor **by any means necessary** if you find yourself and your loved ones in the middle of an attack. Depending on the proximity between your loved ones and the threat, when to engage, if at all, will be a decision that you will have to make. Otherwise, you will need to evaluate your force options, viable exit strategies, putting in affect any defensive or survival options available.

Throughout this book, we have discussed how training, knowledge, and mindset will help you survive the lethal, emotional, financial, and mental aspects during and after a deadly incident. Situational and threat awareness are no less important, and in its own right is a mindset. The good news is that we can reprogram this mindset in order to maximize our ability to monitor our environment intuitively. Towards the end of this segment, you will understand why.

These skills will not only give you a clear advantage, but if you are armed, it could also mentally prepare you and your community beforehand, no matter where you are, placing you and them in a better position to respond and survive.

Let's start with defining situational awareness. **Situational awareness**, in my definition, is understanding the "natural flow" of your surroundings which will keep you aware if and when the equilibrium shifts. In other words, it is the ability to understand and process environmental factors in your area of operation.

Threat awareness, on the other hand, is identifying a potential threat or threats after a shift, or spike, in the equilibrium has been detected. What happens that breaks the silence? What changed the dynamic of the environment and stands out? Did you see it, hear it, or intuitively feel it? Whatever size pebble causes a ripple in the pond, a heightened situational awareness mindset will place the good citizen or police officer in a more tactical and decisive position to engage and survive.

Some would argue that threat awareness and situational awareness are the same. While I believe that they are intertwined and almost inseparable, they are NOT the same. A dollar bill and a quarter as we all know are both forms of currency, but also distinctively different. Assuming everything and everybody is a threat can be dangerous and unhealthy for you and your relationships. This is why police officers have a very low life expectancy after retirement.

Let's discuss the different levels of awareness. The military and some police organizations use a color system from white to red. I encourage you to explore that on your own, but it's not my jam. I prefer to use my own modified system which is a little easier, in my opinion, to relate to and allows me to elaborate in a way that I feel is more effective. **These are Levels of Awareness 1 through 4.**

Unfortunately, the majority of the flock are in Level 1. Somebody in this state of awareness is oblivious to their surroundings and relaxed, perhaps whilst distracted with their mobile device or earbuds. Through complacency, they feel a false sense of safety and security. Complacency has cost officers their lives, and it can kill you too.

As I discussed earlier in the book, a lot of suburbs, especially in the Chicagoland area, went through some major socio-economic shifts that greatly impacted an increase in crime and officer safety. Police officers found themselves in high-risk situations that they'd managed to avoid for 20 years. Complacency is not your friend. I would imagine it is a lot healthier in the long run, but dangerous on the street. You do not want to go through life paranoid, but you sure as hell don't want to always be in Level 1 either.

Level 1 encompasses not only a gross deficiency of situational awareness, but also a weak, unconfident posture. This takes us back to Section 2. When you carry yourself through life, do it with just enough confidence to keep the predators in check but not so much that you draw too much attention to yourself. This balance is important. An aggressor will surely see that you are oblivious to your surroundings, but perhaps the deciding factor of him making you prey will be whether or not he thinks you are weak. Why do you think many of these tragic active killing events happen in gun-free zones? It's because there is a vulnerability and the aggressor knows it. People are busy studying, eating, or praying in these venues. Furthermore, they're likely unarmed and in a Level 1 state of awareness.

From a civilian perspective, blending into your environment and becoming what some would call "the gray man" is optimal. Adapt to the people and their mannerisms around you. Do not stand out or wear clothing that has loud, bright, or patterned colors, writing, or logos. If you are from the East Coast and go to a festival or public gathering in the southern states, your dialect will stand out and draw attention. Be aware of where you are at in contrast to where you are from. Again, be confident but strike that balance by blending in and keeping a low profile. Do not be that pebble in the pond! This brings us to Level 2.

Level 2 is being relaxed, but aware of your surroundings, melting into your environment with good positioning and being prepared to engage a lethal threat if necessary. When I go to a restaurant, an event, or even a theater, I don't always face the doors and the windows, but I'm aware of everybody in my immediate area and my situational awareness is heightened. This elevated level of awareness happens automatically and subconsciously, which we will get into ahead. I also make sure I know where at least two of the exits are. Don't be paranoid, but just be prepared. At this point, while in Level

2, your situational awareness should be a steady flow of normality and an undisturbed equilibrium that will allow you to act immediately.

We know what a reasonably safe environment looks and feels like. As a police officer, I used to automatically get into a "flow state" whilst subconsciously becoming tuned into the area of operation during patrol as the sun was setting and the police radio was chattering away. Ironically, there was a certain level of serenity among the chaos, but that serenity was my equilibrium. Even in the wintertime, the patrol vehicle's windows are cracked in order to hear gunfire or any other unusual sounds like shouting, screaming, vehicles, running, or "pebbles." I was able to detect instinctively or through observation any disruptions in what I call the "equilibrium of normality." It's amazing how much we are able to detect through instinct while on aggressive patrol looking for drug dealers or gun-toting gang bangers at night in pitch darkness. They stand in the alleys between buildings and many times, with a trained eye, an officer can detect a slight movement or shadow, even through his peripheral vision. At that point, the chase is usually on.

Observing, or feeling a criminal's fight-or-flight kick in is interesting. As I pursued them, in a weird way, I felt it, and they knew it. I suppose some call this instinct. I called it hunting. Whatever you call it, it was invigorating. I signed up to chase bad guys, not to write parking tickets. I figured that there were enough officers who were afraid to get out of the squad car that enjoyed writing them, so how can I possibly compete with that? Besides, turning predators into prey always sounded like much more fun.

I apologize for offending those pacifists who may be reading this book, but you have to remember we cannot run from our instinct, and even more importantly, we cannot allow those warriors in blue to lose it. But honestly, I suppose I wouldn't call that an apology, so I shall digress. Let's move on.

Speaking of tickets, I never liked to take the money from folks in the underprivileged areas by writing parking tickets. They have enough to worry about and very little money to pay the fines with, which can build up to the point that their vehicle is eligible for impoundment. I don't know about you, but that sounds like the real crime to me. I've been there. Before I started the police academy, I had close to $1,000 worth of parking tickets that accumulated and doubled while I was going to college in downtown Chicago.

I couldn't start the police academy until I paid them all with the receipt in hand, and you can bet that they got their money! They always do!

Getting back on point, a potential aggressor's behavior is predictable and detectable with the proper training and also when utilizing the RAS, or the Reticular Activating System, as we will discuss ahead.

This takes us to Level 3, which I also call the Threat Awareness Level. In this level, you are at a steady heightened level of situational awareness. You are consciously aware of potential threats which may or may not be identified, and you are prepared to engage. In other words, you are concerned! The equilibrium is fairly steady but looks a little shaky. You may see someone suspicious or your intuition kicks in. Depending on how the potential threat presents itself, this is a great time to start to commence your tactical breathing exercises and to discreetly direct your family or friends to the exits or cover. If possible, notify the police of a suspicious person or group along with a full description. As you learned in Section 2, tactical breathing will lower your heart rate, and allow you to not only maintain your situational awareness but logically figure out your next course of action, including deploying deadly force with precision should it be necessary to engage a lethal threat. Slowing your heart rate may even help you avoid the incident altogether or making the wrong decision. Be aware of your cover, which in theory will be any barricade, wall, or obstacle that is capable of stopping a bullet. A brick wall may stop a bullet, but a wall made out of drywall certainly will not.

Police officers operate, or should operate, between the Levels of 2 and 3. Some of the tougher areas of America that are patrolled by our finest in blue push these warriors into a constant state of Level 3 which will increase their survivability in the short-term, as unhealthy as it sounds. When you get shot at enough times, or when you know that those armed perps in the alley ways are within range of your patrol vehicle, it's a little hard to sit back and relax. Trust me, the anxiety is there, and it is constant. As we discussed, what stress does to our bodies is irreversible. With good training and a plan of action, both police and civilians alike should be able to maintain a steady Level 2 state of awareness.

The last level is Level 4. The equilibrium has been clearly disrupted. The threat has been identified due to the actions of the aggressor or circumstances, and an immediate response is imminent due to the fear of death or great bodily injury. At this point, the acute stress response likely kicks in. With proper tactical breathing, you would be able to mitigate this response because of the reasons discussed in Section 2. Be mindful of your family members, friends, or coworkers that do not have the same training as you. At this point, whether you are in a dark parking lot walking to your car and an aggressor is walking towards you with a knife or you are in your office at work and you hear rapid gunfire in the hallway, you are going to have to make a decision.

If you are armed, you will need to assess the threat and decide whether or not to deploy deadly force. Again, pay attention to your exits, target acquisition, your cover, and where your loved ones or other citizens are in proximity to the aggressor and his line of fire (or yours). If you are unarmed, we will discuss later in this section some of my recommendations on how to survive these attacks and others.

So, I'd like to briefly recap a few things as well as discuss a couple of tips and clues to keep in mind in respect to situational and threat awareness. Again, be confident but blend in. You want to be low profile. Try to maintain a Level 2 state of awareness with the ability to identify any abnormalities from the "equilibrium of normality." Be mindful of the exits as well as cover and concealment within your immediate area and listen to your instinct because it's usually never wrong. I'm not saying to deploy deadly force if your instinct tells you to. I'm just saying to be aware of the potential threats when your gut tells you to do so. Your intuition is your best friend, and when the threat is immediate and necessary, decide whether or not you are going to engage it.

Get into the habit of practicing your observation skills while in Level 2. Pay attention to who is around you, your immediate environmental factors we mentioned above like cover, concealment, and at least two exits. In terms of who is around you, pay attention to their mannerisms, gender, race, clothing, height, and weight. Also, pay attention to their waistband or places where they may keep a firearm or a weapon. Many times, I have asked citizens what weapon they are carrying because they usually have some part of it sticking out or they bring attention to themselves while readjusting it. At that point, as their face turns beet red, I usually offer them a free copy of my book. Be discreet but watch those who are not because they will falter. To a trained eye, somebody with a weapon or who has bad intentions is like a bull in a china shop and easy to spot. This is not always the case, but many times, it is.

Practice taking mental snapshots of people, license plates, and vehicles, then try to go back and see if your recollection was correct. It takes a little time, but eventually you'll be on point with the skill set. The ability to utilize RAS, or the Reticular Activating System, in order to enhance what we have discussed is invaluable and can also change your life in other ways, which we will examine ahead.

When you are at home, work, or other places like a place of worship where you generally have the same people attending, pay attention to the foot traffic and unknown vehicles within proximity of the location. The bad guy knows how to work the environment and you should also. Know what's supposed to be there and what seems to be out of place.

When traveling either on foot, bike, or vehicle, pay attention to who's in back of you. Generally speaking, if I'm suspicious, I like to utilize the three-turn test. I casually make three turns a couple of blocks apart. If the vehicle or the person in back of you maintains a visual on your position, you may have a problem. The clandestine world is a unique existence altogether as many operatives reduce the risk of being compromised by taking precautions while utilizing various strategies for these types of operations. Counter-surveillance is a valuable skill to have, but for the regular citizen and an untrained aggressor, the three-turn test will do the trick and expose them.

Another thing that I think is important to mention with the sex trade not going away anytime soon (for obvious reasons) and the large number of sexual predators lurking within society, be cautious of vans—especially the white vans—that are in proximity of your home, parks, etc. Try to avoid walking past them. These predators like to park and wait for their prey to walk by who is usually in Level 1. Remember, kidnapping is a forcible felony and in many states is a viable reason to justifiably deploy deadly force by any means at your disposal.

Now, in terms of threat awareness, there are usually signs that are present before an attack that you may be able to intercept which will help during your decided course of action, whether it's the use of force or avoiding it altogether if possible. Guns don't kill people, the finger on the trigger does; pay attention to the hands. What's in them? Do you see someone perspiring and fidgeting with something on their waistband, backpack, or pocket? Are they wearing a jacket, sweater or a loose long-sleeve shirt over his beltline in hot weather? This may signify that he's carrying a weapon.

Pay attention to eye contact. Eye contact is an interesting beast on its own. This is slightly related to posture, discussed in Section 2. A potential aggressor senses your fear when you avoid eye contact, which may cause him to attack you. If you look at him too long, that might also cause him to attack you because then you look provoking. If you're getting stared down by a potential aggressor, look at him for about 3-5 seconds and then break contact, but don't look down, because it comes across as submissive. Watching the eye movement of a potential aggressor will not only let you know when he is about to attack, it may let you know if he has other associates in the area who very well may be surrounding you before the attack. Now, as a police officer, even off duty, it's hard to break eye contact, especially for the more aggressive officers always in Level 3. As a civilian, acknowledge the potential threat with 3-5 seconds of eye contact, then break eye contact, and look straight ahead while still utilizing your peripheral vision, focusing on the hands. Trust me, as funny as it sounds, the bad guy will know you are side eyeing him, which is a good thing.

Years ago, I was on the train heading towards downtown Chicago while off duty. A few minutes into the trek, there was a very tall and muscular man who boarded the train and suddenly became aggressive. The train was full of timid professionals hoping to make a difference in the world by working for Corporate America, most likely in some small cubicle. They were just trying to get to work on time to make the big man richer. As luck would have it, this unhinged man walked down the aisle of the train and sat next to every citizen who looked down while avoiding his eye contact and began to threaten them. Sure, a mental illness may have been the culprit, but I know an asshole when I see one. I glanced at him for a few seconds and then began to check emails on my phone, hoping he would get off at the next stop, while maintaining my peripheral on him. Instead, he got up and sat next to me and asked me, "What the fuck are you going to do?" I felt my heart rate go up because I knew where this was going. I chuckled and looked at him while smiling, thoroughly explaining in detail what was going to happen to him if his tail didn't get off at the next stop. After this fine taxpayer exited the train, I could not help but look at all these snowflakes who rapidly repositioned their seats away from me. I couldn't believe it. I think they had me mixed up with the wolf, but this is a good example of how fear distorts reality!

The next segment will dive into RAS, or the Reticular Activating System, so let's get to it!

4.3
The Reticular Activating System

The RAS or the **Reticular Activating System** is an amazing part of the human body that is paramount to our existence in many ways.

I decided to insert this in Section 4 instead of Section 2 because I felt it would be more useful from a situational and threat awareness perspective. The RAS is an extensive topic, but I will try to simplify it the best I can to give you the most benefit when it comes to environmental safety and cognizance.

The RAS is located in the hypothalamus and brainstem region in the base of the brain and has several impressive functions. In a nutshell, the RAS controls our attention, our goal achievement, and threats in our immediate area. It also regulates the motor system that optimizes our responses during the Acute Stress Response (fight or flight).

Furthermore, it is where the conscious and the subconscious merge to flawlessly filter through loads of unnecessary data, allowing us to focus on what matters to us the most. Of course, I was not hunting for parking tickets or traffic violations unless I needed it for the purpose of probable cause for the initial stop, but I subconsciously put RAS to work in other ways. It allowed me to observe any deviations from what I would have perceived as normal in my area of operation. During patrol, it enhanced every aspect of my physiology, senses, and intuition in order to complete the mission, which was to hunt down the bad guy and keep the community safe.

More specifically, RAS filters needless data in order to help us get to our objective faster, while isolating only the tastes, smells, sights, and what we hear or perceive that we feel are mission essential. It only allows in the data that paints the picture of how we actually see the world. This is impressive but also frightening.

Fundamentally, let us discuss the RAS at work. The classic example is when you are looking for a new car. Let's say it was a red Toyota Corolla. The day after you obsessively look for this vehicle online, you will spot every red Toyota Corolla on the road as you are driving. We program ourselves to see only what we think we want to see. If I decide to change the keychain on my car keys, the next day I'll probably walk past it two or three times looking for them before I realize it's on a new keychain. Consciously, I am looking for the keys, but subconsciously, I am looking for the keychain, which is now different.

The RAS can be a blessing and a curse. One way or the other, our subconscious finds a way to remind us of our priorities. Sometimes it pushes us further away from them with the distorted vision of the life we think we have. We could be our worst enemy, so think big. Create the reality that you want by prioritizing your goals and looking at the good with the people you care about or interact with.

In any type of relationship, sometimes we focus just on the bad because that's what we subliminally program ourselves to focus on. Teachers, supervisors, and parents do it all the time. This can be that one kid who talks too much in class or that team member who is always late to the meetings. This is the RAS at work. It's also a powerful tool that reinforces what we see through our experiences in order to influence our belief system or how we view the world.

Looking at the bad in ourselves or others will never let us, or others, see the good. Remember that. Sure, we are talking about threat and situational awareness, but it's important to be happy as well because at the end of the day, that's really what we all want, right?

4.4
Tips for Enhancing Situational Awareness

There are some strategies to help enhance situational and threat awareness. To start, you can practice taking mental snapshots and then recalling the data. This will get you used to focusing on your equilibrium of normality and identify any spikes, deviation, or anything that stands out in any way. The potential threats operating within it or things that just seem out of place will stand out and you will be able to identify it. Get into the habit of scanning your immediate environment and remember that people who carry weapons wear certain types of clothing or behave differently with their mannerisms. I encourage you to "people watch" which, I have to admit, can be entertaining. Pay attention to their clothing, their mannerisms, their dialect or accent, the way they carry themselves, who they're with, and even try to figure out what level of awareness they are in. Are they confident? Are they readjusting an object along the beltline? Are they a predator or the next victim? For a short period of time, I was assigned to downtown Chicago which was full of tourists from all over the world. Oftentimes, I would see many of these tourists in Level 1 state of awareness, and within proximity of them, I would see a predator watching them. It is interesting to watch this play out, especially when we slowly creep up in our patrol vehicle and give the predator a little eye contact to let him know that we know his intentions. Usually at that point, the unsuspecting tourist walks one way and the would-be robber, thug, or thief abruptly turns around and walks the other.

If you are used to detecting or striving to observe these types of behaviors, eventually, you will be able to filter out everything else around that subject naturally and subconsciously.

As a police officer, detecting somebody's "fight or flight" is usually an indicator something is wrong, which sometimes is enough to initiate a field investigation, or at the very least, observe them. At times we would see teenagers driving cars that were stolen while displaying this behavior. They would start to swerve or move their head rapidly in order to look for an escape route. Many times, after they realized that we spotted them, their fine motor skills would diminish, and often, the vehicle crashed which subsequently ended up as a foot chase.

Other times, my partner and I would drive slowly past a group of gang members to scan their behavior, looking for one of them to frantically look for an escape route, which usually meant he had drugs, a warrant, or a firearm on his person, based upon our experience on the street. The simple act of rapidly opening and closing the squad car door was usually enough to watch the thug drop his firearm and attempt to flee from the scene. As a civilian, any deviation will provide an opportunity for you to prepare yourself or others around you should that potential threat progress.

One helpful way to get you into the habit of this is by using my ASAP system: Absorb, Scan, Assess, and Prepare. **Absorb** into your environment, **Scan** those within the environment, **Assess** their appearance, actions, proximity, mannerisms, and associates, and then **Prepare** to take action, if necessary. It is easier said than done, but after time, you'll be a natural.

Before we exit this segment and dive to the next, it's important to realize that criminals and aggressors also utilize this system to pick their prey, as hinted above. Whether they are criminals or an extremist with dangerous ideologies, they are likely trained and understand exactly the type of person, organization, or community they want to terrorize. Their brain is programmed to hunt the weak, and ours should be programmed to hunt them.

The youth in many of the economically deprived areas of America have a warped perception of what they think is normal. This is, once again, the RAS at work. This prevents them and their community from succeeding, which often leads them to a life of crime. It is a vicious cycle and those few pulling the chains of chaos wouldn't have it any other way. Our perception of our environment in the world we live in is influenced by our life experience, what we see in the news, and other factors that dictate the boundaries of our perception as well as how we treat others.

How many wars have been fought and lives lost in the name of God? I wonder what He thinks about that, but that is an entirely different book that I do not plan on writing. With extreme ideologies inspiring foreign and domestic terrorism, the value system of our youth distorted, violence influenced by social media, partisan media outlets, and politicians manipulating entire populations, perhaps I jumped the gun on that statement. It really makes you wonder if we are free, or do we just have the perception that we are? The jury is out on that one, literally. As for me, I feel that we have the ability to pave our path and live the life we want to live. I also feel that if we have certain dark forces attempting to take our life or those around us that we love, we are obligated to do something about it. I have faith in humanity, and something tells me that the big man upstairs just may as well.

4.5
Tainted Soil

There must be a comprehensive approach to the active killer phenomenon, from influential factors that shaped them as a child up until the point they decide to wreak havoc in the world that they perceive to be their adversary. Are they purely evil or do they have political or extreme religious ideologies that motivate them to commit such carnage? Perhaps they have an undiagnosed mental illness that progresses undetected by those close to them who have grown numb and blind.

As I said earlier in the book, unmonitored, addictive social media exposure as well as highly effective partisan media outlets influencing entire populations have contributed greatly because it has dehumanized the human experience.

In 1973, Martin Cooper made the first phone call to a competitor with a cell phone. Since then, our existence has been inflamed in every respect including our emotional, mental, and physical well-being. People text each other from the same room, they check messages within minutes of waking up, and the numerous accidents as a result of distracted driving while talking, texting, or checking social media has changed the course of our evolution emotionally and physically, creating a new type of addiction. Child obesity is at a record high as mobile devices, social media, and gaming have taken the place of sports or playing outdoors with friends.

Our military now has "fat camps" in order to get recruits ready for basic training, and even then, the standards in every respect have drastically changed and will continue to go downhill. Traditional social engagement for both adults and children has plummeted in every respect. Online dating or social gatherings have replaced organic gatherings of such, with no help from the Covid-19 pandemic.

I am sure Mr. Cooper had nothing but good intentions to better his fellow homo sapiens. Due to the drastic changes in society, I often wonder if his opinion has changed. From the little I know about him, he seems like a very intelligent, personable guy with a traditional value system, and at 94, the visionary may just be getting started.

I would be especially curious about his perspective regarding social media, including those who created it. It's been said that the mobile cellular phone has been the greatest contribution to humanity since the wheel, but I'm not sure we can say the same for those who created social media, which has waged war on our value system during this pivotal crossroad of mankind.

Social media, in all forms, offers a voice to the darkest souls of society. Not only has social media possibly influenced a number of active killer attacks and the emotional health of our youth, but it has also influenced crime in urban America, as many crimes have been live streamed. It has silenced the masses, ignited mass psychosis, then divided our once unified country at the will of a few.

It also takes us away from who we are as a species. I feel that if we were more in touch with who we are as a human race and not addictively engaged with our mobile device, we would be more connected with ourselves, our fellow humans, and our planet. We have drastically changed and, in my opinion, regressed as a society with lasting evolutionary implications. Modern-day technology has not been distributed responsibly, which encourages a pathway for other technologies like AI to flourish at the expense of our future. If AI evolves to the point of sentience, combined with the means to act, it may not work out well for us. I don't know about you, but I see a pattern.

Moving on, limited eye contact with those we love, sleep deprivation caused by undisciplined use of mobile devices and hormones like dopamine that is artificially induced due to social media and gaming engagement takes us far from where we are supposed to be.

Recently, some schools have banned mobile devices during school hours, which I think is a step in the right direction. Regardless of how amazing the students' grades are, if they do not have the means to emotionally engage with their peers or staff, how will they develop the ability to succeed in society or cope with life's circumstances?

Take a look around, my fellow anthropoids. Does this look normal to you? I would suspect that not only does social media dehumanize the human experience, I feel it also contributes to the elevated mental health crisis of our youth, which is directly connected to the violent targeted attacks we see today.

Another layer of madness is our educational system that our children are exposed to from elementary school to university. Many of these organizations nurture an unhealthy educational environment that promotes a sense of entitlement and a lack of coping skills or consequences, subsequently taking away power from the parents. Unfortunately, I learned about this the hard way, but that's a story for another time. Parenting a child within a school system that has extreme ideologies designed to decimate the value systems that parents fight so hard to instill in their children is almost impossible.

How much control of our children do we really have when they walk out the door to go to school with their mobile device in hand? Remember, our children go to school to receive an education, not to have a political agenda spewed upon them. As a centrist, I see the dangers of the blue and the red in its extreme form. Save the politics for the ballot box and keep it out of our schools.

I truly feel that children who are immune to consequences and lack coping skills paired with a high level of bullying, including cyberbullying, also places children in a vulnerable position to make the wrong decision, as the NTAC study we discuss ahead suggests. In recent times, there have been numerous accounts of active killers returning to the school they went to or where they were bullied with the intention of murder. Bullying, in any form, has contributed not only to targeted violence but also suicide.

Many schools with the collaboration of local police departments have started to create anti-bullying campaigns, which I believe is a good start. These programs teach children various strategies to use in order to fend off these types of bullying attacks and make it easier for other students to intervene or notify the proper authority.

Being bullied at school is bad enough, but then going home and watching the attacks continue on social media brings this to a whole different level of abuse. When your teenager is in their room with the door closed on their mobile device, do you really know what's happening? You should! Do not turn a blind eye. Monitor their social media and take action, if necessary. The parental controls available on these platforms are useless, and our politicians need to step it up in order to protect our youth.

Transparency while at school and their interaction on social media must be enforced, and the only way to do this is with the appropriate legislation in place. How many organizations, friends, and families have failed the child, friend, or loved one before it gets to this point of violence or suicide? Even worse, how many saw it coming? No folks, it's not just the guns. Somebody's going to have to tell the great minds of academia it's a little more than that.

When I was a freshman in high school, I was not only about a year younger than my peers, but I was also a lot smaller. Being new to the community and having a lack of muscle at that age, I was bullied by a 6th year senior who did not appear to be going away any time soon. Thankfully, I decided to become friends with the toughest kid in the school and most of my problems stopped. What if I was 13 years old today?

I would likely lack coping skills whilst being coddled into and during adolescence, exposed to easily available pornography, violent movies and video games, bullying, and unmonitored social media. I would have likely attended a school system that preaches distorted ideologies instead of teaching me the tools I need in life to succeed. All of this, of course, would happen as my parents helplessly watched. One or all of these factors would change the trajectory of my life, and likely my metabolism. These are real conversations our lawmakers on both sides of the aisle need to have.

As I said earlier in the book, this unprecedented violence that has plagued society did not happen overnight, and it'll take time for humanity to get back on track. We are in a new era, and the decisions we make today as a society will not only impact our children of tomorrow but the survival of the human race.

I encourage parents and lawmakers to unite in order to create transparency within the educational system and advocate for legislature that forces social media platforms to be accountable for the content that our youth are exposed to. As I have mentioned earlier, this includes violent video games and movies.

A 14-year-old boy can't go to a bookstore and buy an adult magazine, but he could go onto social media platforms and have access to porn in real time, many of whom are victims of the sex trade themselves. That same boy can then walk past a cannabis dispensary into a gaming store and buy a video game that entails killing police officers or stealing cars. Sounds like good, old-fashioned wholesome fun, right? Apple pie, anyone? No thanks, Mr. Jinping (leader of the Chinese Communist Party), I'll opt for the space cake instead, or perhaps the fentanyl. As disgusting as it sounds, this is the tip of the iceberg and American culture has taken some dark turns.

Aside from ruthlessly holding educational administrators and social media platforms accountable, putting stronger term limits on politicians may give us a little more control over these overpaid, white-collar criminals, don't you think? And for their professional survival in the hustle called politics, shorter terms may even force them to actually do their jobs!

4.5
The Blind Eye

As the Mandalay Bay Hotel mass shooting proved in Las Vegas in 2017, the threat can come from anyone or anywhere. A 64-year-old obsessive gambler methodologically brought 24 firearms with ammunition into the hotel throughout several days in multiple suitcases during the course of a well-planned operation.

This quirky high roller grew up in poverty, but despite his tough childhood, he would not only grow up and become extremely wealthy, but systematically plan and execute the deadliest mass shooting in American history. On that dreadful October day during a country music festival on the Vegas Strip, the shooter fired over 1,000 rounds of ammunition into the audience with multiple weapons from the 32nd floor window from his hotel suite that faced the festival. This aggressor's actions killed 58 and injured over 800. Upon the police making entry into his hotel room, multiple rifles and ammunition were found scattered as the coward lay deceased from a self-inflicted gunshot wound. To this day, investigations have yet to reveal his motive for committing such a heinous act of terror. Some elements of the investigation revealed that the shooter became obsessed with weapons while distancing himself from family and his girlfriend well before the shooting. As past cases have shown, this is a common behavior and did raise the alarm amongst his closest associates. Yes, folks, it takes a village to raise a kid, but only one unhinged aggressor or an extreme ideology to destroy both the kid and the village.

As this shooting demonstrated, we can't always control the circumstances of these types of situations, but there are a few things that we can control.

This includes having risk and threat assessment and response strategies in place that can identify and manage the risks, prevent, stop, slow down, or neutralize the lethal threat until the responding police arrive. This especially pertains to locations that are gun-free zones like schools, churches, hospitals, and places of business such as retail establishments or an office environment.

4.6
The Bedrock of Risk and Threat Assessment

The concept of threat assessment is a vast, multifaceted, complex space that requires a team of professionals from law enforcement to forensic and clinical psychologists to create the guidelines or deploy such an initiative in the actual organization. Furthermore, those professionals that create these models and guidelines are just one piece of the puzzle. We'll get into this further ahead.

This comprehensively includes behavioral detection strategies and management, or risk assessment, and the physical site security precautionary measures that a property must necessitate. Although this realm of responsibility usually falls into the hands of administrators and leaders of organizations that are susceptible to these types of attacks, it is important for all of us to understand the foundation of the threat assessment space. You may not be a hospital or school administrator, but you may work at one of these or other vulnerable organizations or have a family member that does. When you're at your child's school board meeting, you will be armed with the power of knowledge, ensuring the organization that is responsible for those you love has a balanced threat assessment and response plan from prevention and detection to initiating the proper procedures should an active killer enter the grounds or building. Most of these organizations in the larger metropolitan areas, including its adjacent suburbs, usually have the resources available to take steps in the right direction. This is not always the case in small-town USA where many of these tragedies happen. Many of its organizations, including schools, are under-resourced, complacent, and if a tragedy does occur, first responders from the local police department may not be trained or equipped to handle it. Many folks in these sleepy communities leave their doors unlocked at night and the keys in their car.

You need to understand that it does not take a tremendous number of resources to put a plan in effect. It takes research, knowledge, training, and determination! Appropriate protocols should not only expose the underbelly of potentially lethal threats, including suicide, but it should also include data collection when these indicators are observed and a plan of action when a fact-based threat is detected. Throughout this discussion, I am going to recommend resources that you will be able to reference to remain diligent in this space.

Before we move any further, I want to ensure that you know the difference between risk assessment and threat assessment. Many of those in the industry that are responsible for training organizations for these types of threats do not explain the difference, which causes confusion down the road. As a rule of thumb, the primary goal of risk assessment is to detect and manage potential violent aggressors, and the goal of threat assessment is to protect the potential victims. Let's discuss this further.

Risk assessment is designed to identify, intervene, and manage the potential aggressor based upon the detected behaviors or actions. In other words, an organization that identifies the red flags must have a system in place to do so, then have a decisive plan as to when to step in either to provide the proper mental health or other support, manage the individual before violence occurs, or even at what point to notify law enforcement. Furthermore, if these red flags or behavioral indicators have been identified, the organization must have a management plan in place to minimize chances that the individual will act.

Threat assessment is fundamentally different. The Texas School Safety Center, an official university level research center, is a centralized hub in Texas for research and deployment of safety and security information regarding violence in Texas schools from the elementary to the junior college levels. I like their definition of threat assessment as a **"fact-based, systematic process designed to identify, inquire, assess and manage potentially dangerous or violent situations."** I personally like this definition because it fits within the scope of my position regarding risk assessment and threat assessment being intertwined, yet distinctly different. The Texas School Safety Center offers a variety of resources and training for schools as well as law enforcement. Even if you are not in Texas, you can take advantage of this valuable resource.

Simplifying this further, identifying potential red flags based upon a behavioral analysis (risk assessment) is a lot different than an actual threat made on social media about shooting a teacher in a school or an employee in an office. Remember, people are emotional and love to vent or let off steam. The corner is turned, however, when they are **specific** about the actions they will take, and start **researching** the logistics of potential targets, times, location details, or weapon systems (delivery methods) needed. When such threats or actions are clear, these undisputed facts have enough substance that justifies further investigations or actions by law enforcement.

When the red flags are identified, on the other hand, this is the organization's chance to not only prevent the tragedy from occurring, but to provide the proper support to those involved, including the source of the threat. Know the difference and have a plan for both the indicators of a potential threat and set protocols should a fact-based threat be identified.

It's also important to understand that any risk or threat assessment and response plan can and should differ depending on the organization or functionality of the location like a school, company setting, or church, for example. Such a plan should not only be tailored to your industry, but also to your specific organization, members, and specific locale.

As we push forward, I want you to keep the previous discussion regarding situational and threat awareness at the forefront of your mind because targeted attacks in public venues such as a place of worship, a store, a public gathering, a restaurant or even a theater usually happens immediately and unpredictably. Understand and be familiar with your environment!

In a school or work environment, the same skills are also crucial for the reasons we previously discussed. Yes, the risk or threat assessment plan may be set in place to detect potential aggressors or threats, but many times, it is the students or staff of the organization that is the first to observe these disruptions in the "equilibrium of normality." These are crucial skills to have and will greatly parallel this discussion and most of the remaining content of Section 4 when we dig deeper.

Let's be honest. Throughout this book, we have discussed the importance of neutralizing a lethal threat because it's vital that we do it not only within the boundaries of the law but rapidly and without hesitation. Now, what if we were able to detect and avoid the entire incident from happening before it transpires? The science is there, and this is a conversation we must have because responding to the threat, although necessary, is only one part of the equation. Deploying deadly force during an active killing incident is merely a life jacket while drifting in the sea of mayhem. Yes, it will stop the immediate lethal threat in its tracks, as it should, but it will not address the underlying cause.

Sure, you're a well-trained, off-duty police officer or armed citizen with a tight shot group that would make some of the finest instructors jealous, but what if you get a phone call that there's an active killer in the building who happens to be your only child, your best friend going through a horrific divorce, or your 70-year old uncle with mental health issues? It happens more often than you think, folks. Good people are not immune to things like this happening around them or to those they love. How will you respond then? Many of the loved ones of the attackers are stellar law-abiding citizens who missed the warning signs. In a sea of chaos that the world is currently experiencing, it is easy for it to happen.

It's no secret that love, in any form, is blind. I would guess that's why many of us are divorced. Will we see the warning signs, in any form, from those we love or to whom we are closest? Even more frightening, if we do, how do we avert tragedy and support them? There is an alarming number of active killer incidents that could have been prevented had something been said to the proper authority or those who could have intervened beforehand, especially at home, in schools and the workplace. The warning signs are almost always there. The Mandalay Bay shooter had absolutely nothing posted on social media but did display behavioral changes that alarmed some of his closest associates, who said nothing. What do you do if you hear that passive, yet detailed threat from a fellow student in the university hallway, observe that alarming social media post from your ex-girlfriend or the violent manifesto found in your husband's clothes as you are doing the laundry? Does your organization, community, or family have a transparent strategy for communication should such a threat be detected? They should. We'll dig a little deeper into this shortly.

So, I'd like to lay out a few things before we push through the next few segments. As I have mentioned, every organization, industry, and location present its own challenges, which should be evaluated and tailored to that specific locale. That aside, many of the guidelines presented by mental health professionals, private threat assessment consultants—like me—or federal agencies like the U.S. Secret Service and The Department of Homeland Security can be applied to workplace and school settings, although management and intervention strategies tend to be very different.

Now, a school may have two plans: one for the students and one for the staff because although many of the dynamics are similar in terms of risk and threat assessment, managing the child is much different than managing a grown man in the workplace, even if they are in the same location. A location like a place of worship may have staff or employees but is also open to the public, which requires a heightened sense of situational and threat awareness due to the variables always changing like new congregant membership or potential attackers entering during the service.

Below, we are going to briefly examine a couple different studies presented by NTAC that I feel are important to understand not only from an organizational leader's perspective, but also as a teacher, parent, or member of the community.

4.7
An NTAC Study Overview: Mass Attacks in Public Spaces: 2016-2020

The U.S. Secret Service has been extremely proactive in the behavioral threat assessment space. Historically, the United States Secret Service's mission was to protect and investigate as well as safeguard the nation's most prestigious elected officials. As history has shown, it's not an easy task, but their mission didn't stop there when the country needed them.

In 1998, they created the National Threat Assessment Center. This was the year before the horrific Columbine shooting, which unfortunately set a dangerous precedent for what we see today. After Columbine, schools were required to have some form of threat assessment and response plan, finally giving this domain the attention it deserves. The mission of NTAC is to provide research and guidance for the purpose of Public Safety. This component of the Secret Service consists of a wide range of multidisciplinary team members that support not only law enforcement, but schools and both public and private sector organizations in order to confront targeted violence, like active killers, in the United States. With the active killer phenomenon not going away anytime soon, they have their hands full, and from the looks of it, so do we.

The **Mass Attacks in Public Spaces: 2016-2020** is a 70-page, open-source study that examined 173 attacks that took place in a variety of different locales including businesses, schools, places of worship, military bases, nonprofit service providers, residential complexes, public transportation, as well as open spaces, and was published in 2023. Yes, currently, as this book is being written, it is 2024, but it's important to establish a baseline and these studies do exactly that. Furthermore, the data collected through this study and others like it is invaluable and extremely useful. They did a good job. As I have said, knowledge is power, so it's important to learn as much as you can from a variety of different resources so you can apply it to your family, community, or organization.

The data from these 173 targeted attacks were studied from 2016 to 2020, taking note that 51% of the cases were in businesses, 35% in open spaces, and only 8% in schools from kindergarten to university level. The study is data driven yet heavily dives into some of the concerning behaviors displayed by the attacker years before the attack as well as the behavior displayed leading up to the attack, including communications. Bear with me as we dive into some of the numbers and then we'll segue into some of the more interesting findings. Dealing with studies can be a little bit frustrating, so I've tried to condense it to get the most out of it. Let's dive right in.

The majority of these attacks were conducted by males using handguns that were legally purchased, illegally purchased, or purchased by a close associate of the attacker for the attacker. Many of the attackers also had a variety of mental health issues like suicidal thoughts, depression, delusional episodes, or psychosis.

Overall, 126 of the attacks were conducted with firearms, but here are the other weapons used:

- 28 with bladed weapons
- 18 with vehicles
- 6 with blunt objects
- 3 were incendiary
- 3 with explosives
- 3 with other forms of weapons, such as hands or feet.

Regarding the ages:

- 44 of the attackers were between the ages of 14 and 24
- 63 attackers were between the ages of 25 and 34
- 36 attackers were between the ages of 35 and 44

- 21 attackers between the ages of 45 and 54
- 11 attackers between the ages of 55 and 64
- Only 5 attackers were over the age of 65. The oldest was 87.

Most attackers were classified as white, followed by African American, Hispanic, then Asian. One hundred and fifteen had a past criminal history, which I thought was interesting, but not surprising. What also was not surprising was what I have been talking about throughout this book, which were the pre-attack indicators. Their motives and their drastic behavioral changes in most of the cases happened well before the attack was carried out, which means it could have been prevented.

I truly feel that studies like these point out the importance of how this is a team effort that starts well before the attack occurs. We cannot always prevent these types of attacks, but the signs are there well in advance for us to take the necessary steps to identify, intervene, and manage before the organization or community comes under attack.

The study discusses motives with **51% of them pertaining to grievances** that were personal, domestic, or workplace related. Of this, 46 of the cases were personal motives, which included bullying, financial, or health-related stressors or feelings of victimization. **18% of the cases encompassed the motive relating to extreme ideologies** in any respect, and **14% related to psychotic symptoms**.

Even more disturbing, 32 of the attackers did target-related planning which entailed researching and photographing the location of the attack online and in person. Next came weapons planning with 29 cases. This includes acquiring the weapon, doing research on the type of weapon best used for the attack, and even practicing with the weapon or securing the proper permits in advance. **Many of these attackers were not able to legally obtain weapons due to mental illness, domestic, or other criminal history factors but were able to obtain the firearms in other ways.** This included online purchasing, a friend or family member purchasing the firearm for the attacker, 3D printing the weapon, or stealing an unsecured firearm from a friend or household member.

In 9 of the cases, the attacker prepared hit lists and maps of the targeted location. In 7 of the cases, the attacker researched prior attacks from school shootings to international terrorist incidents. What is more frightening, they researched what tactics worked and what did not work. In other words, they conducted an AAR, or After-Action Review of the incident to learn from it and not make the same mistake.

Six of the attackers researched logistics, which entailed law enforcement response times, capabilities, and tactics as well as the capability of the ammunition they chose to use. Lastly, they researched gun store rules and the types of suspicious behavior that would be reported to the authorities. That's right, folks, they do extensive research, much of it online and traceable, prior to the attack.

One last crucial note regarding the planning conducted by the attackers: **fifty-one of the attackers made final communication or displayed behaviors that indicated that the attack was going to happen and that it was imminent.** This included calling loved ones, social media posts, farewell videos, journals, or manifestos that detail their plans and reasons for the attack.

This entire study directly or indirectly involves the unusual behavior or stressors of an attacker beforehand. Let us take a more precise look at some of the indicators that the attackers displayed throughout this study.

These red flags include but are not limited to:

- Extreme interest in violence, pornography, or weapons
- Interest in military or law enforcement careers but failure of acceptance into those fields for several reasons
- Social isolation
- Bullying or being bullied
- Financial, relationship or health issues
- Recently fired from their job
- Behavioral changes in appearance, mood, religious beliefs or ideologies, substance abuse or actions that are uncharacteristic of their normal being
- Changes in performance and work, grades, or attendance

Concerning, fact-based threats or behaviors that were prior to an attack that would have required law enforcement involvement or intervention included:

- Detailed communication on social media to friends or family, goodbye calls, journals, or written manifestos detailing the attack
- Threatening, harassing, stalking, or other violent behaviors were displayed prior to the attack
- Unusual statements, bizarre behaviors, increased anger, and a deeper interest in violence warranted documentation and mental health intervention prior to law enforcement involvement
- Direct threats, physical violence, and an intense escalation and anger
- Firearm, explosive, or other weapon related inquiries or online searches, especially when other concerning behaviors are also present
- Interest in extreme ideologies like hate-related groups, misogyny, or terrorism
- Fixations that become obsessive

The responses, or lack thereof, toward the concerning behavior and communications of those who detected this behavior prior to the attacks in the study I thought was a little alarming. Once these behaviors were detected, 116 took direct action, 73 were cautious expressing concern asking others for help, protecting themselves or others, and 29 took no action at all.

Those that took direct action with the attacker took the position of positive reinforcement recommending mental health assistance or an evaluation. Many organizations attempted to communicate with the attacker and asked him to stop the behavior or leave, which was not enough. Other organizations notified law enforcement, terminated the employee, or suspended the student.

Some of the more proactive responses involved developing escape routes, securing a safe house, getting a guard dog, or sharing photos with staff, family, or friends so they know what the aggressor looks like.

It is important to understand that within this study, 73 of the attackers displayed "concerning communications" to their family members which included parents, siblings, children, or extended family as well as romantic partners. Coming in second was "peripheral contacts," which took up 71 of the cases that included law enforcement or other local organizations like Child Protective Services or the court system.

If this study showed anything, it showed us that an attack could come from anyone at any time. There is not one specific profile that would determine what type of person would commit such an attack, although a little intuition goes a long way. This study is a clear indication that a strong plan must be created and managed to minimize these risks. The data shows that the red flags are almost always there well in advance. As the shooting in the Mandalay Bay Hotel proved, we may not always figure out why the killer decided to commit murder, but the warning signs were clear, whether we are blind to them or not. The next segment will dive into an overview of the second NTAC study I have chosen to discuss, which focuses on targeted violence in schools from levels K-12. Let's move!

4.8

An NTAC Study Overview: Protecting America's Schools | A U.S. Secret Service Analysis of Targeted School Violence

This study focuses on targeted violence in school levels K-12 between the years 2008 to 2017 and looks at 41 incidents while examining the motives, stressors, and behaviors of the attackers before and during the attack. **Keep in mind that the stressors and behavioral indicators and changes are similar to the first paper we discussed prior.** Obviously, when you're dealing with children, circumstances are very different because they find themselves in the middle of situations like divorces, financial turmoil that their parents are dealing with, homelessness, the foster care system, or a school that doesn't address the bullying that takes place or fails to provide the proper mental health support should the student be under emotional duress.

Whether the students are capable of carrying out such an attack or not, it is in the best interest of the organization, the child, and the community, especially within an educational environment, to provide a stable and healthy atmosphere for the student to flourish and receive the proper emotional support if necessary. Although we will get into threat assessment guidelines ahead, it is crucial for the school or organization to create a positive climate and transparent atmosphere. This includes a <u>fluid communication pathway</u> regarding the duress a student may be experiencing, or potential threatening indicators or communications as detected by friends, family, staff, or teachers.

Listen. Educators, like law enforcement, have a tough, underpaying job. Most teachers take the job because they want to make an impact on the lives of the most important asset of our society, which is our youth. It is hard enough to teach children, regardless of their age, in today's dysfunctional ecosystem, but then having to offer the emotional support that they may not be getting at home brings this dynamic responsibility to a whole new level. Like any other public service job, it eventually weighs heavily on the heart, creating a cynicism that tends to mask some of the most important aspects of their job, which is not only teaching, but promoting the emotional nourishment the child needs. This to the side, many teachers have become masters of their craft, systematically identifying some of these red flags, but still, proper protocols are not put in place to streamline the communication regarding these observations so the child gets the proper support. **According to the study, only about 17% of the schools had reporting mechanisms in place.**

Although I feel threat assessment and response plans should be well-rounded, including physical site safety measures put in place, this study stresses that the best way to prevent a targeted school shooting is identifying, intervening, and managing the students in distress because the indicators for such potential violence are present well in advance.

Protecting America's Schools | A U.S. Secret Service Analysis of Targeted School Violence study showed that most of the schools that were victims to these targeted attacks **did** have physical safety protocols in place, including student resource officers. Being an optimist, I still feel compelled to do everything possible to make sure that if the day comes that an active killer steps on the grounds of a school system or other location, that there are protocols in place to prevent a breach, neutralize or slow down the progression of the actual attack. I understand the data tells us that prevention is the key, and although I do agree, I also feel that the proper physical protocols should be part of the threat assessment and response plan because it is the right thing to do.

The findings from the study can paint a picture whilst helping sway us in the right direction regarding the creation of a solid threat assessment and response plan. If you are in the threat assessment industry in any capacity, or are a business or educational institution leader, I strongly recommend that you not only read this report and others like on the NTAC website but use their other resources that they offer. This includes a document called **Enhancing School Safety Using a Threat Assessment Model: An Operational Guide for Preventing Targeted School Violence,** which is a straightforward threat assessment guideline for schools to utilize and parallels this second study that we are discussing now.

Some of the primary discoveries according to this study include the following:

- There is no student profile or type of school that was targeted.
- Most students who conducted attacks had multiple behavioral characteristics and motives.
- Most attackers used firearms that were obtained from the home.
- Most attackers displayed neurological, psychological, and behavioral symptoms.
- Half of the attackers had interest in violent topics.
- All of the attackers had social stressors stemming from peers or domestic and romantic partners.
- A negative and unstable home life affected every attacker at some point in their life.
- Most of the attackers were bullied and even more alarming, students and staff who observed this happen had failed to intervene and report it in many cases.
- Many of the attackers had law enforcement interactions as well as disciplinary measures against them from the school at some point.
- All of the attackers had behavioral indicators that warranted intervention, which in some cases included detailed communication prior to the attack.

The frightening reality learned from this study is that although there's no way to profile a student, **there are indicators** that can accumulate and cause the student to cross these lines of morality and then attack. The good news, if there is any, is that almost every attack could have been prevented from a risk assessment perspective. According to the study, this should entail strong policies, the proper tools and reporting mechanisms in place as well as the proper training to assess, identify, and manage those at risk.

The research conducted by the attacker as well as the operational planning that usually happens at home falls into the laps of the parents, loved ones, community, or partners. As caretakers, we have to be diligent about what our children are exposed to, how they interact with their peers, who their friends are, their interests, monitoring social media and online activity, and ensuring that the school has the proper system in place to assess, identify, and manage those in need.

Let's jump into some of the other interesting findings that this report shows. Seventy-three percent of the attacks occurred in high schools whereas 22% occurred in elementary schools, with most of the incidents happening in the suburbs. Although the majority of these schools had lockdown procedures in place, only 17% had alert systems available to notify members of the school community, which I find unacceptable. Fifteen percent of the schools employed unarmed security guards, although nearly half of the attacks had school resource officers on the premises, which opens up another conversation regarding training, site security management, and lockdown protocols.

Only 22% of the schools had procedures in place to intervene and support students displaying concerning behaviors, although some of the schools did have some variation of threat assessment teams. Sixty-one percent of the attackers used firearms, and 39% used a knife with three of the attackers using a Molotov cocktail, a bow staff, and a hammer.

The majority of the attacks took place during morning classroom hours, with 24% of the attacks happening before school. Something to keep in mind is that most school doors and entry points are locked or are supposed to be locked when class starts. Obviously if the attacker is a current student, he is already in the building or in class. However, schools are extremely vulnerable to attacks before school starts because of the numerous tasks parents and staff are performing during drop off. Everybody is in a hurry to get to class, and parents are in a hurry to drop the children off and go to work. Furthermore, the entry points are more active due to students or staff arriving late. For those of you who drop off your children in the morning, you understand that this can be a chaotic part of the day with lots of moving parts, and because of this, schools need to be more diligent during this time.

I thought it was interesting that 75% of the attacks tend to happen during the morning hours or before school begins, but what is also interesting is another aspect of the timing. **It was also learned that many of these attacks happen within a week of the students coming back from a suspension, expulsion, holiday vacation, illness, or any other break in attendance.** This is important to remember.

Most of the attacks lasted less than 5 minutes with over 50% lasting less than 1 minute. This does not leave a lot of time for external law enforcement officers to respond if the threat was not successfully engaged by the SRO. Even more surprising, most of the attacks stopped without on-site or external Law Enforcement engagement, because of the attacker leaving the premises, weapon malfunctions, or suicide. The response times for the on-site SRO's and external law enforcement responding officers were not impressive and leaves room for improvement.

Most of the attacks occurred in classrooms or outside the premises with some of the attacks occurring in cafeterias, administrative offices, and hallways. Locker rooms, gymnasiums, and restrooms were less common places for the aggressor to attack.

In terms of demographics, the majority of the attackers were white males with 17% of the attackers being female from grade levels 7-12.

Next, we are going to discuss in a little more detail the motives, stressors, and behavioral characteristics of some of the attackers. Keep in mind that some of the findings overlap with the first study that we discussed above.

Grievances were most of the reasons why these attacks occurred, which included bullying, staff engagement, and romantic components. The desire to kill was at 37%, and suicidal motives were 41%.

Sixty-three percent of these attackers were bullied, which includes verbal, physical, social, and cyber. Verbal came in number one at 74%, which did not surprise me, but cyberbullying came in last at only 9%, which I must admit took me a little off guard. I was expecting a higher number with this, but I am interested to know if any more studies will come out which encompass the Covid and post-Covid era which I think has drastically changed the trajectory of this and other factors. I'd also like to reiterate the fact that most schools did next to nothing regarding the bullying with these attackers.

The study recommended that students should be taught more extensive coping skills, which is obvious. This responsibility should fall on the parents, but as I have said, parents have little support and recourse in this day and age, and this is tragically affecting youth—but do not get me started.

Other prominent factors included stressful encounters with parents, failing grades, suspensions, and even insecurities like personal hygiene or appearance. Almost half of the attackers had a history of substance abuse or use, and 77% had a history of using, practicing, or had a strong interest in firearms or knives which also includes hunting or weapons familiarity learned in JROTC. I am surprised that video game usage was not mentioned in this study, which I think is extremely influential in these attacks and how they are carried out with precision.

Forty-one percent of the victims were attacked randomly, with 15% targeted groups such as jocks, goths, or bullies. Eleven percent of the victims were collateral, which means they were not the intended victim.

Over half of the attackers planned the attack prior. This information that NTAC learned was based upon several sources including interviews with the attackers, their social media activity, and journals, among other things. Like the first study noted, they conducted weapons research, weapon practice, surveillance of their target, logistical research, documented their intentions, researched previous school attacks, researched tactics, and analyzed police response times as well as other calculated steps to help them conduct their attack. Half of the attackers concealed the weapon in their backpack prior to entering the school whereas others used methods like a guitar case, golf bag, or gym bag.

Disturbingly, about 23% had a strong interest in the Columbine massacre, and 20% expressed a strong interest in Nazism ideologies.

One hundred percent of the attackers displayed one or multiple forms of concerning behaviors prior to an attack. This study revealed several of these behaviors as:

- Some type of communication reiterating the intent or targets
- Increasing anger and aggression

- Strong interest in weapons, as mentioned above
- Spoke of or displayed depression, sadness, and isolation
- Drastic changes in appearance, hygiene, behavior, or apathy
- Communicated self-harm, suicide, or being bullied

I feel that studies like these validate why it is imperative that threat (and risk) assessment teams are essential for every school, enterprise, church, and hospital. It offers a stratagem to not only these organizations, but for threat assessment professionals in order to better support those in need of intervention and prevent targeted violence, regardless of the locale. It also ensures that the proper mechanisms are in place to assess, identify, and manage behavioral indicators that could lead to these types of attacks. As I have mentioned, many of the behavioral indicators and stressors are homogeneous, regardless of the organization that the attack takes place in. The way that you intervene and manage the persons involved, however, are very different. The next segment will discuss an overview of my Hybrid Threat Assessment and Response Guideline. Again, remember that this space is extremely extensive, and the segment ahead is designed to give you a solid foundation from which to grow. Let's move!

Hybrid Threat Assessment and Response Guideline Overview

4.9

Every threat assessment plan should be not only balanced, but tailored to the specific organization, location, community, or occupants that are being protected. More specifically, the primary focal points should be, but not limited to, **Detection, Assessment, Management, Targeted Violence Response, and Survival Strategies during an attack.** There is not one plan that can fit the needs of every organization, industry, or locale, and it is important to realize that my model, like any other model, is just that—a model from which to build.

Many mental health professionals are understandably focused on the behavioral approach, whereas plans created or influenced by law enforcement seem to focus more on threat awareness, site security, and survival or response strategies in some form because that is what they do. This approach is, in my mind, equally important, regardless of what studies show. Yes, it is crucial to make sure that we, as a society, mitigate this unprecedented increase in targeted violence, especially in its earliest stages of development, but solely relying on this approach seems incomplete to me. The failures in Uvalde proved that a "balanced" approach is crucial from the organizational threat assessment perspective to the law enforcement response. Being that this is the case, I have created a comprehensive guideline that may give you more of a bird's eye view of what to consider when implementing or discussing such a plan. This segment provides a loose overview so you will be able to ask the right questions, no matter what your connection is to the organization, locale, or community.

The foundation of this guideline entails the following:

A. *Create a balanced threat assessment team.*

B. *Establish a communication strategy for the TAARS team, staff, or students, support assets, parents, loved ones, those at risk and those being protected within the organization, including documentation or notifications during or after an attack.*

C. *In detail, establish what specific thresholds, red flags, or behavioral indicators would dictate law enforcement intervention or mental health intervention, including management strategies.*

D. *Conduct a site safety assessment for breach points and weaknesses in and around the building, which also includes vulnerable times during hours of operation.*

E. Establish a response and survival plan which includes lockdown procedures for the organization prior to or during an attack for the team, staff, and those being protected.

F. Establish a mental health intervention plan for staff, students, team, families, and community in case a targeted attack occurs.

Let's break these steps down.

A. Create a balanced threat assessment team.

First and foremost, regardless of the industry you are in, you need to form a well-balanced, multidisciplinary team. In a hospital or company, human resources and security directors ideally can facilitate and organize the team with the support and supervision of the administrator or leader of the organization. Most of these organizations are well-funded, so there is absolutely no excuse not to have some form of threat assessment team and plan in effect. Smaller companies, schools or organizations will have to improvise depending on the resources they have available to them, but an effective team is possible and necessary!

Equally as important, you must establish consistent meeting times. If you learned anything throughout this book, you have learned that consistency is important. Furthermore, the team meeting times, stakeholder training, and any other progressive steps within the plan must be well-documented to prove that the organization was responsibly prepared prior to and during an attack. I can assure you that if an attack occurs and your organization cannot prove through documentation that preventative and responsive protocols were implemented, they will be grossly liable.

If the team members cannot meet in person, the post Covid-19 world gifted us with the ability to function remotely. Make it happen and ensure your team members show up. If they do not take this responsibility seriously, then they are not right for the task, and move on to somebody else who is.

This team should include but is not limited to:

- Law enforcement representatives or security specialists who have a strong rapport with law enforcement
- Mental health professionals and/or social workers (depends, but can be remote)
- Medical personnel or staff specifically trained for such attacks and injuries
- The leader of the organization, including managers who are in direct contact with the staff or employees
- IT professionals to assess or monitor emails, social media platforms, behavioral or risk assessment applications used, communications of staff, potential attackers, students or customers (remote)
- A legal team to evaluate policies, privacy concerns, and other legalities (remote)
- Community, nonprofit, volunteer and religious leaders should also be involved.

With the exception of a school setting, most of these team members don't always have to be on the premises, but a rapid response security team (especially in a hospital) with staff that is trained in mass casualty incidents including field triage is highly advised. Below are my recommendations for the school threat assessment team that I feel is imperative to have on site.

A school Threat Assessment team should include but not be limited to:

- An SRO (school resource officer)
- Teachers
- Administrators
- School nurses specifically trained in mass casualty incidents involving injuries sustained by sharp instruments, explosives or firearms
- IT professionals to assess or monitor emails, social media platforms or staff and student communications, or early warning indicators (remote)
- A legal team for policy, privacy concerns, and other legalities (remote)
- Parents, faith leaders, or community members

Most schools, regardless of the available resources, are able to create some variation of a threat assessment team. There are ways to reduce the resources a little. For example, the lawyers and IT professionals do not have to be onsite, but it makes sense that an SRO (school resource officer), a mental health professional, and other team members are within the building and trained. Once again, unarmed security is not the answer, but ensuring that they are at least trained with less lethal weapon systems is better than nothing. If you do opt for security, they must be masters of situational and threat awareness, understand the vulnerabilities of the location, and must be able to confront an attacker with enough force to stop the threat. No exceptions. Many retired or off-duty police officers perform these functions and are more than capable, but the SRO is the best option, in my opinion. Municipalities are always trying to find a way to save resources.

I have heard rumors that in Chicago the police will no longer be assigned within the schools in the near future. This is extremely irresponsible but does not surprise me. What is more precious than the safety of our children? I can assure you that the person who makes this decision has his own security (police) detail, compliments of those high taxes and parking tickets paid for by those who are not getting the same protection. I would love to see how the politicians justify that. Let's move on to the second step but pay attention and challenge your community leaders to ensure they provide the proper resources to keep your schools and community safe!

B. Establish a communication strategy for the TAARS team, staff, or students, support assets, parents, loved ones, those at risk and those being protected within the organization, including documentation or notifications during or after an attack.

This step is extremely crucial because it is the foundation of every aspect of the plan. This includes documentation in all forms including training, as noted above. Your team must establish specifically **how** to document and disseminate the warning indicators of the potential attackers amongst their team, staff, employees, students, parents, or community members under the direction of their legal team or advisors. Furthermore, what system will be used? There are a number of risk assessment applications available that can be monitored by IT team members or, in many cases, mental health professionals or outsourced services.

Another aspect of communication involves how the team members directly communicate with each other, so you need to establish this method of communication as soon as possible. Whether it's via email, a call, or an app, developing a communication strategy is imperative.

As I discussed earlier in this section, most targeted attacks could have been prevented if the communications of the attacker were conveyed to the proper authorities. An organization must create the proper atmosphere, or "climate," for transparency and open communication to take place. Furthermore, they must establish communication strategies amongst those who are operating within the organization or school.

For example, students need to feel comfortable enough to be able to open up to a teacher or faculty member about any stressors that they or their classmates may be having, or after observing an alarming comment on social media. Then, the teacher must be able to quickly relay that concern to a member of the threat assessment team so they can document, assess, and intervene, if necessary. Some examples of communication strategies can be with a hotline, an email, website, or even a smartphone application and, in my opinion, there must be multiple options to use. Most states do have reporting systems in place that are free and available to those interested. The best tool that any organization can have at their disposal is an open dialogue with those within the location and a rehearsed course of action.

Also, you need to establish the specific way that you will notify the police, whether it is during an attack or requires law enforcement intervention through the risk assessment process, whether the SRO or security professional is involved or not.

Do not limit your lines of communication to those within the building or the threat assessment team. Parents, loved ones, previous schools or employers, and community members should also have the means to express their concern should there be any behavioral indicators or red flags that should be addressed. I personally feel that every organization should have a smartphone application used for the sole purpose of communicating alarming behaviors of those about whom they are concerned. With virtually everyone having immediate access to mobile devices, there's no excuse not to have a mobile app in the hands of every citizen that is tailored to every specific organization or industry. Communication should be rapid and fluid at this place in time. No excuses.

Another crucial component of communication also includes how staff will communicate with each other to initiate lockdown protocols, summon external law enforcement, and notify the TAARS team or other stakeholders during an actual targeted attack, a cyberattack, a natural disaster, civil unrest, an attack on the water supply, or internet and power outages.

Although telephone landlines are still very reliable, we cannot say the same for internet connections or mobile devices. Considering radio communication options with a direct line to external law enforcement and the onsite security or SRO makes sense.

It also makes sense to provide radio communication options for the staff to communicate with each other on a day-to-day basis. This will ensure the radios are practiced with, the direct channels to law enforcement are known, and the system is charged and always available. It's quick, cost-effective, reliable, and simple to use.

Although we have briefly discussed alarm systems, keep in mind that if the organization opts for an alert system, many of which are provided by the state or private enterprise, the staff must understand how to use the system and also understand, as with all technology, things can go wrong. Glitches, internet issues, power outages, and user errors due to the Acute Stress Response or unfamiliarity with the operation of the platform can happen while using these alert systems during an attack. Keep it simple so the lockdown and response plan can be successfully initiated under a violent targeted attack and lives can be saved.

C. In detail, establish what specific thresholds, red flags, or behavioral indicators would dictate law enforcement intervention or mental health intervention, including management strategies.

When we discussed the studies above, we listed several stressors in behavioral indicators that can and have led to targeted violence in locations like churches, schools, and the workplace. Your threat assessment team must establish, in detail, the specific indicators and behaviors that would dictate what action to take. This also ensures accountability.

Some indicators may just require counseling and other indicators may require a more intense mental health intervention with a coinciding management strategy. In its extremity, some indicators may even require law enforcement involvement, depending on the situation. This may entail an investigation of the alleged threat or concerning behavior or perhaps a more aggressive police response, depending on the circumstance.

D. Conduct a site safety assessment for breach points and weaknesses in and around the building, which also includes vulnerable times during hours of operation.

Law enforcement or a security specialist should assess the physical location, focusing on not only the actual building but also the grounds leading up to the building. Your objective is to prevent entry, first and foremost. If this fails, the next objective is to slow down the attack so the attacker is neutralized by onsite or responding officers.

During the site assessment, consideration should be taken regarding where the police or fire station is in relation to the property of interest, demographics, and socio-economic factors within the surrounding environment, crime statistics, potential attackers based upon validated threats or risk factors, and the registered addresses and visual familiarity of registered sexual predators. Obviously, this is the tip of the iceberg, but also a great place to start. Although all breach points and weaknesses should be identified and corrected or fortified, let's spend a little more time on this step and discuss this and more ahead.

Special consideration should be given to building design, fortifying breach points, and the use of technology. Regarding building design, many underestimate the importance of a good architect. I am sure the great Frank Lloyd Wright would agree, but the challenges of modern society have called upon these draftsmen to take a new direction. With the weather intensifying at unprecedented levels, these factors must be considered and built into the design for the building to sustain nature's fury. The same holds true for modern-day targeted attacks! Have you ever looked at a police station? Many of them have large open windows facing the entrance or very large cement flowerpots in the front that add to the mystique of the building that the local taxpayers work so hard to pay for. Well, the large windows are to see any oncoming threats and the gigantic flowerpots are barricades designed to stop vehicles. Most police stations are built like fortresses and for an incredibly good reason.

Fortunately, there are architects that are expanding their markets in these types of proactive designs. The design of a police station, in most respects, is more aggressive than that of a school or a university. For a school, a corporate building or hospital, the key is to strike that balance. You want those in the building to feel safe and in fact be in a safe building, should a threat arise, but still be conducive for learning, healing, or working.

Some architects have designed smaller lockers so students can see over them or even clear walls or offices, which leave a little room for debate. Ideally, you want to see the threat coming and you want to slow it down or stop it during the attack. Some buildings have barricades within the building that perform other functions but provide good cover from gunfire. If your organization is in the position to redesign a building or in the process of planning a new development, I strongly recommend placing security protocols into the design by seeking out both specialized architects and specialized consultants.

If a building is already built, you could add the same features that provide the same protection through some aftermarket options.

You want to pay attention particularly to the access points, including the locking system. Consider using fobs, swipe cards or even biometrics for entry. This will not only limit who enters a certain area, it will provide intelligence to responders if a tragedy does occur.

The building exterior and the interior walls should be made of durable materials for construction that will stop a bullet or provide cover from gunfire.

Ensuring the line of sight from all points within the area of operation is also imperative. If you see the threat coming, you can react, lock down the building, call the police, and initiate your response plan. Your line of sight should also include from before the point your property begins until entry into the building. You want to be able to have a field of vision yet have some cover.

There is an amazing business called Armored One. They provide an array of interesting products which includes bullet resistant glass windows as well as a special film that sticks onto the window to provide some level of gunfire resistance. Are these solutions bulletproof? Not yet, but it will slow down the bad guy long enough for first responders to arrive and neutralize him. With the windows being reasonably priced, it's an option worth exploring. Keep in mind that I rarely endorse businesses unless I truly feel in my heart that they are worth mentioning. They are passionate about what they do, and they have made a difference. Furthermore, it is surprisingly economical.

Moving on, you want to have layers of security from the design of the building to the response plan should a breach occur, which includes threat specific alarm systems that are auditory, alerts that sync with a company app, or perhaps even upon activation, it isolates or secures the common areas to which the public or the aggressor has access. Extensive thought should be placed into not only early warning detection systems, but the manner in which occupants within the building or facility are notified of such a threat.

Pulling a fire alarm with an active shooter in the building places more victims in the line of fire, especially if the aggressor is in the hallway or attempting to make entry into a room or building. Some advisors in this industry have recommended this protocol, but I highly disagree with it. There must be a method of communication with staff so the response plan can be safely initiated. Pulling the fire alarm is not the answer.

In December of 2023, a 67-year-old man applied to be a professor at UNLV but was denied employment. The armed and distraught professor entered the University and began to hunt and murder those he felt were responsible for his rejection. During the course of the rampage, the fire alarm was pulled, and the aggressor located and killed the targeted university staff until confronted and neutralized by responding university officers. Luckily, the students safely exited the building, but how would this have ended if this killer did not have specific targets and randomly fired at will towards students flooding into the hallway after the alarm was pulled? I would bet that the casualties would be much greater than three.

During an active killer incident, **do not pull the fire alarm.** Consider having an alternative alarm that is specific to the type of threat or an app that not only allows communication amongst staff, but also the police. Possibly even an intercom, a landline in the rooms that simultaneously calls to notify staff, and other clear communication protocols that will expedite the initiation of the lockdown and response plan. Remember, lockdown and response protocols of an elementary school is much different then that of a university.

Finally, let's discuss technology. Currently, in 2024, the numerous video surveillance options available on the market are unprecedented. With artificial intelligence gaining ground rapidly, I foresee this technology enhancing the industry as well as with the alert systems for such attacks. Many municipalities have cameras watching the traffic lights to monetize from those who are barely making ends meet. Furthermore, many police departments have camera systems strategically placed throughout their jurisdiction in order to surveil known gang and drug spots. It makes sense to me to add schools or locations that are at risk of targeted attacks into the mix. This does not imply replacing the law enforcement or security assets in lieu of a surveillance system.

In a school, having that extra support from a bird's eye view is invaluable as an SRO. If the shooter is approaching the school or it is already under attack, the SRO and the external responding officers will have a tactical advantage prior to engaging the attacker, revealing weapon systems used, current location, number of attackers or wounded, and other needed intelligence required to neutralize the threat. Using drones and training the school resource officer, security specialists in an organization, or other members of the threat assessment team with this technology seems viable as well. Again, having a live feed of an incident taking place in real time is invaluable to those on the premises, responding officers, and emergency medical services.

Another amazing technology is the emergence of gunfire detection systems used not only for high crime areas but within schools and other vulnerable gun-free zones. These systems detect gunfire, then alert law enforcement so they can immediately respond.

Just recently, firearm identification and detection systems through video surveillance using AI has also been introduced. This technology actually detects, isolates and identifies a firearm, then notifies law enforcement and the stakeholders so they can initiate their response protocols. This technology is advancing at a rapid pace, and I strongly recommend exploring these systems if you are tasked with enhancing the safety of a specific location. I feel that if we utilize AI to remotely detect a firearm through a video feed and infuse this technology with the ability to monitor the biometrics of a potential aggressor, or victim, this will drastically affect the outcome of a planned targeted attack well in advance.

I truly believe that eventually biometrics may take center stage in this industry, powered by artificial intelligence - AI. As we have discussed, the Acute Stress Response is a powerful part of our human physiology and is detectable, either by using situational awareness skills or technology.

Many schools, especially in urban America, use metal detectors which have proven to be useful, including handheld systems. There are more discrete metal detectors currently being developed, but I do feel that the more traditional looking detectors do act as a deterrent to some extent, at least in the actual building. Again, I do feel that having the ability to detect a potential aggressor's biometrics like heart rate near a point of entrance is crucial, and I feel that onsite detectors prior to entry should have this ability.

Before we move on to the next step, allow me to circle back to a what I mentioned earlier regarding timing because it is vital to understand. We mentioned the times potential attackers tend to act, such as within a week of returning from a break, a suspension, or any other extended time away from the organization or at the beginning of the day, specifically in regard to targeted violence in schools. I would also like to reiterate that morning drop-off times are chaotic as well as lunch hours, as children or staff tend to leave the facility and return shortly after. Again, I do feel that these are vulnerable times of the day that are susceptible to these types of attacks that warrant an enhanced sense of awareness.

E. Establish a response and survival plan which includes lockdown procedures for the organization prior to or during an attack for the team, staff, and those being protected.

Civilian response is a crucial part of this overall plan. The vast majority of this book provides the tools to create a good foundation for this to happen. Whether you are trained to neutralize an active killer or you are a teacher at a school, civilian response protocols and survival training must be part of your TAARS plan. **This step also should include a specific training** schedule regarding all aspects of the plan as well as the communication protocols discussed above.

I'd like to briefly refresh your recollection regarding a couple of vital topics we've already discussed that are pertinent to this step, and then we will discuss some critical knowledge that can be the difference between life and death.

First of all, an organization's targeted violence civilian response plan must entail situational and threat awareness training which may identify attackers prior to, during, and even after the attack. The proper training may even enable them to intercept the potential attacker during his preparation phase as well as detect other behavioral indicators previously discussed. **Situational and threat awareness training is imperative for all involved.**

Next, your team and those to be protected should also understand the dynamics of the Acute Stress Response as discussed in Section 2. It's important to understand this so they're able to function under stress, dial 911, detect other active threats, take directions from staff or law enforcement, run to safety, or perhaps even fight, as we will discuss ahead. As I have stated, like a broken record, if you are not able to mitigate these primal gifts of our ancestors, your odds of surviving any attack are low. If you are reading this book, you'll have the tools and the knowledge to disseminate this information to where it needs to be. Even if your place of employment, your place of worship, or child's school has a threat assessment plan, chances are a proper civilian response and survival plan has been overlooked or is incomplete. Knowledge is power, as it is also your survival.

Avoid, Deny, or Defend

In the past, those in the midst of an active killer attack have been instructed to run, hide, or fight. You need to forget everything you think you know because although running and fighting are viable options, **hiding and hoping is a death sentence**. The bad guy will find you and when he does, he will kill you and those huddled next to you. Only under special circumstances does hiding make sense, but we will not discuss that here. In the recent past, law enforcement has encouraged a different approach, which is **AVOID, DENY, or DEFEND.**

Regardless of where you find yourself during an attack, your actions must be intentional, and your mindset must be firm. Remember that conversation? Yes, even if you are unarmed, the warrior mindset will not only give you an advantage, but it will also throw off the well-planned attack, requiring the bad guy to physically and mentally readjust, creating an opportunity to stop him, as the OODA Loop suggests. Remember, if you stay a victim, you will die as one. Before we discuss this, let us talk about the lockdown.

The Lockdown

Fundamentally, a lockdown refers to the restriction of movement within a building or community. This can also refer to a "secure and hold" strategy if the threat is outside of a building. Remember, if the threat is outside of the building, depending on the situation, the doors and entry points into a building will be restricted or completely locked. If the threat is already in the building (although every circumstance is different) it is likely that the entry points would have to remain accessible to law enforcement or other first responders to engage the threat or render medical attention, so keep this in mind. Many organizations provide entry codes or keys to law enforcement, so they can have access in case of an emergency. You want to make sure the police can gain entry to neutralize an attacker, but having the entry points always secure will prevent the attacker from even entering the building in the first place. Sure, it makes sense to have pre-designated access points discussed with law enforcement, but in the heat of the moment, they need to enter the building as quickly as possible should the attacker successfully breach the location.

The Initial Shock

When you first hear gunfire, your mind will play a few tricks on you, whether you see the attack unfold in front of you or hear it from a distance. You will second guess what you are seeing or hearing, and when you realize that you are in fact in the middle of an attack, that is when your Acute Stress Response kicks in. It is at this point that you will have to assess your options and decide what actions you will take depending on your function, training, or proximity to the attack. This is a lot of processing for someone who is not trained under this type of stress, and it is for this reason that an organization must inoculate and train those involved so when, not if, an attack happens, auto pilot or ingrained memory takes over and the right decisions are made as we discussed in detail during Section 2.

Now, let's break down the AVOID, DENY, and DEFEND strategy. This strategy pertains to civilians who are under a targeted attack (active killer or terrorist). I know we already discussed this, but I thought I would offer a friendly reminder that if you are law enforcement or armed, your objective is to locate and neutralize the attacker with speed and without hesitation, by any means necessary.

So, first we have **"Avoid."** If at all possible, avoid, escape, or run from the attack by exiting the vicinity, location, or building as quickly as possible. Sure, this makes sense, but not everyone has the opportunity to escape, depending on where the attacker is, their reaction to their stress response, or their physical limitations. During the situational awareness segment, we talked about paying attention to the exits. Under stress, people tend to frantically leave in the same way they entered, usually in droves, which can be deadly. Furthermore, when the stress response kicks in, as we discussed, it can limit your ability to hear, use your limbs, and may even cause you to freeze, among other hindering effects. If mitigated correctly, with the help of some tactical breathing and training, this stress response can enhance your speed, agility, and awareness.

Avoid open areas like cafeterias, hallways, and even bathroom stalls if possible. Upon successfully escaping the danger, call the police and provide as much detail as possible for responding officers. If responding officers are arriving as you are attempting to leave, listen to their instructions. You may be experiencing auditory exclusion so keeping your hands visible and over your head is advised. Remember, in their eyes, you may be a threat.

Next, we have **"Deny."** This is referring to denying entry to the attacker into the building, classroom, office, or any other space where he is attempting to continue the attack. In other words, the occupants of the room need to barricade themselves within the space by any means necessary and then relocate to the proper cover (an obstacle, wall, or structure that can stop a bullet). This includes staying away from interior or exterior windows, shutting off the lights, closing the shades or curtains, silencing mobile devices and keeping quiet. Shutting off the lights will help conceal potential targets and give the occupants an advantage as their night vision will acclimate to the dark. If the attacker enters a dark room from a bright space, this may create an opportunity to neutralize or subdue the attacker because his vision will be temporarily impaired.

The entry point of the room or space must be locked and barricaded in order to provide another obstacle for the attacker to negotiate. There are door stops and locks created by companies like Nightlock that are specifically meant for this type of purpose. I encourage you to explore these options. If the door has the ability to lock, use it. Moving furniture to block the entry and path, as well as securing the door by using ropes, belts, or a little muscle can also help prevent entry to the attacker and buy a little time until he is neutralized or the attack has ceased. DO NOT open the door until law enforcement has given the "all clear" and you are confident that it is, in fact, the police, and NOT THE ATTACKER. Utilizing codes or phrases only known by the staff and the police is an option but is not fool-proof.

If you or the other occupants are confronted by the attacker or he gains entry into the space, you need to fight, or **"Defend."** Now, this is an uncomfortable conversation because the last thing you want to do is bring a pencil to a gunfight, but that's exactly what you may have to do. Get into the unorthodox habit of understanding your surroundings and pay attention to what you can weaponize immediately.

This can be a knife, a pen, a letter opener, keys, specialized key chains, a pencil, a screwdriver, or those long nails attacking sensitive areas like the eyes, throat, and arteries under the armpit, adjacent to the groin area or the heart region. Again, less lethal weapon systems would be useful under these circumstances, especially within gun-free environments. Understanding and initiating steps within the OODA Loop and Hicks Law, discussed previously, during this phase of an attack is crucial and will place the attacker in a vulnerable position to be overrun and neutralized by any means necessary! If the attacker has a firearm, you want to control the muzzle (where the bullet exits the firearm) and attempt to disarm him as quickly as possible. Understand how to use pressure points in places like the side of the neck or pushing the nose back with the palm, which will create an instant reaction that may provide a chance to disarm him.

There is another concept that you should be familiar with, which is understanding the difference between a **"timer"** and a **"switch."** During an engagement, the location on the body that the attacker wounds you, or where you wound the attacker, is vital, and can determine how long either would remain in the fight, or survive. In other words, when deploying a knife or firearm, for example, hitting a "switch" will immediately stop the attacker, resulting in his instant demise. The eyes, the soft area just under the larynx (voice box), center of chest, or places where the main arteries are populated will induce this type of reaction.

With a "timer", the wound may be severe but will take time for the person to bleed out, enabling them to stay in the fight longer. Wounds to the shoulder, legs, and arms are examples, although, it does depend on where within those regions.

You have to understand a couple things. First of all, this is a fight for your life, the lives of others around you, and the life of your loved ones who are waiting for you to come home. Remember, even if you are unarmed, you may deploy deadly force, depending on the circumstances, by any means necessary if you or others around you are in fear of immediate death or great bodily injury, especially during an active targeted attack. The engagement will be ugly and unsettling. The last thing you would expect when you wake up in the morning is your students or co-workers watching you violently lunge and neutralize an armed attacker with a sharpened pencil as he is attempting to commit murder. The two things I know for sure are that you most likely will save countless lives and your students or coworkers will never look at you the same.

One final thought. I strongly advise incorporating self-defense instruction as part of your response and survival plan, including soft and hard control tactics as well as basic firearms training. As mentioned above, if firearms are not an option, consider kits that contain less lethal weapon options at your disposal like a CEW device (tasers), ASPs, pepper guns, or chemical sprays while ensuring your team is trained under stress in order to deploy them during an attack if fighting is their only option.

Figure 4A This is a popular less lethal called the S2 Pepper Spray Gun produced by Salt Supply Co. Go to www.saltsupply.com to learn more!
Courtesy of Salt Supply Co.

Furthermore, it is important to have emergency medical kits that include a CAT, or Combat Application Tourniquet, a chest seal, and other emergency medical supplies that can help sustain life until proper medical attention arrives. Let's go on to the last step.

F. Establish a mental health intervention plan for staff, students, team, families, and community in case a targeted attack occurs.

As a wise man once said (about four times in this book so far) if the bad guy doesn't kill you, the stress just may. It is imperative that the mental health professionals on your team, organization, or in your community establish and coordinate a mental health crisis plan should an attack occur. Targeted attacks not only affect those that were in the line of fire, but the family members, law enforcement, emergency medical personnel, and other members of the community.

Previously in this book, I touched on the Highland Park shooting. Despite this tragic act of terror inflicted upon the community during a 4th of July celebration, the Highland Park, Illinois, leadership did a phenomenal job providing resources and support to the community within hours after the attack. Taking it a step further, they created The City of Highland Park Resilience Division along with a web page that provided (and still does) not only resources for the community but also an opportunity to pay tribute to the victims, donate, provide information regarding vigils, and much, much more. I was impressed and strongly recommend those tasked with creating a crisis plan to explore this resource as a model that they provided to their community after that dreadful day. The healing process takes time for the community, and for those who lost loved ones to this type of senseless violence, it never ends.

Let's now take a glimpse at the DOJ report ahead regarding Uvalde as we creep towards the end of Section 4.

Department of Justice Uvalde Report Brief

In January 2024, the DOJ finally released the long-awaited report regarding the 2022 Robb Elementary School massacre. Most professionals in both the law enforcement and educational community nationwide understood well in advance that the horrific tragedy that unfolded that day was an epic failure at face value, but the report proved that this failure was multifaceted well before the day of the attack.

Unsurprisingly, the NTAC findings in past attacks discussed earlier in this section seem to be right on point in terms of school preparation and response. This 500-plus page content-rich report was the product of countless hours of these dedicated investigators, many of whom suffered emotional consequences during and after the investigative process. Not only should our prayers go out to the families of those affected but to the responding law enforcement who neutralized the threat as well as the investigators of this report and others of the past.

The Robb Elementary killings, unfortunately, was an epic failure from law enforcement involvement to the school's response protocols. It was, cumulatively, the flagship of failure and grossly exposed the vulnerabilities in respect to everything we have discussed throughout this book and what can and will go wrong amid an attack. Although this report is extensive, I feel that we should not only briefly discuss the elephants in the room but some main points that reiterate many of the topics we've discussed thus far throughout this book. My brief analysis is an overview, but with all due respect, it deserves its own book, which very well may be my next project. Let's start with the police response.

What made Uvalde unique was that the school district had their own Police Department, of which there were none of its officers at the school prior to the attack. Nonetheless, the police response was rapid as nearly a dozen officers arrived within minutes of the attack ready to engage the killer. **The deadly mistake they made is that they then stopped,** assuming the incident became a barricade situation that would dictate another method of response. The police were not familiar with the property, the school lockdown and response procedures, the entry points, or how to quickly access the property. Poor training, lack of coordination with the school prior to the tragedy, poor leadership, and poor policies were highlighted as having a direct impact on how law enforcement responded once they arrived on scene. These findings are on point with what I have mentioned throughout this book, but where were the other failures? The report strongly suggests that the responsibility also falls within the domain of the school.

The newer internal alert system that the staff were not familiar with was activated less than a minute prior to the attacker entering the school and lockdown protocols commenced. The problem was that not all the emails, texts, and notifications were immediately received, possibly due to internet issues or operational knowledge of its use. Shockingly, 27 minutes after the attack commenced, another communication was sent stating that the children were safe and in the classrooms.

Furthermore, although some form of a threat assessment team was established, it was not active. As a result, the proper communication strategies and lockdown procedures were not available among the staff, the community, and responding law enforcement. If there was a strong threat assessment team in place, or what I like to call a TAARS team, there may have also been better coordination with the police, so they were familiar with not only the response protocols but the details like how to enter the location to stop the attack.

The doors were unlocked, although a staff member did attempt to lock the door prior to the attacker gaining entry. Yes, it was an old building, but

I would have to also guess that the Acute Stress Response may have been understandably present as well. I do feel that if the doors were locked, there would have been more opportunity for the police to immediately engage the killer outside of the building, but at this point, we will never know. Also, if the doors were inadvertently locked after the attacker made entry, the police may not have had the ability to enter the building to engage the killer. This is another reason protocols should be understood and rehearsed by the TAARS teams, law enforcement, affected members of the community, and even elected officials.

Lastly, I would like to talk about complacency. Uvalde is a tight-knit community and has a small-town feel. The paramedics responded and worked on their own children, police officers had family members within the school during the attack, and it was known as a police friendly community. Also, being that Uvalde was close to the Mexican border, at times, Border Patrol commonly pursued violent migrants, resulting in school lockdowns within their area of operation.

Among many things I have discussed throughout this book, I have stressed to always expect the unexpected. This preparation should be reflective of the training, the coordination, and the response plans implemented from law enforcement, community leaders, and any organization that is expected to ensure the safety of those we love.

Although numerous components in Uvalde was negligent well before the attack took place, we can use it as an unsettling model in order to prevent and properly respond to these targeted attacks, wherever they may happen.

Rumination

So, although the Hybrid Threat Assessment and Response Guideline discussed above is an overview within my TAARS model, it creates a foundation to grow from and ensures that you have the ability to ask the right questions to those responsible for the safety of whom you cherish.

As the world changes, the way that we identify, mitigate, and respond to a targeted attack like an active killer incident will change as well. Use all the resources available and regardless of your budget, a little research and a good consultant can get the ball rolling. We must remain vigilant and open to new ideas as well as responsibly embracing emerging technologies, such as AI, to keep us ahead of the curve and allow us to innovate. Perspective is everything, whether it's how we see our at-risk loved ones or how we implement the protocols to protect them. As I have said, love is blind, and if we do not pay attention, this obscurity can be deadly.

Walking through these uncertain streets of the "free world" will take perseverance. Successfully neutralizing an active killer or terrorist during a targeted attack will take training, and changing this downward spiral of America will require a collective consciousness of not a few, but all. Arming citizens with this knowledge is my mission as the blood of my fellow Americans has stained the very soil our Founding Fathers fought and died on. However, do not be fooled because this virus is deeper than you think.

As this targeted violence is spreading across the globe, our adversaries from both afar and native, continue to penetrate deep within the minds of our youth through social media platforms and other dehumanizing strategies, which has greatly encouraged carnage only seen in war. The only weapon greater than the sword is destroying the minds of the youth of your nemesis. While some strategists may call this brilliant, I call it a call to duty. Pandora's box is now open, and the question is how far will humanity go to close it.

EPILOGUE | THE TRUDGE FORWARD

First and foremost, it has been my privilege to walk with you on this pitted road that very few have dared to tread. The topics discussed were painful with circumstances that our ancestors would have deemed apocalyptic. Americans have been numbed by the slow and consistent progression of this chaos as we, the old souls of this world, open our eyes to an unfamiliar place. The only way is relentlessly forward as America is the last great experiment of what is still called democracy. There is nowhere else to go.

In closing, **Battlefield America** has discussed my strategies to detect, mitigate, confront, respond to, and survive a violent targeted attack regardless of where it may happen upon disclosing my theorems of what brought us to this pivotal crossroad of not only our nation but this unsustainable plague of humanity.

Moreover, I have attempted to expose the profuse underbelly that is strongly supported by the NTAC studies discussed, which is the tip of the iceberg.

We embarked onto the pathway of the warrior mindset, strategies for mitigating the effects of our primal gift of ancient man, as well as the mechanics to consider while making the decision to deploy deadly force in self-defense and in the defense of others should you be forced to confront an attacker, thickening that thin blue line. Such humans, regardless of their mission, eternally believe in the cause and understand that the greatest tool is that of the mind.

This being the case, the function of the modern centurion may not always involve confronting an attacker but still a battlefield in its own right. This can be the mom who lost her son at the hands of an active killer that is fighting for new legislation to make schools a safer place or the administrator of an institution who is calmly and collectively guiding his subordinates to safety while under heavy gunfire. The warrior could be that school principal, faith leader, or CEO systematically ensuring their organization has a strong TAARS plan in place to detect, mitigate, respond to and survive a targeted attack, or the aftermath, should that dreadful day ever come. Sadly, it can also be those that perished in the midst of violence inspiring us to take action or ensuring the mental health of our youth is protected by dismembering one social media platform at a time.

Amidst this fog, there is hope. In May of 2023, due to the "indicators" affecting the mental health of our youth and adolescents, Surgeon General Dr. Vivek Murthy issued a public advisory encouraging policymakers, technology companies, caregivers and families to come together to minimize the impact of social media, its excessive use, and the toxic content that is easily accessible. Regardless of where you stand politically, Dr. Murthy took the first critical step in the right direction!

Furthermore, in early 2024, lawmakers started to hold those in charge of these toxic social media platforms responsible for the damage inflicted upon our youth that has resulted in targeted violence and suicide. Lawmakers from the blue and the red, for once, became a vibrant purple, roasting those who have morphed the mental health of our youth. Ironically, certain parts of Europe associate purple with the mourning of death. I think that means something and is truly symbolic.

Even more surprising, one of the first bans may be that of TikTok, as they are under suspicion of gathering data for the CCP from those who have the app downloaded on their device, many of which are the children of our country's leadership. I think this is a good start, but I am gravely disturbed by the fact that the mental health of our youth was not a deciding factor in this first crucial leap forward, which tells me that we have a long way to go. Furthermore, if this does happen, I would imagine the American-developed social media platforms may have increased usage as a result, which I think is futile.

The time has come to roll up our sleeves, as our work has just begun. Our children and their future are worth it. The fabric of this great nation is without a doubt torn, but any adversary, foreign or domestic, can never kill the will of the American spirit—and that, my friends, is worth fighting for.

Let's move!

Bibliography

"2017 Las Vegas Shooting." Wikipedia, the Free Encyclopedia. Last modified November 20, 2023. https://en.wikipedia.org/wiki/2017_Las_Vegas_shooting.

"5.3 Other Use-of-Force Defenses – Criminal Law." Last modified December 17, 2015. https://open.lib.umn.edu/criminallaw/chapter/5-3-other-use-of-force-defenses/.

"7 Takeaways from the Final Police Report on the Las Vegas Shooting." PBS NewsHour. Last modified August 3, 2018. https://www.pbs.org/newshour/nation/7-takeaways-from-the-final-police-report-on-the-las-vegas-shooting.

9 News. "RAW: Security videos show moment of deadly Olde Town Arvada shooting." YouTube. Video. November 10, 2021. https://www.youtube.com/watch?v=c7Seeqg6lg4.

Elise Hammond and Maureen Chowdhury. "April 17, 2023 - Kansas City, Missouri, homeowner faces felony charges in shooting of teen." CNN. Last modified April 18, 2023. https://www.cnn.com/us/live-news/ralph-yarl-shooting-investigation-04-17-23/index.html.

Adams, L. The Second Amendment primer: A citizen's guidebook to the history, sources, and authorities for the constitutional guarantee of the right to keep and bear arms. Skyhorse Publishing, 2013.

Afshar, Elizabeth W. "New Details About 2017 Las Vegas Mass Shooter Revealed in Hundreds of FBI Documents." CNN. Last modified March 31, 2023. https://www.cnn.com/2023/03/31/us/las-vegas-2017-shooting-stephen-paddock-fbi-documents/index.html.

Amir Vera, Artemis Moshtaghian, Holly Yan. "Police Identify Victims, Gunman and Armed Bystander in Indiana Mall Shooting." CNN. Last modified July 19, 2022. https://www.cnn.com/2022/07/17/us/indiana-greenwood-park-mall-shooting/index.html.

"Behavioral Threat Assessment and Management for Educators and Administrators." Texas School Safety Center. Accessed May 21, 2024. https://txssc.txstate.edu/tools/tam-toolkit/defining-tam.

"Benchmark Analytics : Police Use-of-Force Toolkit." Benchmark Analytics. Last modified September 30, 2021. https://www.benchmarkanalytics.com/police-use-of-force-toolkit.

Berger, J. M., P. Singh, L. Khrimian, D. A. Morgan, S. Chowdhury, E. Arteaga-Solis, T. L. Horvath, et al. "Mediation of the acute stress response by the skeleton." Cell Metabolism 30, no. 5 (2019), 890-902.e8. doi:10.1016/j.cmet.2019.08.012.

"Texas School Shooting: Biden Calls for 'action' on Gun Laws After 19 Children, 2 Teachers Are Killed." NBC News. Last modified May 25, 2022. https://www.nbcnews.com/news/us-news/live-blog/texas-school-shooting-live-updates-biden-calls-action-gun-laws-19-chil-rcna30427.

"Black Lives Matter Activists Accuse Executive of Stealing $10 Million in Donor Funds." NBC News. Last modified September 7, 2022. https://www.nbcnews.com/news/nbcblk/black-lives-matter-activists-accuse-executive-stealing-10-million-dono-rcna46481.

"Black Lives Matter Leaders Condemn Allegations of Mismanaged Funds." NBC News. Last modified April 12, 2022. https://www.nbcnews.com/news/nbcblk/black-lives-matter-leaders-condemn-allegations-mismanaged-funds-rcna23882.

"Black teen shot after ringing wrong doorbell is a gifted chemistry student and a 'gentle soul,' former teacher says." NBC News. Last modified April 17, 2023. https://www.nbcnews.com/news/us-news/ralph-yarl-shooting-victim-highly-intelligent-gentle-soul-former-teach-rcna80024.

Bruce K. Siddle and Dave Grossman. Israeli Combat Shooting and Tactical Training. Accessed May 21, 2024. https://www.combatconcepts.info/uploads/4/6/6/4/4664213/effects_of_combat_stress_on_performance.pdf.

"Chicago Board of Education Moves to Pull Resource Officers out of Schools." Chicago Tribune. Last modified February 23, 2024. https://www.chicagotribune.com/2024/02/22/chicago-board-of-education-moves-to-pull-sros-out-of-schools/.

Chowdhury, Maureen, and Mike Hayes. "Uvalde Shooting Report Released to Media." CNN. Last modified July 17, 2022. https://www.cnn.com/us/live-news/uvalde-shooting-texas-house-report

n.d. https://www.cisa.gov/sites/default/files/publications/18_0711_USSS_NTAC-Enhancing-School-Safety-Brief.pdf.

n.d. https://www.cisa.gov/sites/default/files/publications/active-shooter-emergency-action-plan-112017-508v2.pdf.

"City of Highland Park,IL." City of Highland Park, IL. Accessed May 21, 2024. https://www.cityhpil.com/resiliency/index.php.

Collinson, Stephen. "Analysis: Biden's Botched Afghan Exit is a Disaster at Home and Abroad Long in the Making | CNN Politics." CNN. Last modified August 16, 2021. https://www.cnn.com/2021/08/16/politics/afghanistan-joe-biden-donald-trump-kabul-politics/index.html.

"Combat Stress Response & Tactical Breathing - Go Flight Medicine." FAA Aviation Medical Examiner (AME) – Go Flight Medicine. Last modified May 18, 2024. https://www.goflightmedicine.com/post/combat-stress-response-tactical-breathing.

Commonwealth of Virginia v Alan Colie, CR-00038492-00,01,002, Oct 2023. n.d.

n.d. https://portal.cops.usdoj.gov/resourcecenter/content.ashx/cops-r1141-pub.pdf.

"Constitutional carry." National Association for Gun Rights. Last modified June 22, 2023. https://nationalgunrights.org/about-us/key-issues/constitutional-carry/.

"Crimes and Crime Data Search." Free Government Offices Locator and Public Record Search - The County Office. Accessed May 21, 2024. https://www.thecountyoffice.com/crimes-and-crime-data-.

"Critical incident review of the response to the school shooting in Uvalde, Texas." COPS OFFICE. n.d. https://cops.usdoj.gov/html/dispatch/02-2024/uvalde_critical_incident_review.html.

"The Dangerous Expansion of Stand-Your-Ground Laws and Its Racial Implications." Duke Center for Firearms Law. Last modified April 15, 2024. https://firearmslaw.duke.edu/2022/01/the-dangerous-expansion-of-stand-your-ground-laws-and-its-racial-implications.

"Deadly Force." LII / Legal Information Institute. Accessed May 21, 2024. https://www.law.cornell.edu/wex/deadly_force.

Denver 7 News. "Newly released video shows Arvada shooting involving officer, Good Samaritan." YouTube. Video. November 10, 2021. https://www.youtube.com/watch?v=_DN-rvIYjZM.

Dhanalakshmi Harikrishnan. "Reticular Activating System | Definition & Function." https://study.com/academy/lesson/reticular-activating-system-definition-function.html. Last modified November 21, 2023. https://study.com/academy/lesson/reticular-activating-system-definition-function.html.

E. Garcia-Rill. "Reticular Activating System." Encyclopedia of Neuroscience. Last modified 2009. https://www.sciencedirect.com/topics/neuroscience/reticular-activating-system.

Ede, R. "Rest and digest: The parasympathetic nervous system." livescience.com. Last modified March 8, 2023. https://www.livescience.com/parasympathetic-nervous-system-rest-and-digest.

Enhancing school safety using a threat assessment model: An operational guide for preventing targeted school violence. n.d. https://www.secretservice.gov/newsroom/reports/threat-assessments/schoolcampus-attacks/details.

"Fight, Flight, Attachment Cry, Freeze or Submit: Adult Responses to Childhood Trauma." Calgary Psychologist: Help for Professionals Work and Home Life. Accessed May 21, 2024. https://turnerpsychologycalgary.com/trauma/fight-flight-or-freeze-adult-responses-following-childhood-trauma/.

"Fight-or-flight response | Definition, hormones, & facts." Encyclopedia Britannica. Last modified May 5, 2009. https://www.britannica.com/science/fight-or-flight-response.

"Fight-or-flight response." Wikipedia, the free encyclopedia. Last modified September 4, 2023. https://en.wikipedia.org/wiki/Fight-or-flight_response.

"Firearms Services." Illinois State Police. Accessed May 21, 2024. https://isp.illinois.gov/Foid/Ccl.

History Cooperative. "The First Cell Phone: A Complete Phone History from 1920 to Present." 2023. Accessed May 21, 2024. https://historycooperative.org/first-cell-phone/.

French, J. D. "The Reticular Formation." Journal of Neurosurgery 15, no. 1 (1958), 97-115. doi:10.3171/jns.1958.15.1.0097.

Frontline PBS | Official. "Inside the Uvalde Response (full documentary) | FRONTLINE + @ProPublica + @texastribune." YouTube. Video. December 5, 2023. https://www.youtube.com/watch?v=bBofi_etkUo.

Full news conference: Arvada Police officer will not be charged in shooting of good Samaritan. "Full news conference: Arvada Police officer will not be charged in shooting of good Samaritan." YouTube. Video. November 8, 2021. https://www.youtube.com/watch?v=B22Stw2RjKk.

"Full Text of the U.S. Constitution | Constitution Center." National Constitution Center – Constitutioncenter.org. Accessed May 20, 2024. https://constitutioncenter.org/the-constitution/full-text.

Grossman, Dave, and Loren W. Christensen. On Combat: The Psychology and Physiology of Deadly Conflict in War and in Peace. Ppct Research Publications, 2007.

Grossman, Lieutenant C., and Kristine Paulsen. Assassination Generation: Video Games, Aggression, and the Psychology of Killing. Columbus: Little, Brown, 2016.

"How the fight or flight response works." The American Institute of Stress. Last modified August 21, 2019. https://www.stress.org/how-the-fight-or-flight-response-works.

"Immediate Response to an Active Shooter." University of Montana | Public Flagship in Missoula. Accessed May 21, 2024. https://www.umt.edu/emergency/active-attack/respond/.

Improving school safety through bystander reporting. n.d. https://www.secretservice.gov/newsroom/reports/threat-assessments/schoolcampus-attacks/details-1.

International Association of Chiefs of Police and the Fraternal Order of Police. CONSENSUS POLICY. AND. DISCUSSION PAPER. ON USE OF. FORCE. International Association of Chiefs of Police, 2017.

"An Introduction to 'The Five F's': 5 Physical Responses to Danger and Threat." Trauma Thrivers. Last modified March 10, 2021. https://traumathrivers.com/an-introduction-to-the-five-fs-5-physical-responses-to-danger-and-threat/.

Jamie D. Aten Ph.D. "Situational Awareness and Survival." Psychology Today (blog). October 10, 2020. https://www.psychologytoday.com/us/blog/hope-resilience/202010/situational-awareness-and-survival.

Jason M. Lindo, Isaac D. Swensen & Glen R. Waddell. Persistent Effects of Violent Media Content. Cambridge, MA: National Bureau of Economic Research, 2020. https://www.nber.org/papers/w27240.

Krieg, Gregory. "What We Know About the Highland Park Shooting." CNN. Last modified July 7, 2022. https://www.cnn.com/2022/07/05/us/what-we-know-highland-park-shooting/index.html.

Lawrence, E. "Hero armed citizen landed 8 of 10 shots at 40 yards to stop mass shooting in 15 seconds." American Military News. Last modified July 20, 2022. https://americanmilitarynews.com/2022/07/hero-armed-citizen-landed-8-of-10-shots-at-40-yards-to-stop-mass-shooting-in-15-seconds/.

"Man who shot Kaylin Gillis grew increasingly bitter about trespassers, neighbor says." AP News. Last modified April 23, 2023. https://apnews.com/article/fatal-shooting-wrong-driveway-new-york-36fd62216cf3d9c20333d760148269a0.

Encyclopedia Britannica. "Martin Cooper." 2013. Accessed May 21, 2024. https://www.britannica.com/biography/Martin-Cooper.

Martinelli and Associates. Last modified January 4, 2023. https://martinelliandassoc.com/.

Martinelli, Ron. "Forensic Force Series | The Return of the Carotid Restraint Control Hold." PORAC, February 2014.

Martinelli, Ron. "Murder or Stress-Induced Hypervigilance." PORAC Law Enforcement News, December 2010.

Martinelli, Ron. "The Forensic Forum | The 21 Foot Rule: Forensic Fact or Fantasy." PORAC Law Enforcement News, 2014.

Martinelli, Ron. ""The Art of Force" - Pre-Contact Threat Assessment." Expert Witness and Business Consultants Directory | Experts.com. Last modified February 2011. https://www.experts.com/articles/the-art-of-force-pre-contact-threat-assessment-by-ron-martinelli.

Mass attacks in public spaces: 2016-2020. n.d. https://www.secretservice.gov/newsroom/reports/threat-assessments/mass-attacks-public-spaces/details-1.

Monahan v. City of New York, No. 20-CV-2610 (PKC), 2022 WL 954463 (S.D.N.Y. Mar. 30, 2022). n.d.

National Threat Assessment Center. Enhancing school safety using a threat assessment model: An operational guide for preventing targeted school violence: Executive summary. 2018.

"New FBI Records Offer Detailed Insights into Route 91 Mass Shooting." Las Vegas Review-Journal. Last modified September 27, 2023. https://www.reviewjournal.com/crime/homicides/new-fbi-records-offer-detailed-insights-into-route-91-mass-shooting-2753200/.

"New York man given 25 years for killing student mistakenly on his property." the Guardian. Last modified March 1, 2024. https://www.theguardian.com/us-news/2024/mar/01/kevin-monahan-sentence.

"Number of People on Terror Watchlist Stopped at U.S. Border Has Risen." NBC News. Last modified September 14, 2023. https://www.nbcnews.com/politics/national-security/number-people-terror-watchlist-stopped-mexico-us-border-risen-rcna105095.

"Nytimes.com." The New York Times - Breaking News, US News, World News and Videos. Last modified November 28, 2016. https://www.nytimes.com/2016/11/28/us/active-shooter-ohio-state-university.html.

"Nytimes.com." The New York Times - Breaking News, US News, World News and Videos. Last modified July 5, 2022. https://www.nytimes.com/live/2022/07/05/us/highland-park-shooting.

"Nytimes.com." The New York Times - Breaking News, US News, World News and Videos. Last modified April 23, 2024. https://www.nytimes.com/2024/04/23/technology/bytedance-tiktok-ban-bill.html.

"Nytimes.com." The New York Times - Breaking News, US News, World News and Videos. Accessed May 21, 2024. https://www.nytimes.com/article/waukesha-parade-victims.html.

"Officials release video capturing the actions of good samaritan during olde town Arvada shooting." Denver 7 Colorado News (KMGH). Last modified November 11, 2021. https://www.denver7.com/news/local-news/officials-release-video-capturing-the-actions-of-good-samaritan-during-olde-town-arvada-shooting.

Osborne, Samuel. "Alan Colie: Man Who Shot YouTube Prankster at Virginia Shopping Centre Acquitted." Sky News. Last modified September 29, 2023. https://news.sky.com/story/amp/alan-colie-man-who-shot-youtube-prankster-at-virginia-shopping-centre-acquitted-12972201.

Pampaloni, Hanna. "Jury Issues Not Guilty Verdict in Dulles Mall Shooting." LoudounNow.com. Last modified September 28, 2023. https://www.loudounnow.com/news/jury-issues-not-guilty-verdict-in-dulles-mall-shooting/article_97d3a774-5e57-11ee-a574-e7c60093e456.html.

"Passing Motorist Shoots, Kills Gunman Who Ambushed Arizona Trooper." NBC News. Last modified January 13, 2017. https://www.nbcnews.com/news/us-news/ambushed-arizona-trooper-saved-passing-motorist-who-shot-attacker-dead-n706381.

"The Payback (song)." Wikipedia, the Free Encyclopedia. Last modified March 31, 2024. https://en.wikipedia.org/wiki/The_Payback_(song).

Perleberg, Mike. "Woman Who Saved Officer's Life Makes Tearful Plea For Immunity Legislation." Eagle Country 99.3. Last modified January 29, 2019. https://www.eaglecountryonline.com/news/local-news/woman-who-saved-officers-life-makes-tearful-plea-for-immunity-legislation/.

Protecting America's schools: A U.S. secret service analysis of targeted school violence. 2019.

Protecting America's schools: A U.S. secret service analysis of targeted school violence. n.d. https://www.secretservice.gov/node/2565.

Rahman, Moin. "Understanding Naturalistic Decision Making Under Life Threatening Conditions." ResearchGate. Last modified March 2009. https://

www.researchgate.net/publication/228299727_Understanding_Naturalistic_Decision_Making_Under_Life_Threatening_Conditions.

"Register for a Local Illinois Concealed Carry Class Now." Concealed Coalition. Accessed May 21, 2024. https://www.concealedcoalition.com/illinois

Robinson, Thomas N., Jorge A. Banda, Lauren Hale, Amy S. Lu, Frances Fleming-Milici, Sandra L. Calvert, and Ellen Wartella. "Screen Media Exposure and Obesity in Children and Adolescents." Pediatrics 140, no. Supplement_2 (2017), S97-S101. doi:10.1542/peds.2016-1758k.

Ruscio. "You May Need a Vagus Nerve Reset. Here's How to Do It." Dr. Michael Ruscio, DC. Last modified April 29, 2024. https://drruscio.com/vagus-nerve-reset/.

Sanchez, R., and B. Gingras. "New York man found guilty of murder after 20-year-old woman was shot and killed when car turned in wrong driveway." CNN. Last modified January 24, 2024. https://www.cnn.com/2024/01/23/us/new-york-man-found-guilty-of-murder-after-20-year-old-woman-was-shot-and-killed-when-car-turned-in-wrong-driveway/index.html.

State of California. ASSEMBLY BILL 392 INTO LAW, MANDATING STANDARD FOR USE OF DEADLY FORCE. 2019.

State of Florida v Curtis Reeves 373 So.3d 625 (2023). n.d.

State of Florida Vs Curtis Reeves. Accessed May 20, 2024. https://www.curtisreevestrial.com/.

State of Illinois. 720 ILCS 5/7-1 | Use of force in defense of person. 2004.

State of Texas. Penal Code Section 9.32 | Deadly Force in Defense of Person. 2024.

State v. Lester, 588 S.W.3d 893 (Mo. Ct. App. 2019). n.d.

"State V. Lester." Case text - Cocounsel. Accessed May 20, 2024. https://casetext.com/case/state-v-lester-2035/case-details.

Surgeon general issues new advisory about the effects social media use has on youth mental health. (2023, May 23).

HHS.gov. https://www.hhs.gov/about/news/2023/05/23/surgeon-general-issues-new-advisory-about-effects-social-media-use-has-youth-mental-health.html

"Surging Violence and Far-Right Extremism: Unpacking Social Media's Role in The 2024 Election." Georgetown Security Studies Review. Last modified April 25, 2024. https://georgetownsecuritystudiesreview.org/2024/04/25/surging-violence-and-far-right-extremism-unpacking-social-medias-role-in-the-2024-election/.

"Texas School Safety Practices Survey Report." Texas School Safety Center. Accessed May 21, 2024. https://txssc.txstate.edu/research/reports/practices/.

Threat Assessment and Active Shooter Prevention. January 23, 2024. https://www.secondsight-ts.com/threat-assessment-blog/active-shooter-threat-assessment.

Treisman, Rachel. "How to Help Those Impacted by the Highland Park Parade Shooting." NPR. Last modified July 7, 2022. https://www.npr.org/2022/07/07/1110286494/highland-park-shooting-how-to-help.

"Trial of Andrew Lester, who shot Ralph Yarl after teen rang the wrong doorbell, set for next year." KCUR - Kansas City news and NPR. Last modified September 20, 2023. https://www.kcur.org/news/2023-09-20/trial-of-andrew-lester-who-shot-ralph-yarl-after-teen-rang-the-wrong-doorbell-set-for-next-year.

n.d. https://www2.ed.gov/admins/lead/safety/threatassessmentguide.pdf.

Understanding the Difference Between 'risk' and 'threat'. March 13, 2024. https://www.riskintelligence.eu/background-and-guides/understanding-the-difference-between-risk-and-threat.

"Averting Targeted School Violence: A U.S. Secret Service Analysis of Plots Against Schools." United States Secret Service. Accessed October 29, 2024. https://www.secretservice.gov/newsroom/reports/threat-assessments/schoolcampus-attacks/details-0.

United States. Secret Service. National Threat Assessment Center. Mass Attacks in Public Spaces - 2018. 2019.

"UNLV Gunman ID'd As Anthony Polito, 67, Professor Who Failed to Get Job at School." New York Post. Last modified December 8, 2023. https://nypost.com/2023/12/07/news/unlv-mass-shooting-suspect-idd-as-anthony-polito-professor-who-failed-to-get-job-at-school/.

Oxford reference. "Vigilante." n.d. https://www.oxfordreference.com/display/10.1093/oi/authority.20110803115833556.

"Violent Media in Childhood and Seriously Violent Behavior in Adolescence and Young Adulthood." PubMed Central (PMC). Accessed May 21, 2024. https://www.ncbi.nlm.nih.gov/pmc/articles/PMC10177625/.

The Washington Post. Last modified June 28, 2021. https://www.washingtonpost.com/nation/2021/06/28/john-hurley-hero-police-shooting/.

"What is the stress response." Simply Psychology. Last modified February 14, 2023. https://www.simplypsychology.org/stress-biology.html.

WNYT.com | NewsChannel 13 - WNYT.com NewsChannel 13. Accessed May 20, 2024. https://wnyt.com/wp-content/uploads/2023/04/Monahan-Criminal-Complaint.pdf.

WUSA 9. "Video of DoorDash driver shooting prank YouTuber in the mall." YouTube. Video. October 2, 2023. https://www.youtube.com/watch?v=3vnPUh_u58s.

"A year after tragedy struck olde town Arvada, a family sues Arvada police and tries to move on." Colorado Public Radio. Last modified June 22, 2022. https://www.cpr.org/2022/06/22/olde-town-arvada-shooting-johnny-hurley/.

www.ingramcontent.com/pod-product-compliance
Lightning Source LLC
Chambersburg PA
CBHW041039050426
42337CB00059B/5068